MW00785246

GAVIN AT WAR

GAVIN AT WAR

The World War II Diary of Lieutenant General James M. Gavin

EDITED AND ANNOTATED BY LEWIS SORLEY
Additional annotation by Keith Nightingale

CASEMATE
Philadelphia & Oxford

AN AUSA BOOK
Association of the United States Army
2425 Wilson Boulevard, Arlington, Virginia, 22201, USA

Published in the United States of America and Great Britain in 2022 by
CASEMATE PUBLISHERS
1950 Lawrence Road, Havertown, PA 19083, USA
and
The Old Music Hall, 106–108 Cowley Road, Oxford OX4 1JE, UK

Editor's Prologue and Epilogue and annotations, copyright 2022 © Lewis Sorley
James Gavin's diary, copyright 2022 © The Gavin family collection
Additional annotation copyright 2022 © Keith Nightingale

Hardback Edition: ISBN 978-1-63624-024-4
Digital Edition: ISBN 978-1-63624-025-1

A CIP record for this book is available from the British Library

All rights reserved. No part of this book may be reproduced or transmitted in any form or by any means, electronic or mechanical including photocopying, recording or by any information storage and retrieval system, without permission from the publisher in writing.

Printed and bound in the United Kingdom by TJ Books

Typeset in India by Lapiz Digital Services, Chennai.

For a complete list of Casemate titles, please contact:

CASEMATE PUBLISHERS (US)
Telephone (610) 853-9131
Fax (610) 853-9146
Email: casemate@casematepublishers.com
www.casematepublishers.com

CASEMATE PUBLISHERS (UK)
Telephone (01865) 241249
Email: casemate-uk@casematepublishers.co.uk
www.casematepublishers.co.uk

Cover: National Archives and Records Administration, 221951747.

Contents

The typewriter that Gavin carried with him in the war, on which he typed this diary.

Foreword

Here is a voice that speaks to us directly from the past. My father kept a personal diary from 1943 to 1945 while he was in Europe with the 82nd Airborne Division. His diary is now shared for the first time.

The diary is an unedited account: immediate, intense, and written without thought of publication. It covers the combat jumps into Sicily and Italy, planning the D-Day Airborne operations, and my father's combat experience in Normandy, Holland, the Battle of the Bulge, and from there through the end of the war. It is by no means a full account of my father's experiences during the war. Readers looking for that should go to *On to Berlin* written by my father and published in 1978.

Airborne operations were an entirely new kind of warfare in 1943, and my father had a unique perspective: he planned Airborne operations in Europe at the highest level and was part of those operations as a commander in combat. A central fact of Airborne assaults, a precedent set by my father and now a tenet of Airborne command, is that the commanding officer is first out of the door of the airplane in a combat jump. Once on the ground, my father faced the same dangers of combat as any other paratrooper. This makes the diary an especially valuable primary source from World War II.

Another important aspect of my father's experience was his commitment to the well-being of his men. The standards of training and leadership he established are the bedrock of the Airborne and his voice resonates with soldiers today as it did in World War II. The strength and power of his leadership are embedded in these pages.

Lewis Sorley Jr reviewed the text for clarity and compiled an index of the text. In addition, he wrote a biographical sketch and chose photographs from the Army History and Education Center in Carlisle, Pennsylvania.

Keith Nightingale added notes about Airborne operations and other important issues to the text. He has an unsurpassed knowledge of the Airborne in World War II and was personally acquainted with my father. His notes bring the diary to life.

This project would not have occurred without Bob Sorley's and Keith Nightingale's expertise and hard work. Sincere thanks to both of them.

Any proceeds from this publication will go to the 82nd Airborne Division Association which promotes the welfare of past and present 82nd Airborne paratroopers and also to the Army Heritage Foundation in Carlisle, PA, in appreciation of its role as custodian of my father's papers and the history of the United States Army.

Chloe Gavin

A Gavin Remembrance by Walter Woods

Walter Woods was aide to General Gavin during World War II. He wrote this letter to Gavin's daughter Chloe around the year 2000.

In 1942 I was 22 years old working in the shipyard in Newport News, Virginia. Most of my friends and buddies had been drafted. Because of my defense job I would not have been drafted. I quit my job and volunteered for service because I felt it was my duty to defend my country. I came home to Clyde, North Carolina and went to the Haywood County draft board in Waynesville, North Carolina and volunteered for service.

I was inducted in the U.S. Army Infantry in October of 1942. I was sent to Fort Jackson, South Carolina and then later to Camp Wheeler, Georgia. After four or five weeks in infantry training a memo was posted on the bulletin board asking for volunteers for the Airborne Parachute School. I went to the headquarters order[ly] room with several other soldiers and took the test and examination for the Airborne. I passed the test and was sent to Fort Benning, Georgia to parachute school. After four weeks of training which included five parachute jumps, I was qualified to become a paratrooper. I was assigned to a base in Phoenix City, Alabama for approximately two or three weeks. I left there for Camp Shanks, New York for deportation to North Africa. I left New York by boat to Casablanca, Africa where I was assigned to the 82nd Airborne Division 505 [Parachute Infantry Regiment] headquarters company. Colonel Gavin (at that time) was commanding officer of the 505 regiment.

After being there for about two months we jumped in the invasion of Sicily. They were all inland jumps. I did not know Colonel Gavin at this time. General Ridgway was the commanding officer of the 82nd Division. The only thing I knew about Colonel Gavin was that he was the commanding officer of the 505 (known as "Slim Jim"). We were there about five weeks.

After the battle in Sicily, we went back to Africa for about two weeks to prepare for the invasion of Italy. We jumped around the middle of August in 1943. The next morning after I jumped in Italy, the acting commanding officer called me to the field which was set up for headquarters. Colonel Gavin had requested that I come to see him. (I did not know him personally or had not spoken to him at this time.) I do not know why I was chosen for the special duty I was assigned. When I went to see Colonel Gavin, he said, "I am Colonel Gavin, your commanding officer."

I saluted him and he said, "At ease." He asked how many rounds of ammunition I had, if I had 250 rounds. He said we are going on patrol, and he wanted me to accompany him as a point guide, which included myself, Colonel Gavin, and about six or eight soldiers and two officers. I cannot recall their names except one was Captain Olson. We left around 8 AM and returned around dusk. He asked me to stay and then dismissed all the other soldiers. They then returned to their regular duties. After this, he asked how many blankets I had. I answered one. He said, "I have two, you take one," and insisted that I take the blanket. He then said, "You bed down here, and I will bed down over there." He pointed to a location about ten yards away. He told me to be prepared to leave at any moment. We didn't go out that night. The next morning, at the break of day, we ate our breakfast which consisted of "C" rations and went from one command post to another that day. We were gone all day. He said, "Son," (he called me son all the time, he hardly ever called me soldier. If he did not call me son, he called me Woods.) "Bed down here" (the position we had moved to that night). The next morning which was the third day he had a meeting with his staff, and he told me the company commander wanted to see me. The commander asked how I liked my new duties. I replied, "The Colonel is about to wear me down." (I was 22 years old.) I asked, "Do I have to do this job?" The commander said, "The Colonel has requested you to do this job," and said, "You don't have to (laughing) but we can make you wish you had." I reported to Colonel Gavin and from that day on I was assigned to him personally for whatever he wanted me to do.

He was a father figure to me, and this became a father and son relationship. We fought battles together. He talked about his personal life to me and about life in general.

From that period, we went on into Italy. We went from front lines post to post regardless of how rough it was, he visited the front lines every day and I was with him everyday.

He was promoted from Colonel to Brigadier General in 1943 and went from 505 to headquarters company of the 82nd. He was promoted to assistant division commander. He was in the 82nd but assigned to the 505. I was also promoted from corporal to sergeant.

We were in Italy about a month. We left Valtero River right out of combat and went to Ireland by boat and stayed there awhile and trained. From there we went to Leicester, England. We still continued to visit every unit each day although just in training. He talked personally to all soldiers he came in contact with regardless of rank. He was loved and respected by all the troops. He did not expect us soldiers to do anything he would not do or have any better food or living conditions than he did. We left England for the invasion of Normandy.

We left for the invasion about 7 or 8 o'clock on June 5, 1944. We jumped in Normandy about 2 o'clock in the morning on June 6. General Gavin jumped first in the string of 12 men. I jumped second and Captain Olson jumped third. This is the way we jumped in all our jumps. We landed in Normandy St. Mere Eglise. I landed in the church cemetery. He landed somewhere close to the church. I did not get in contact with him until later in the afternoon. (I had the privilege of going to Europe for the 50th Anniversary of the Invasion of Normandy and was able to visit the cemetery where I landed.) We started assembling the groups together as soon as possible. By mid-afternoon we had a large group of troops together which General Gavin was commanding outposts. We were in Normandy about two months. From there we went to Sissonne, France where we trained and prepared for the invasion of Holland. At this time General Gavin was the commanding general of the 82nd Airborne Division. On Sunday, September 17, 1944, we jumped in Holland, him first, me second, and Captain Olson third.

General Gavin was a very brave man who had great faith in his men. The battle or the weather never stopped him from going to check the troops. He would go in the rain or snow. If the battle was severe, he would crawl from foxhole to foxhole to talk to his men to let them know he was with them. Words cannot explain the love and pride I had for General Gavin. In case you don't know, General Gavin, Captain Olson, and myself were wounded in battle. This is very touching for me to tell you as there were many things, I could tell you about the battle. After each battle, the wounded and the dead were taken behind the front line. General Gavin would talk with the wounded and at times, would hold their hands. For the ones that were dead, he would go from one to another and just shake his head. In Bergenendal, Holland, where the picture of your father and myself was taken (which I have enclosed), it was a cool rainy day. We had had a severe battle. We won the battle and drove the Germans out of town. That was the worst battle in Holland. We lost a great number of men. After the battle, the wounded and the dead were brought back. General Gavin walked up and down the line, stood and looked for a while, and said to me, "Woods, what a shame." About that time Jack Thompson, the correspondent, walked up and talked to General Gavin. (I do not know what he said.) Then he took pictures of the scene. Just a short distance from there he took the picture of your father and me.

Our last mission was the Battle of the Bulge in Belgium. The weather was the worst of any battle we were in. Snow was four or five feet deep. General Gavin, at this time, was in command of all troops (it was a very unorganized front). General Gavin took over command and soon had all forces under control. As you probably know, he was wounded in the Bulge. That did not stop him from going to all units on the front line. I was also wounded, but I still went with him, except one day. We were going to one of the outposts. I was in front of him and got in too far in the enemy line. We got pinned down from German fire and had to fight our way out and went on to the right place. The only time that he ever said anything to me was the next morning, "Woods, you are getting too brave. You are going to get us killed. I think you should stay at the command post for a few days." I stayed that day. The next morning at daybreak he said, "Woods, let's go." So that was the first and last time he ever said anything to me about it. From then on we were out and going everyday.

If you have the book *Gavin* the pictures after page 40 of the four people in the jeep are your father in the right front, Sergeant Landers as the driver, in the back seat Captain Olson on the right and me in the left with the rifle. In the book *On to Berlin* the pictures of the dead and barely alive, I was there and saw this. Also, I am mentioned in this and several other books.

In our spare time together, he would ask me if I had written home or if I had heard from home. That was important to him, although I did not have the chance to write them very much and although my family wrote to me, I sometimes did not get their mail.

He talked to me personally. He talked so much about [his daughter] Barbara. He would show me pictures of her and wrote to her often. I think I knew him as well as anyone or maybe better.

After the Battle of the Bulge the war was coming to an end. We were having a lot of encounters with the Russians. After the war was over, we returned to Sissonne, France, to prepare for the move to Berlin as the honor guard. I had enough points to come home for discharge. General Gavin asked me if I would stay as his orderly, which consisted of taking care of all his personal property which included his books, clothes, and to prepare it for the move to Berlin. The last day I was with him was when he flew to Berlin with all his belongings. When I left him in Berlin, I flew to Camp Lucky Strike in France for my return to the States. I saluted him, he

shook my hand and said, "Good luck, Woods." I returned to the States and was discharged in September.

Sometime after I came home, he sent me pictures and three citations. After serving personally more than two years with General Gavin, I feel very honored to have done this. The only regrets I have is I didn't keep in touch with him until he was not doing too well. I did correspond with him, and he knew I was well and doing good.

There is so much to be said between the lines, I could never tell you. In this small brief summary, I hope some of these things will give you a greater understanding of my time with your father.

He was a great man.

Editor's Prologue

James Gavin was a soldier through and through. Tall, lean, smart, and ambitious to lead, he moved up quickly in the expanding American forces as World War II impended. Still a captain in late 1941, he was, just three years later, a major general in command of the storied 82nd Airborne Division, self-styled the "All Americans," with AA the centerpiece of their bold red, white and blue shoulder patch.

Noted historian Carlo D'Este got it just right: "Jim Gavin was the real deal: an authentic hero whose life was marked by exemplary courage, leadership, and great accomplishment."[1]

In March 1907 Gavin was born James Ryan in New York City under difficult circumstances. His mother was a recent immigrant from Ireland, his father's whereabouts unknown. Soon after his birth his mother placed him in the Convent of Mercy in Brooklyn, where he remained until about the age of two.

He was then, under auspices of an entity known as the Catholic Home Bureau, put with foster parents, Martin and Mary Gavin. He was given their name and lived with them in Mount Carmel, a small town in the coal fields of eastern Pennsylvania. "Orphaned before he was two" is the way Gavin described it in an author profile many years later.[2] When Gavin was about ten years old his foster parents formally adopted him.

In a draft memoir written many years later Gavin provided an explanation for his middle name of Maurice, which had not appeared on his birth certificate. "I recalled very vividly the discussions that I had with my foster mother. She was the one who told me, when I was to be confirmed at the age of 12, that I was to take the name of James Maurice." When Gavin asked where Maurice came from, "she said that the Catholic Home Bureau had told her to give me that name. I assumed that my mother must have so advised the Bureau, so I accepted the middle name."[3]

"The Gavins were characteristic," James Gavin later wrote. "Like all Irish, they were religious and hard workers ... One of my earliest memories is being impressed with the need to work and to contribute to the support of the family. Education was not considered important."[4]

Martin Gavin worked as a coal miner. It was a hard life, and an often dangerous one. Wages were low, so other family members were expected to work and help support their families.

Gavin developed considerable sympathy for his foster father. He remembered him as kind and generous, hard-working, gentle. But along with this Gavin became determined not to end up as a coal miner himself.

Gavin's foster mother was another matter entirely. She was a heavy drinker, eventually a full-blown alcoholic, and often beat Gavin for whatever he did or didn't do that displeased her. (During such violence Gavin's foster father would leave the house.) Gavin craved his foster mother's approval and affection, but to no avail. He said later that he did not ever recall her having put her arms around him or hugging him, but he remembered the whippings she administered aplenty.

In a later oral history Gavin surprisingly gave a much more positive account of life with his foster parents: "I had a great upbringing there," he maintained.[5] The reality, though, seems to have been as Gavin described it to his close friend and literary agent Sterling Lord: "As a foster child, I had a very rugged upbringing."[6]

The schooling Gavin received as a youth was somewhat haphazard. Initially he was enrolled in a Catholic elementary school, going through the first three grades and a semester of the fourth, then moved to the public school. In sixth grade he returned to the Catholic school for that grade and the next, finally returning to public school, and the end of his formal education, for eighth grade. Meanwhile he was reading every book he could lay hands on, including those he was able to borrow from a local Presbyterian church. And somewhere along the line he had been well schooled in penmanship. As an adult he wrote a fine hand and had a distinctive signature.

The Gavins proved far from ideal foster parents. Neither could read or write, and education meant little to them. The result was that when Gavin finished the eighth grade they pulled him out of school. That was, as far as they were concerned, all the education he needed. Now he could go to work full-time to help support the family.

From the age of six or seven Gavin had begun part-time work, starting as a newspaper delivery boy. By the time he was in fifth grade (at age 11) he had both morning and evening routes and was the local agent for three out-of-town papers. At 13 he had cornered two Sunday routes and had a couple of boys working for him.

He filled in what free time he had with various odd jobs. One involved hauling a neighbor's coal supply from where it was delivered at the curbside to his basement coal chute. Gavin did this, bucket by bucket, for 25 cents per ton of coal moved. Whatever he earned, Gavin recalled, he gave to his foster mother. "The Irish were brought up like that."

During Gavin's teen years the situation at home grew progressively worse. Mary Gavin was frequently drunk and abusive, neglecting the home and not preparing meals, constantly quarreling with her husband. Later, Gavin would describe his boyhood as a rather harsh and severe upbringing, and it certainly was that. "It wasn't milking cows on Sunnybrook Farm," he once observed.[7]

Thirsting for more education, and for a better quality of life, Gavin ran away from home early in the morning of the day he turned seventeen. Making his way by train to New York, virtually penniless and with only the clothes he wore, and unable to find other work, he enlisted in the Army. While he was underage at the time, some "arrangements" were made that enabled him to do so.

Almost right away Gavin's life, and his future prospects, improved dramatically. He liked the Army from the beginning and was thankful for the educational opportunities it provided.

After recruit training he was sent to a Coast Artillery unit stationed at Fort Sherman in the Panama Canal Zone. There he encountered a friendly first sergeant who took an interest in him, plus he gained access to an excellent post library. Soon he was made battery clerk and after only a few months promoted to the rank of corporal in Battery E, 2nd Coast Artillery.

One day the first sergeant, described by Gavin as an Indian and known (inevitably) as "Chief" Williams, summoned Gavin to his orderly room. There was a memorandum posted at headquarters, he was told, and he should go up there and read it. The subject was competitive entrance examinations for enlisted men aspiring to enter West Point. Gavin took the preliminary test, passed the physical examination, and qualified to attend an Army prep school. That school, conducted at Corozal, on the Pacific side of the Canal Zone, began on September 1, 1924. Similar schools were established throughout the Army, an effective means of preparing aspiring young soldiers to gain admission to the Military Academy.

Right away the dozen or so students in Panama—all, like Gavin, Army enlisted men—took a comprehensive written examination, sort of a "Where do we stand now?" kind of test. Gavin's heart sank when the results were published. He had done very poorly in mathematics, never having studied algebra and the like. They kept him anyway, probably because gaps in prior education were precisely what the prep school was designed to make up for.

Gavin remembered their "wonderful" instructor, First Lieutenant Percy Black, describing him as a patient and intelligent gentleman.[8] Lieutenant Black would meet with his students each morning, taking them through an hour's instruction each in algebra, geometry, English and history. The rest of the day they would study on their own to prepare the next day's lessons. Gavin was finding it hard going, often studying until midnight, but he stuck with it.

Gavin received word in late May that he had passed the entrance examinations and would be admitted to West Point. His First Sergeant immediately took him out of ranks, suggesting that he use the remaining time before reporting to West Point for further study.

On July 1, 1925, Gavin entered West Point on an Army competitive appointment as a member of the Class of 1929. Later he would acknowledge the fundamental importance of that opportunity: "It is fair to say that, more than anything else, West Point molded my mind and body."

Meanwhile Gavin's achievement was enthusiastically reported by his hometown newspaper, the *Mount Carmel Item*: "From a newsboy to a cadet in the United States Military Academy at West Point, the story of the life of 18-year-old James M. Gavin, whose home is at 543 West Fig Street, Mount Carmel, reads like the sensational rise of a picturesque hero in an Alger book." Gavin still had that clipping more than 60 years after it was published.

Shortly after being sworn in Gavin and his new classmates were taken to a conference room and issued a questionnaire. One of the first items to be entered was one's age. This posed a problem for Gavin. When he enlisted he had entered his age as 18. Since then, a year and a half had elapsed. What to do? He put down that he was 21, a decision that later puzzled him and caused him no end of worry.

***

The West Point academic curriculum in those days was demanding. Every cadet took the exact same subjects (the only exception being foreign language, in which there were several options), with heavy concentration on mathematics. At the end of his first (plebe) year Gavin stood 249 in his class academically. The next year he was 208. Next after that 192. And for the final year he was 113. Each year he had improved his class standing. That yielded an overall standing of 185 of 299 on the Graduation Order of Merit List, a truly spectacular performance for someone whose previous formal academic experience had ended with the eighth grade.

His fellow cadets respected Gavin's character and judgment as well, electing him their company representative to the Honor Committee.

Gavin had the usual cadet struggles with the Tactical Department. Some of his more interesting "quills" were for overcoat on wrong hook (1 demerit), Battalion Adjutant marching out of step with music while taking post at parade (3 demerits), and holding young lady's hand in East Sally Port of South Area (3 demerits). But he not only persevered but prospered, being made a cadet corporal in the third year and a cadet lieutenant and battalion adjutant as a First Classman.

Many years later Gavin wrote of the pervasive and lasting influence of the ethical teachings he encountered at West Point. "Cadets are taught to be honest in all things," he recalled, "and there is a resoluteness about their honesty that grips a man to the marrow. Once a matter is resolved into right or wrong, then the right must be chosen, and always the harder right rather than the easier wrong." There he was drawing on the Cadet Prayer for his phrasing. "Even the Academy itself is a monument to this principle, as it stands on a granite mountain that alters the course of the mighty Hudson River on its way to the sea. So must her sons adhere to the right when the issue is drawn. May there never be compromise when our Country and our Honor is at stake."[9]

***

Gavin branched Infantry upon graduation from West Point, entering an Army about to experience a long stretch of what were later accurately described as "the lean years."

After three months in flying school at Brooks Field in San Antonio, Texas, Gavin washed out and was reassigned to Camp Harry J. Jones near Douglas, Arizona, quite near the border with Mexico. There he joined the 25th Infantry, an all-black regiment with the exception of white officers. Gavin had no previous experience with black people—there being none where he grew up—and no prejudices. He enjoyed that assignment, working with experienced non-commissioned officers and troops who typically had several years of service, and later said many of them became his friends for life.

In late 1932 Gavin received orders to the Infantry School at Fort Benning, Georgia, one of the Army's grand old posts, to take a course of instruction concentrating on weapons and tactics. During this course he was exposed to an officer known throughout the Army as "Vinegar Joe" Stilwell, then heading up the school's Tactical Department. Gavin found him a demanding but superb officer from whom he learned the importance of an officer's being able to do himself anything he asked his troops to do.

Soon after graduating West Point, Gavin had married Irma Baulsir, also known by the nickname "Peg" or "Peggy." Irma did not, as it turned out, much like Army life. Just before leaving Fort Benning Gavin learned that Irma was pregnant. She was then on an extended visit with her parents in Washington, D.C., where she decided to remain and have the baby there. Meanwhile Gavin moved on to Fort Sill, Oklahoma, and the 38th Infantry, then a few months later to the 29th Infantry at the same post.

On Armistice Day in 1933 a beautiful baby girl arrived. They named her Barbara Margaret. Unfortunately, the telegram informing Gavin that he was now a father went astray and it was not until two days later that he got the news. His wife and his mother-in-law were not amused.

Gavin's next assignment after Fort Sill was to the Philippine Islands. Before sailing he took a brief leave to visit his foster parents in Mount Carmel. Mary Gavin was out of town somewhere. Martin Gavin was by then living in a home for senior citizens, where Gavin visited him. He found the old man content with his circumstances and desirous of remaining there. Gavin gave him some money, then headed for New York, where his long voyage to the Philippines would begin. In later years Gavin said he often thought of his foster father, a good and decent man who did not have much of a happy life and felt very sorry for him.

***

In the Philippines Gavin joined the 57th Infantry, a regiment of the famed Philippine Scouts, at Fort William McKinley, where he would serve for the next two years. He was impressed by the professionalism of the troops at all levels. Years later, during World War II, they would give a splendid account of themselves on Bataan.

After two years in the Philippines Gavin returned to the United States, in the autumn of 1938, for assignment to the 3rd Infantry Division. He commanded Company K of the division's 7th Infantry Regiment, stationed at Vancouver Barracks, Washington. Midway through that tour of duty he was promoted to captain, about a decade after being commissioned.

In later years Gavin would remember with gratitude the mentoring he received from First Sergeant Max Roth, with whom he served in Company K. Roth had been in the same outfit for 16 years, not unusual in the between-the-wars Army. During World War II he was commissioned and reached the rank of lieutenant colonel.

Roth and Gavin stayed together through the winter of 1939–1940, during which time the regiment was gradually shifting to a war footing. At one point they made an amphibious landing in Monterey Bay, then went into camp nearby. During that time Gavin lived in a small wall tent pitched on a sand dune, described by him as a dreary setting. Maneuvers and tactical exercises took up most of his time, reading the rest.

***

In the spring of 1940 Gavin got orders to West Point, where he was assigned to the Department of Tactics. This assignment was very much to his liking, an opportunity as he saw it for further study and to learn through teaching. And, rather than the usual assignment as Tactical Officer for a company of cadets, Gavin was assigned to the staff of the Commandant of Cadets, where he was able to devote most of his time to study and matters related to instruction.

By that time, of course, the war in Europe was dominating headlines everywhere. Gavin, like others in the military establishment, was convinced that American involvement in the war was inevitable. And they all knew that American forces were lamentably unready for that.

Teaching tactics gave Gavin an excellent opportunity to learn all he could about the combat underway in Europe and to teach and discuss that in the classroom and with fellow instructors. Gavin, for one, was very much aware that the cadets he was teaching were very likely to soon be fighting the war he was describing.

Of course, the blitzkrieg, with its powerful waves of armored forces, was a prime topic of interest. Then there appeared another innovative form of warfare, illustrated by the German airborne invasion of Crete. This caught Gavin's attention and imagination in a big way. He saw in airborne operations the potential to counter enemy forces in an imaginative and highly effective way. He thirsted to be part of such an effort.

In April 1941 Gavin applied for airborne duty and parachute training. The West Point Superintendent disapproved that application, specifying that Gavin could not be released unless the Military Academy were provided an officer of equal ability. Over the next weekend Gavin drove to Washington to see a friend who was assigned in the Pentagon working Infantry assignments. With his help an officer acceptable to West Point was offered up and Gavin was granted his request. In July 1941 he was assigned to airborne duty and the following month graduated from Parachute School.

***

While he had been assigned to West Point Gavin began to do something he later said he had wanted to do all his life, begin a search for his birth mother. Having long ago read his adoption papers, he knew that he had been born James Ryan, and that he had subsequently been placed for adoption through an agency in New York City known as the Catholic Home Bureau.

Gavin now went to New York, where he talked with people in the famous Burns Detective Agency. They took his case and assigned an agent, viewed by Gavin as a very capable person, to it. They were able to verify that he had been born at the Holy Family Hospital, located at 155 Dean Street in Brooklyn.

In the spring of 1941 Gavin visited the hospital. He asked to see the birth records for the month of March 1907. A large register was brought out and laid before him. There he found his entry: Born on March 22, 1907. Delivered by Dr. Eugene Cronin. Mother's name Catherine (Katie) Ryan. Residence 692 Dean Street. Gavin immediately went to that address, only a few blocks from the hospital, but found no trace of his mother there or anyone who knew anything about her. The neighborhood had obviously changed in the intervening years. People he spoke with told him it had once been populated almost entirely by Irish immigrants, but now they were nearly all Italians.

City records, Gavin found, did not include anything about a Catherine Ryan being married at about that time. His search thus came to an end, at least for the time being, as he was fully absorbed with his new assignment and preparations for going to war.

***

Creation of American airborne forces began in 1941 at Fort Benning, Georgia, with establishment of a platoon of volunteer paratroopers. Gavin, then a 34-year-old captain, aspired to join those pioneers. "I was teaching tactics at West Point at the time," he wrote, "and it seemed to me that the tactics of the blitzkrieg and the use of an ever-larger scale of armored formations would not be enough, and that we would have to find a new dimension of warfare."[10]

Upon graduation from Parachute School Gavin was given command of Company C of the newly activated 503rd Parachute Infantry Battalion at Fort Bragg,

North Carolina, soon moving up to become the battalion executive officer (second in command). Then Brigadier General (later Major General) William C. Lee—taking command of what was called the Provisional Parachute Group, headquartered at Fort Benning, Georgia—brought Gavin up to his staff. Gavin—a "dynamo of intelligent energy," said Lee—became head of the Plans and Training Section of the Provisional Parachute Group at Fort Benning, and later of the Airborne Command at Fort Bragg, writing much of the basic training doctrine and the first textbooks on airborne training and tactics. It was, said Gavin, one of the most exciting and interesting periods of his life.

Since they were building the new units from scratch there were almost no aspects that were not under development. The list included doctrine, loading of aircraft, formations, operating procedures, weapons, uniforms, combat rations, methods of issuing orders and engaging in combat. There would be no "front lines" as in traditional combat. The important thing, they determined, was to seize their objectives at once, then expand as the tactical situation required.

Said General Lee of Gavin, "His friends spoke exceedingly well of him, and he impressed his associates with his quiet dignified bearing, his appearance of lean physical toughness, and his keen and penetrating mind."[11]

Gavin, with his wife Irma and daughter Barbara, was attending a movie in Columbus, the town right outside Fort Benning, when suddenly the film was stopped, and the theater's owner came on stage to announce the Japanese attack on Pearl Harbor.

***

In February 1942 Gavin, by then a newly minted major, was sent to Fort Leavenworth, Kansas, where he attended a short course at the Army Command and General Staff School designed to qualify those enrolled to function as division staff officers. Gavin found his fellow students—from the Regular forces, the National Guard, and the Army Reserve—highly motivated, as the nation was by then at war.

Back at Bragg in April 1942, Gavin and his associates wrote the first training manual on employment of airborne troops. They had by then formed the first airborne regiments and were contemplating an airborne division.[12] Such divisions, they speculated, would be formed of two parachute infantry regiments and a glider regiment, the latter to be for delivery of artillery, signals, reconnaissance, medics and other elements constituting heavy loads.

An exception to this latter provision was the possible use of 75mm pack artillery, whose pieces could be broken down into seven loads. Experiments proved the feasibility of this. Gavin later reflected that they used parachute artillery in all their important operations in the war. In Holland, he said that was the only artillery he had for the first 24 hours, and it made a tremendous difference.[13]

In the spring of 1942 Gavin accompanied General Lee on a visit to Headquarters, Army Ground Forces, in Washington. The purpose was to discuss organization of the first airborne division. The idea was to convert an existing division to an airborne-capable one. But it was stipulated, the division chosen must not be a National Guard one, because after the war that division would return to the state with which it was affiliated, and the active forces would no longer have an airborne capability. The division to be chosen, then, would be one from the Organized Reserves, one that had already completed its basic training and was located near one or more airfields.

The division that met these requirements and was chosen was the 82nd Infantry Division, then stationed at Camp Claiborne, Louisiana, and commanded by Brigadier General Omar Bradley. Brigadier General Matthew Ridgway was its assistant division commander. That certainly sounded like the beginnings of an all-star lineup. Soon Bradley was sent to take command of the 28th Division, which seemed to be struggling and needed someone like him to straighten it out. Ridgway moved up to command the 82nd.

Gavin later commented on what an astute decision it had been to choose the 82nd Division on which to build the first airborne division. Given its stellar leadership, the division was well trained and had high morale, just right for what they had in mind. Plus, it had an admirable history, in World War I having spent more consecutive days in combat than any other American division. One of its commanders then had been General Jonathan Wainwright, later a hero at Bataan and recipient of the Medal of Honor. Even more famous, though, was its Sergeant Alvin York, who while on patrol led the seven surviving men of his platoon in the capture of 132 Germans.

General Ridgway established the division headquarters at Fort Bragg. The parachute regiments to man it came from Fort Benning. Then the 82nd cadred the second such division to be formed, the 101st Airborne Division. In the meantime, two constituent elements of the new division, the 504th and 505th Parachute Infantry Regiments, were being trained at Benning. Gavin assumed command of the 505th in August 1942. By late 1942 he had been promoted to full colonel and, with his regiment, was soon to enter combat in the early stages of American involvement in World War II.

In February 1943 Gavin moved his regiment to Fort Bragg, where they became part of the 82nd Airborne Division, along with sister regiments the 504th Parachute Infantry Regiment under Colonel Reuben Tucker and the 325th Glider Infantry Regiment commanded by Colonel Harry L. Lewis.

In April 1943, the division was alerted for movement to Africa, leaving by way of Camp Edwards, Massachusetts, and the Port of New York and arriving in Casablanca on May 10, 1943. Gavin later noted that his greatest concerns at that time were training and the readiness of the troops and what impressed him most were the spirit and ability of the young paratroopers.

In July 1943 Gavin commanded the airborne combat team—designated the 505th Parachute Combat Team (Reinforced)—that spearheaded the American assault on Sicily. "I went into the war with great pride in my country and a determination to excel in the crucible of war," said Gavin. In that he succeeded admirably.

Gavin continued in command of the 505th Parachute Infantry Regiment when it took part in the parachute landing at Salerno Bay on the night of September 13/14, 1943.

Then, promoted to brigadier, he became Assistant Division Commander of the 82nd Airborne Division and, shortly after that, was placed on temporary duty as airborne advisor to the Supreme Allied Commander (Dwight Eisenhower) in London. When the plans for Operation Overlord, the Normandy invasion, were essentially complete, on February 1, 1944, Gavin resumed his post as Assistant Division Commander of the 82nd Airborne, then based at Leicester, England.

Gavin led the division's parachute assault echelon into Normandy. When the division's commander, Matthew B. Ridgway, was elevated to command of an airborne corps, Gavin was promoted to major general and took command of the 82nd Airborne Division (just three years after, as Captain Gavin, he had reported for duty with that first parachute platoon at Fort Benning).

All this he writes about with insight, charm, and intelligence in this combat diary, including not only the combat itself, and those alongside whom he fought, but observations on the very senior officers, both American and British, he encountered, on the war's grand strategy and battlefield tactics, on the Germans, and even his girlfriends (notwithstanding his young wife Irma waiting at home). It is a remarkable document, now fortuitously made available for the soldiers of a later day.

***

During the war years Gavin came into close contact with virtually all the leading airborne commanders and many others who would advance to the top levels of Army leadership in combat and then in the post-war Army. They were, as might be expected, an aggressive, ambitious and controversial collection of colorful personalities. Both the alliances they (sometimes) formed, and their rivalries were key factors both in and out of combat.

During his extraordinary service Gavin made many friends and a number of enemies, and it might be said that he was very proud of both. General Dwight Eisenhower was to Gavin a disappointment, later to be severely criticized by him. General Matthew B. Ridgway was a superior, a mentor, and then a rival, but always much admired. General Maxwell Taylor earned Gavin's disdain and harshest criticism.

Taylor had been division artillery commander in the 82nd Airborne when Gavin was a regimental commander. Both soon advanced to division command, Gavin of course of the 82nd Airborne Division and Taylor of the 101st Airborne Division (where, due to an accident of fate, he was in Washington on some errand when the 101st had its days of greatest fame while surrounded by German forces at Bastogne during the Battle of the Bulge).

Of particular interest is Gavin's view of British Field Marshal Montgomery, which is all over the map. In his MHI oral history Gavin notes that, on Sicily, "when he got into Messina, there was a great undercurrent of feeling on the part of the Americans that Montgomery wasn't all that great. He refused to take chances. He certainly wasn't a brilliant battle leader…"

Later in that same document, referring to the recently revealed account of special intelligence in Group Captain F. W. Winterbotham's book *The Ultra Secret*, Gavin is highly critical of the senior commanders who had access to this extraordinary source and failed to fully exploit it, including especially Montgomery. Winterbotham's book, says Gavin, "does make it convincing that they should have done better than they did in many cases. Montgomery chasing Rommel all the way across North Africa, reading his daily situation reports every day, his troop dispositions, troop strength, logistic situation, tank strength and so on. It seems inexcusable, due to the fact that we controlled the Mediterranean pretty much, too."

***

Beginning in early April 1943, when he was commanding the 505th at Fort Bragg, Gavin began compiling the typed diary of events and observations here published, a project he continued through the first day of September 1945 in Berlin, producing more than 200 entries overall and a manuscript running to more than 66,000 words. As will be seen, those entries vary in length, frequency, and especially content. Sometimes there are entries on several consecutive days, but more typically they appear once or twice a week. Longer gaps understandably match with the pace of operations and the combat situation.

After the D-Day jumps on the night of June 5/6, 1944, it took Gavin until July 14th to tell that story, but then he does so in arresting detail in one of the longest entries in the entire journal. During the more than two years this self-appointed task continued Gavin advanced from command of a regiment to division command and finally command of U.S. forces in Berlin. It is extraordinary how, given the demands of those assignments, he could summon the energy and self-discipline to stay with it.

For many years no one save Gavin knew of the journal's existence. Only when it was discovered in his effects after his death did the family become aware of it. Now, at the initiative of Gavin's daughter Chloe, this edited version is being published for a wider audience. It is, like its author, good soldierly stuff.

Notes

1   "Jim Gavin: The General Who Jumped First," History Net.
2   Gavin, *Crisis Now.*
3   From Chapter 12, "The Search," p. 428, of draft manuscript in family's possession.
4   *War and Peace in the Space Age*, p. 23.
5   Gavin Oral History, U.S. Army Military History Institute, 1975.
6   Gavin August 31, 1981, Letter to Sterling Lord, GP Box 8.
7   Gavin August 31, 1981, letter to Sterling Lord, GP Box 8.
8   Black (West Point Class of April 1917) won a Silver Star in World War I and a Legion of Merit, Bronze Star Medal, and Purple Heart during World War II.
9   *War and Peace in the Space Age*, p. 34.
10 Gavin, *Crisis Now*, p. 16.
11 Major General William C. Lee, "Introduction," Gavin, *Airborne Warfare*, p. ix.
12 Eventually five airborne divisions were formed during the war. The 11th served in the Pacific theater, the others—13th, 17th, 82nd, and 101st—in the European theater (although the 13th saw no combat).
13 Gavin, *Airborne Warfare*, p. 103.

Editor's Note on the Text

The text from which this account was derived has some deficiencies. Related material on file at the Army Heritage and Education Center also presents some problems.

Some of the lines on various pages run off the right margin, depicting partial words or obviously missing words. In some cases, the context allows the substance or meaning of the missing text to be derived with relative confidence, but in other instances what is missing is not apparent, only that there is something lost.

General Gavin never got around to editing what he had written. We know from his many other published works, however, that he was a highly literate and articulate writer, someone who could—and would—have put this text into finely crafted and punctuated language before sending it to press.

We have thus, in the process of reproducing and annotating the diary, edited it as we feel confident General Gavin would have done before submitting it for publication. This includes breaking up often very long segments into more readable shorter paragraphs. The text does reflect language and attitudes that were common at the time of writing but are no longer acceptable. Whether he might have adjusted these in editing, we will never know, but we have chosen to retain these sections.

But in all those instances where it is not readily apparent how the omissions should read, we have not guessed, simply shown that there are gaps in the text as it was available to us. Thus [++] is our indication of a word or words missing that we cannot with assurance supply.

Acknowledgments

Chloe Gavin Beatty, youngest daughter of General Gavin, was the sparkplug for this project. She supplied the typescript text of her father's journal, provided insights into family relationships, and contributed valuable photographs.

At the West Point Association of Graduates what is known as a Cullum File is maintained on each graduate. That file contains useful biographical information and, especially for persons as prominent as Gavin, can amount to a considerable treasure trove of information. Marilee Meyer is the highly competent and dedicated Memorials Editor on the AOG staff. She helped a lot by providing the rich contents of General Gavin's file.

The Army Heritage and Education Center in Carlisle, Pennsylvania, ably led and administered by its Director, Col. Geoffrey Mangelsdorf, is the repository for General Gavin's papers, some 44 archival boxes of them. Over many weeks working with those files, and especially the very valuable correspondence they included, I was helped by many members of the AHEC staff. I owe special thanks to Duane Miller, who was unfailingly helpful during an extended period when the coronavirus pandemic forced restrictions on the access researchers usually have to the holdings of the Center.

The Army Heritage Center Foundation is the fund-raising entity supporting AHEC. Its very able long-time Executive Director, Colonel Michael Perry, was an always reliable source of information on where to go in the AHEC staff for whatever help was needed. We are most grateful to him and to Amanda Neal, the Foundation's exemplary office manager. In recognition of the importance of AHEC both to this project and in its stated mission of "telling the Army story, one soldier at a time," any royalties generated by this work are being donated to the Army Heritage Center Foundation.

All would have gone for nought were it not for Joseph Craig, the superb Director of the AUSA (Association of the United States Army) Book Program, who found an outstanding publisher for the work and had it designated an AUSA Book.

Lewis Sorley

CHAPTER I

Going to War

Fort Bragg, NC, April 8, 1943

Better late than never. The regiment [505th PIR] was activated at Fort Benning July 1, 1942. Moved to the Alabama training area in October, to Camp Mackall at Hoffman, NC March 7th, and was assigned to the 82nd Division and moved to Fort Bragg two days after arriving at Mackall.[i]

About two weeks ago we were alerted for overseas movement. We haven't been given our movement date yet, but I believe that it has been set and Division has it. Probably about April 22nd.

The most pressing administrative problem at the moment is the AWOL situation. Five days ago, the Regt had a total of two AWOLs, the low[est] to date. We have been averaging about ten. Today at reveille we had 61. Godalmighty what a mess. By now, 9:00PM, it is down to about 40, but it has been a trying day. Army Regs and the Courts Martial manual do not provide sufficient latitude to enable a conscientious commander to adequately punish a man. AWOL at this time can be a most serious offense. If permitted to get out of hand, as it has in some industries, the Regiment will never get into combat.

Upon their return or apprehension, the men are removed from jump status, heads shaved, placed in the guardhouse if the case is aggravated, and made to wear a blue denim uniform with a six-inch yellow stripe up the back. They are not allowed to eat at a table. Instead, they are given a mess kit and required to eat sitting on the ground. They stand at attention while all other men eat and, when they are through, the AWOLs are permitted to go through the chow line for what is left.

They come to work at four AM and work all day. Those who are not in the guardhouse pitch pup tents in the company streets and are not allowed to associate

---

i   The 82nd had just been converted to airborne but had no qualified forces. The independent 504th PIR and 505th PIR were just assigned under the command of Major General Ridgway. At this point it was not a cohesive unit and would not truly be until the Sicily campaign.

with the other men in barracks except to go to the latrine. In addition, they are punished as authorized by the 104th Article of War.

The regiment is in good fettle and mentally it is ready. These people will fight. There have never been soldiers like them. Parachuting is a good test of a man's courage for combat. A man who will jump regularly with equipment will do most anything.

We do [not?] need more training. Much more intensive training at this time would definitely make us stale. They have been working very hard, regardless of the day or hour, since the date of activation. Drill call now is at 7:30. The day usually ends about 5:30, with chow at six. It is a rare day, however, when there is not some night work. Schools, conferences, equipment checks, inspections or night problems.

My night has never, or very rarely, ended before 10:00. The type of training that we need most is that that we will get in the theatre of operations. A few men killed, a few air attacks, and an exchange of gunfire with an enemy force will do wonders to drive our lessons home.[i]

Sunday, April 10, [1943]

Prop blasted[ii] the novices last night and evidently some of them have not fully recovered. A morning like this morning is maddening.

Being at war makes no difference. The entire cargo shipment to the Port of Baltimore awaits the 24-hour-late report of several indifferent company commanders. In peace these company commanders would be relieved at least, [but] in war the best must be made of what I suppose is a normal wartime situation. If all these wartime officers were relieved for every grossly or even slightly inefficient act, we would have no officers nor army in short order.

I talked to General Ridgway for quite some time about our coming entry into combat. He explained that we will have a major role, an airborne effort to be made in conjunction with the British airborne division. He spoke at some length on the attitude of the British and the necessity for our cooperation with them. Said that we

---

i Gavin has identified key elements of making an infantry unit effective that were not understood throughout the Army and often overlooked by many—clear discipline, tough physical conditioning, live fire tasks, and an appreciation of the soldier psyche. He knew when enough was enough. He also understood that nothing conditions soldiers to "get it right" more than combat and casualties. Much of his training wisdom has since been embedded in Army training doctrine.

He further identifies the personal elan of airborne soldiers that allowed him to press harder and demand higher standards—a condition he continuously encouraged and used as is done today.

ii A Prop Blast is an Airborne tradition where new officers are hazed to the extreme by those that have gone before in the unit as a rite of passage. It is a ritualistic bonding that adds to the unique cohesiveness of Airborne forces. The methodology may be alcohol fueled (WWII to Vietnam) or extreme physical stress events (contemporary). Regardless, it is a point of pride to be Prop Blasted. The term refers to the sudden rush of air when a jumper exits which propels him backward and opens the chute.

were always the tail on the British kite. He spoke with such fervor on the subject that I suspected him of trying to get me to commit myself on my "Anglo-cooperative" factor. There are so many Americans who can't get along with them and have no desire to do so.[i]

Although I have definite convictions on the subject, I can still cooperate fully at any time with them. Their soldiers are good and are not afraid to die. What more could one ask? Any hostility based on a feeling of inferiority I have long lost. We have a lot to learn from them and they have a great deal to learn from us. Separately we cannot survive long in this war. Together we can win.

The operation in which we are to play a part is, I was led to believe, all planned. I suspect that it must have something to do with crossing the Mediterranean. Today the press reports that Rommel has given up Sfax. This is just about in keeping with, or perhaps a bit ahead of, the allied timetable.

We are to have six weeks to train in the theatre before commitment. If he is driven out sooner than they figured, we may not be given much training time.[ii] Although we were activated July 1st, looking back it seems to me that we could use considerably more time before combat. I know from history, however, that we have had plenty of time. What we need most is the real thing, then perhaps a lull to absorb the lessons and lick our wounds.

I was assured by Gen. Ridgway that the part of the 505 is a prime one. It is exciting and stimulating to realize that the first regimental parachute operation in the history of our army is to be taken by the 505. It is going to be very, very tough to do well, but if we fail it will not be from lack of effort. I know the regiment will fight to the last man. They will fight as American troops have never fought before. With a little luck in the weather, so that we can have good air support, and enough application on the part of every soldier in the regiment, which is presumed, we will do a good job.

Gen. Ridgway expressed an interest in the maintenance of continental and world peace by having in the U.S. a large airborne striking force. This is a natural [step to take]. Gen. Browning has also mentioned it.[iii] Why send a cruiser to an affected area a week after the shooting starts when several airborne divisions could be flown in

---

i   U.S. officers noted the condescending attitude of the British military to their U.S. counterparts. They considered them amateurs at this stage and did not hesitate to make the point.

ii   This is the first hint of friction between Gavin and General Ridgway concerning working with the British. Ridgway wanted to ensure complete cooperation by Gavin, whereas Gavin was more reticent about their potential performance.

     It is important to understand at this juncture that the 82nd Division, while formally converted to airborne, was still not the cohesive entity it later became. The 505th PIR and the 504th PIR were independent airborne regiments newly assigned. Organizational loyalties had not yet been established. The cohesion that existed at this point was largely restricted to the individual PIRs.

iii   General "Boy" Browning was the head of British Airborne Forces.

and reinforced in 24 hours? If the 505 does well in this coming effort the airborne project in our army will get the green light.[i]

Fort Bragg, N.C., April 17, 1943

This has been a busy week. Everything is shaping up nicely. Our first units are to leave Tuesday morning, the 20th, destination Camp Edwards, Mass. Never having been there, it may not be too boring, but at this stage anything short of the actual thing is not very entertaining. Everyone is anxious and on edge. It appears now as though we will bivouac and train by combat team.

I am not sure of the efficiency of the 456th FA Bn yet. Although we have worked one problem and Col. Hardin appears to be quite capable, the men of the battalion have not (sic) appeared none too well disciplined. I spoke to Boyd, Division G-3, about being made responsible for them after arriving in the theatre of operations and yet not having an opportunity to check them nor their equipment while they are still here where corrections can be made. Not especially interested, as usual.[ii]

Rommel is being pushed into the last corner of Tunisia and the entire theatre shows promise. We are going to have a good show. This regiment is going to do well. All it needs is opportunity. If they fight as well in Africa as they fight in Fayetteville, we have nothing to worry about. The AWOLs are down to an even dozen.[iii]

Camp Edwards, Mass., April 24, 1943

The division moved in 18 trains, the 505 being spread over four. Took five days and closed here Friday the 23rd. Everyone has worked hard. Under present circumstances, being at war, anxiety to get overseas etc., makes a move of this sort easier than it would be in peacetime. Hours of work mean nothing for anyone and if everyone is on the ball, as they are in these parachute units, then things all click.

The secrecy discipline, which is most important since this is the first airborne division committed, is very good. All troops have been restricted for several weeks now, no phone calls, telegrams, visitors. Here on Cape Cod the situation is ideal. MPs are at the canal crossings, and no one can leave nor communicate with the outside world. I believe it is being very effective.

Shoulder patches are covered, jump boots and qualifications badges are not worn. "Parachute" is omitted from all unit designations, even in official communications.

---

i   General Marshall was a major supporter of the airborne concept and constantly urged his theater commanders to use the capability. Other subordinate generals were not so sure.

ii   Boyd was a holdover from the 82nd Division before conversion. He was soon replaced by General Ridgway.

iii   Gavin knew that the AWOL rate was a direct reflection of soldier satisfaction with the unit—bad units have high rates and good ones low.

This is a terrific job for the personnel adjutant and supply officer. They should be on their jobs for quite a while before they hit this place.

The "Port of Embarkation" type of inspections should be normal and frequent for all units expecting to go overseas. Completeness, marking, neatness, and a systematic display arrangement are essential.[i]

I am to leave here with the CT 505 advance party, probably in the next 48 hrs. Gen. Keerans will be on the ship CT 505 has been assigned. That will not be so good, as we are in for a rough time. As I understand it now, I am to be the troop commander of all troops aboard, a few over 7,000. That will be a new experience and a good one. I am looking forward to it. That is one thing I have learned to seek and get a lot out of—troop command. I'd give anything to command a division.

This overseas movement will probably be the largest in the nation's history, if not the world's history. Some ships will very likely be sunk by submarines. I hope not too many. We all have confidence in the efficacy of the army and navy planning and protection for these affairs. We'd better have.[ii]

At sea, 2nd Day out of NY, April 29, 1943

The advance detail of the combat team left Edwards and arrived in NY Monday 26th. Boarded the *Monterey*, former Matson liner. Arranged for reception of troops, which started at 1000 [on] the 28th. 5,388 officers and men boarded ship by 1815. The ship sailed at 0415 today, the 29th.

The entire convoy consists of 23 transports, eight destroyers, one aircraft carrier, and the battleship *Texas*. Total shipment about 58,000 men. Destination: Oran. Object: murder.

And the morale is very high. Aboard ship with me is Gen. Keerans. I have been designated by Gen. Ridgway, however, as Commanding Officer of troops. It is quite an experience. The ship is very much overloaded. 688 men do not have bunks and must shift sleep with others. The mess is of course very much overcrowded. Two meals a day are served.[iii]

---

i   Here, Gavin notes a key indicator of unit quality is the "small stuff"—uniformity of all things, cleanliness, and attention to detail.

ii Brigadier Keerans was the deputy division commander and was MIA, presumed killed in Sicily, after his plane was shot down by friendly fire. Gavin hints of some disregard for Keerans' qualities and may have resented someone between him and Ridgway. Gavin had little regard for Keerans due to his drinking.

iii Gavin is describing the massive sea lift required to move the Army from the United States to Africa. The troop transports were generally a mix of Navy vessels designed to move troops and commandeered civilian liners and transports. Troop space was exceedingly cramped with minimal amenities. It was not unusual to have a hold outfitted with eight stacked canvas racks from deck to ceiling in tight rows. In the most overcrowded, hot bunking was necessary, as he describes.

Many of the units aboard lack organization and discipline, particularly the replacement units. This makes for a difficult job of control and police.[i]

The transport commander is one Lt. Col. Truscott. He seemed to be a bit under the weather last night. Didn't mind that, but I didn't like him to talk to the officers in that condition, which he proceeded to do with obvious difficulty.[ii]

The accompanying Navy ships have been test firing their guns for the past hour and it is very reassuring. Gen. Keerans told me this morning that the 505th Combat Team would be sent to Oujda (?), the headquarters of the Fifth Army, for training.[iii] Gen. Ridgway is to be there with Div. Hqrs., so we should get plenty of supervision. Miss N.

About 900 miles East of NY, May Day [1943]

All units seem to be getting under control. Another few days and we will be in good shape. Finally had to detail Col. Batcheller and Maj. Krause in charge of the replacement units EGB 385 and 497. The condition in which they arrived at the boat is rather unbelievable. Officers did not join units until just before boarding the train for the boat. No organization nor control, ordnance neglected, and the men not only very green but scared. They were obviously relieved and pleased when someone stepped up and told them what to do. Sixteen new second lieutenants and 500 recruits. 516 helpless waifs.[iv]

Chief Officer Davis and Purser Hutchins quite pleasant. I am enjoying their company. Hutchins told me that we were the best unit that they have had aboard since the Marines on the way to Guadalcanal. It took no time at all to point out that that was no compliment, that parachute troops are as good as Marines at anything any time.

The *George Washington* dropped back for awhile yesterday, luckily, she was able to regain her place in the convoy. The alternatives appeared to be to have her turn back to NY unescorted, which would have been very dangerous, or to transfer all of the troops and overload the other boats in the convoy, permitting her to go back to NY empty except crew. Since Gen. Ridgway is aboard the *GW* there is little

---

i   These were units composed of personnel who would be the replacement pool for casualties of many combat units. As such, there was no real chain of command or cohesion.

ii Alcohol consumption was allowed with officers receiving a liquor ration and the troops a beer ration. Overuse was a constant problem, especially with many of the pre-war service callups and within the National Guard units. Use or limitation was a matter for each commander to determine.

iii Oujda, Morocco, would be the base of the 82nd prior to Sicily.

iv Here, Gavin is describing elements not in the 82nd, but just placed on his ship. Batcheller and Krause were members of the 505th. Both would later command airborne battalions. Batcheller was a particular favorite of both Gavin and Ridgway and succeeded Gavin in the 505th only to be relieved in the UK for disciplinary reasons.

doubt but that the latter course would have been followed, as much as it would have overcrowded us.[i]

Gen. Keerans is giving me a free rein on running the troops aboard, which is the way I like it, either that or he actively command the troops. He told me today of the Division Staff becoming parachutists, probably drawing pay right now. I didn't miss the opportunity to ask that they please jump and be active parachutists if they are rated as such. It will rest poorly with the troops if they do not. This entire damn situation in the division must be straightened out. It would be fine if an entire unit were parachutists.[ii]

We swung cargo nets over the aft booms today for exercising. Should work well.

400 mi E of Casablanca, May 8, 1943

This time tomorrow we should be in sight of land. It has been a very uneventful voyage so far. The stretch of water that we are now crossing is known as "submarine alley," so we may yet see action on water.

The days have been occupied with inspections, training, boxing, shows, etc. A language class for all on board has been conducted over the public address system. War Dept.-issue records are played. At the same time troops follow the broadcast in texts. A good idea. Keeps them out of trouble. They don't learn much Arabic.

General K back to normal after a three or four day drunk. I dislike that in anyone. After recovering they invariably act tough and act as though everyone has been loafing during their lapse. I thought that he had given up those habits. I never want to serve in his division if he gets one. I may have to, but I hope that I can avoid it. With no one to whom he would be accountable it is probable that he would be drunk most of the time. Out of loyalty to him his next senior would really have a job. Even when he is sober his judgment is not entirely sound. I am tired of tolerating his drunkenness for days at a time and then defending my policies the remainder of the time.

I have that anxious feeling again. I want to get going. Tunis and Bizerte fell into our hands last night. It may mean that we will get into this in less than six weeks, which is what the plan originally called for.

The skipper of the boat says that these are the best troops he has ever carried. Very flattering and satisfying, but rather hard on the troops. They have really been harassed and have spent most of their time scrubbing, mopping, brushing, and policing in general. I suppose that it will all pay. This housekeeping is never to my

---

i   The *Washington* was a new battleship and it was used as both a troop transport and escort vessel.

ii   Here is a key comment identifying the lack of cohesion between the "leg" division headquarters and the Airborne 505th. The airborne elements from Gavin on down had little regard for the senior headquarters. This would change over time and be eliminated after Sicily, in no small part due to Ridgway's driving personality and the growing bond between him and Gavin.

liking, but it seems to be one of the things that we must do well. Field operations and combat are the objectives. It is so easy to lose sight of them, especially aboard ship. Everyone wants his particular interest emphasized.[i]

Just finished making a debarkation inspection of a company in an EGB (replacement) unit under Krause. Of 150 men, 15 had lost their leggings aboard ship, several had lost their helmets, and God knows how many have lost mess kits, knives, forks, tent poles, pins, etc. It is certain that a great deal is lost. There is a huge pile of unclaimed articles in one of the foyers.

Yet these men are to be combat replacements. From the day a man becomes a soldier he must learn the lesson of watching and caring for his property. It is a responsibility of command that is frequently, all too frequently, shirked.

On every occasion make the man pay out of his pocket for every item lost, officers also. That gets results. It may hurt in the training area, but it certainly adds up to combat efficiency.

Gen. K allowed as to how Gen. Ridgway probably will be promoted if the coming show goes over. I feel quite certain that I will also get an opportunity for advancement if I survive. I may not. I am going to keep the parachute tradition in mind. Chances will be taken, risks run, and everything ventured. If I survive, well and good. If I am killed, at least I have been true to myself, my convictions, and the Military Academy and all that it has taught me. At the moment I haven't the slightest fear. Jumping long ago removed all of that. All that I want is opportunity. I'll take the calculated risks with a minimum of calculation.[ii]

Capts. Ireland and Vandervort are doing a splendid job. They are excellent Div Staff material. Maj. Krause looks like an exceptional combat officer. Gorham will go far, but I believe Krause may pass him. Batcheller's future is limited. Gray is inexperienced and unambitious. Zaj will go along with me on supply matters. He knows it. The most promising young officer in the regiment is Capt. John Norton. He could handle a battalion very effectively right now. If he survives his first fight he is on the way to fame. The Academy will be proud of him. I have some splendid officers and the troops are tops. Not having sent anyone to OCS since last September, we have many men of excellent officer qualifications. I'll commission them as soon as I can.[iii]

---

i   Gavin here notes the difficulty in keeping the troops engaged and not losing their edge, a constant problem for a long crossing with no space to operate.

ii   This is a foundation piece in Gavin's ethos and beliefs—the airborne has a special capability and qualities that only they possess. He understood this intuitively, and in so doing laid the basis for today's airborne spirit and belief in themselves.

iii   Gavin is building his roster of top combat leaders. Ireland would be a key part of Ridgway's staff and Vandervoort and Krause would command within the 505th: Krause the 3-505 in Sicily and Vandervoort the 2-505 in Normandy. Norton would quickly be his "go to" guy, organizing the pathfinders and later as the S3 of the 505 and G3 of the division. He later retired as a lieutenant general. Zaj was the S4 responsible for logistics, especially difficult in an airborne unit.

10 mi N of Oujda, French Morocco, May 16, 1943

Landed at Casablanca May 10th, 3:15PM. Moved to staging area N of city and remained there three days. Troops moved by truck, rail, and short marches to Oujda. I flew in a C-47, arriving 4:15PM May 12th. Gen. Ridgway called myself and Col. Tucker up to orient us on our probable combat task. It has been directed by the GHQ, is to be known as "Husky," and is to be executed July 10th. It contemplates the seizure of Sicily. The 505th CT is to spearhead the amphibious landing of the 1st or 45th Divisions. Our jump is to take place in moonlight the night of July 9th, 11:30PM. The exact mission is yet an issue but should be settled shortly.

From an analysis of the probable missions, it is clear that the effort will be a very risky one and a costly one. It is nonetheless a typical parachute operation. The risks are great, but the rewards are greater. Many lives will be lost in a few hours, but in the long run many lives will be saved.

May 13th Col. Tucker was called to town and alerted on a plan involving CT 504 to seize Tangiers and Ceuta airdromes in the event Hitler marched into Spain. We are to be ready to follow on this plan.

A study of the G-2 information at the division war room in town indicates that there are 12,000 Luftwaffe troops on the island, plus about 35,000 Italian troops. It may be a mean and nasty fight. The softening up has started already. We have made one great and irretrievable mistake so far. We are all wearing our wings, boots, etc. Everyone here knows that we are parachutists. This will cost us lives.[i]

Our training is to start tonight and from now on will be conducted mostly at night. We have one hell of a lot of work and not enough time. Our present billets are exposed to German attack, but so far have been spared.

Yesterday I took the battalion COs down to the war room. This afternoon I am going to take the CO of the 456 Para Arty, Col. Hardin, down. The proposition of substituting mortars for artillery was broached by Gen. Ridgway. I dissented.

My engineer company, commanded by Capt. Gurfein (41), appears to be of very doubtful combat capabilities. I plan on taking them anyway for demolitions work, mine planting, and some wire.

Gliders will not participate at this calculation because of the transports being turned over to the British the first day after our drop. We are now trying to standardize our jumping technique with that of the British.[ii]

---

i   The Luftwaffe had several infantry and armor units independent of the Army. The existence of the Luftwaffe Hermann Goering Armored Division was not yet appreciated. This unit would be the greatest challenge for the 505th, especially at Biazza Ridge.

ii   The standardization issue, especially as it regarded formation flying, was a constant friction that persisted through Normandy. Both elements simply trained separately and argued over flight formations tactics. The British wanted a single file flight pattern where the U.S. opted for the V of Vs. Ultimately, both sides flew as they wished.

Oujda, May 21, 1943

There is in this area an Airborne Training Center which is in theory responsible for the airborne training of all such units nearby. In addition, the 82nd Division has, and appreciates that it has, a responsibility for its own training. Since Chuck Billingslea is in the ATC, I have been inclined to use his help. This is decidedly not au fait. Yet without his help it is next to impossible to get training going for lack of aids, personnel, materiel, etc.

Division very jealously watches its prerogatives, and well it might. In addition, since our, the 505th, rise to tactical operational prominence, it has been unusually critical of everything we do. The entire staff has been most difficult to get along with and seems to go out of its way to find things to criticize.

If I fought back as bitterly as I feel like doing, I would soon lose out, since they are in the driver's seat. Husky is still going ahead, and my position is still strong in top circles. I will make about any sacrifice to be permitted to take the 505th CT into this affair.

About all of the Div staff resents our participation. This slow displacement of the glider people by parachutists is just becoming obvious to them. Anything that could be done to discredit the parachute effort in favor of the glider effort at this time would not be overlooked. Their position is a difficult one in that, if this plan goes through, as it appears as though it will, then their only opportunity to claim credit will be in remotely fostering the participation of our unit in the show. Many are desirous of using the parachute effort as a ladder. They have been doing well. Now, however, it has become obvious that they are not parachutists.[i]

The division had a review for Lt. Gen. Clark on the 19th. Afterwards he had the entire staff and COs to his villa in town for tea, followed by dinner at the Terminus Hotel. He spoke very nicely and has not changed much in technique except to be more of a disciplinarian. It is obvious that he needs a good airborne staff officer.

Had a review for Lt. Gen. Spaatz yesterday, the 20th. Ordinary affair. Only significant in that we are losing very valuable training time.

Had a long talk with A-3 of the 52nd Wing, Majs. Crouch and Brown. The pressing training problem facing them is the insistent British and probиli[++] American pressure on them to fly us in single ship "formation." This is a big question and one that means a lot to us. All of our training will be thrown out.

---

i   This point is in regard to the friction between the non-jumping staff of the 82nd Division that became the 82nd Airborne Division. The staff did not understand airborne needs or support requirements and resented the newly assigned 504th and 505th PIRs. The inclusion of the 325 GIR did not go smoothly with the airborne who viewed them as inferior troops based upon performance. This would not change until airborne personalities went to Division HQ and the 325 performed well in Normandy.

These people have never seen transports flown in formation. No one around here has ever been able to do it. I argue that, even if I lose half of the transports through formation flying, at least the half that gets through will be together and land at the same place. The question is yet undecided. We will soon have to know. Our Air Corps property is due in starting today and soon we will be able to practice our jumpmastering.

It is annoying to encounter these officers who, because of the recent British successes in this theatre, must continually extol the merits of the British system, especially contrasted to ours. Even the British admit that, with even numbers and materiel, the Germans would not have been beaten. A year ago, it was the Germans who everyone wanted to emulate. Compared to the Germans our organization was wrong, our staff wrong, and fighting technique worse. Now it's the British. It is high time that the American system be given some credit. Our soldiers, especially our parachutists, are as good as any. If they lack anything it is effective leadership. No part of effective leadership consists of continuously harping on how much better the British system is than ours.[i]

Oujda, May 25, 1943

The largest part of the past few days has been spent in preparing plans for Husky. Gen. Ridgway had a conference Sunday night at which time each G [primary staff element chief] gave his estimate of the situation and I gave the 505th CT plan. I like the mission and am satisfied that we can do the job effectively that has been assigned to us. Our casualties are hard to predict. Many of us suspect that the Italians will fold up at the first blow, but that is too dangerous a supposition to let creep into our planning.

Yesterday I got a ride in a Cub [aircraft] with Maj. Farr to make a reconnaissance for an area for a rehearsal of Husky. It is difficult to find ground that approximates the layout in Kansas. We will have to take anything close, keeping in mind that the primary purpose of the jump is to test the combat loads.[ii]

Col. Eaton told me yesterday that, on their return from the staff conference of two nights ago, he and Gen. Ridgway agreed that after this coming show I am to be recommended for BG. I am very glad and will feel that in a way I have repaid some of my debt to the Military Academy. I want to do well because of what I learned

---

i   In later post-war discussion, Gavin often talked about the senior British generals having a very poor view of the U.S. military and its leadership. They were rarely interested in U.S. techniques, regardless of success. Gavin rightfully resented this.

ii By this he means the individual loads and airdropped supplies in Parapacks. The issue was that even a basic amount of ammunition and materiel grossly overloaded troops. He was constantly trying to find ways to lighten loads without unduly risking the men. This is a problem that persists today.

there and what it means to me. Gen. Lee told me months ago that I would be coming up for promotion very soon, so I have in fact been expecting some boost. I have worked hard for it, anyway.

This present "promise" I do not entirely trust. Gen. Ridgway is most ambitious. Eaton is not unambitious. The combination is dangerous to work under. They are inclined to keep personal interests foremost. At the moment Majs. Mulcahy, McKellum, and another are in serious CM difficulties at Casablanca and the Gen. refuses to touch it and has forbidden us to have anything to do with it. His attitude apparently is that by taking an interest he condones the crime. Since he is new in the theatre and still working at making a reputation, there is something to this attitude. Unfortunately, the reaction of the officers of the division is not too good, especially those parachute officers who have felt all along that the Div. CG and staff are not looking out for parachute officers.[i]

Talked to Gen. Browning of the British AB yesterday. Nice to see again. Seems to have lost some of his pep. We are having a struggle with him over the ultimate command of the combined allied AB effort. Gen. R[idgway], I understand, was adamant.[ii]

Found a place where an excellent bath with hot water could be obtained for 20 francs. Got one.

Miss reading, light to read by, music. The latter primarily.

Billingsly [Billingslea] and Ryder paid a visit yesterday. Both want to come with us on the big affair and I would like to have them. Ryder said that he was going back as soon as the show is over. I hope that I am permitted to, for a short time anyway. I rather like this field life. If I only had books and music to balance my diet, I would feel much better.

The troops are in fine fettle. I have never seen tougher troops. This damn atabrine is causing some casualties. They call it the GI shits.[iii]

---

i   This is another indication of the distance between the division staff and the parachute infantry regiments. Gavin felt that the staff was looking out for its own interests to the detriment of the troop line.

ii   General Browning was the "father" of British Airborne and always wished to place the U.S. Airborne under his command. He continuously mounted a back-door campaign to gain control and was only partially successful as the erstwhile Corps Commander for Operation *Market Garden*. Ridgway and Gavin fought for an independent U.S. Airborne force within the Airborne Army commanded by Lieutenant General Brereton. Both elements essentially fought as independent entities.

iii Atabrine was the primary preventative medicine for malaria, which was a major issue in Africa, causing significant troop loss. It had a common diarrhea effect and its administration required constant supervision to ensure consumption.

Oujda, May 25, [1943]

A year has made a lot of difference. At this very moment I question my suitability to continue to command a regiment efficiently unless I change my manner and attitude. I am testy and a crank. It seems that most people in this army are putting in time, following a schedule of calls with frequent periods of rest and indifference. There is never time enough to get everything done, and there are few people who are working hard continuously. One thing after another comes to my attention that requires immediate correction and few seem interested in doing anything about it.

In this division Gen. R wants certain things. Gen. Keerans comes around and wants something else. Gen. Taylor calls and wants something else. Each thinks his requirements the most pressing. The Div staff is spotty when it comes to application. Occasionally they are on the ball, but frequently we are left holding the bag. Perhaps more than anything else I need a few minutes rest or change. Too much pressure and no opportunity to let off steam. I must be getting very difficult to work with.

Yesterday I accompanied some of the Div staff to Oran and Mostaganem in connection with air support for our coming show. Conferred with Col. Hickey, ASO of the I Armd Corps. There is not a great deal that can be done just now except make tentative plans.

The routine bombing of Sicily is underway, with the more thorough bombing of Pantalleria getting immediate attention.[i] The AS plan calls for all ships to be under immediate control of Task Hqrs, with little or no opportunity for calls for close support by the unit COs. This is evidently necessitated by the distance of the bases and the little time that aircraft will have available to spend over the objective area. Until we get bases it will be impossible to have air alert ships over the area.

Prior to our drop the entire area will get a thorough going-over. We asked for an alley to be blasted through the coastal AA defense installations and for fighters to accompany us to knock out searchlights. The latter did not seem entirely feasible to them, although they stated that it was one of the things taught in our service schools.

Tomorrow I hope to go up to the II Corps and the 1st Div[ision] for more direct, and what I am sure will be more beneficial, contact. Operations at the I Corp [sic] do not seem to have any of the "pushover" idea that is somewhat prevalent here. I am very glad. I learned that the II Corps, commanded by Gen. Bradley, is to be under the I Armd Corps commanded by Gen. Patton. This is rather unusual. Spoke to Patton. I would estimate that his corps is to be made an army, probably the Seventh.[ii]

The raison d'etre of the Fifth Army is not entirely clear. It is not like Gen. Clark to sit and let things go by. It may be that he is pinning his aspirations on the

---

i   Pantelleria was an island adjacent to Sicily with an Italian garrison and viewed as a significant threat. It was secured by a British commando squadron.

ii   This is exactly what happened.

worthwhile-ness of the airborne effort. He has set up an airborne training center. Patton appears to have the training and use of ground and armored troops sewed up.[i]

Oujda, May 29, 1943

Time flies. May 27th, I accompanied Gen. Ridgway, G3, and some other staff officers of the Div to Relizane to the Hqrs of the II Corps. It was most interesting, since the corps had just finished a tough fight up in Tunisia. Gen. Bradley commands the corps. He was as nice as ever and as unimpressive in appearance as ever.

Bill Keen is a BG and his chief of staff. Of his capabilities I am not aware. He is a politician, appears to turn his charm on and off, and can appear tough when necessary. We talked [about] the Sicilian operation. The 505th CT will be definitely detached from the Div and attached to the Corps. They will then in turn attach it to the 1st Div.[ii]

Late in the afternoon Gens. Terry Allen, Ted Roosevelt, and Andrews of the 1st Div came to the CP for a conference. Terry Allen is a tough-looking soldier, makes a damn good impression, and no doubt is just as good as he looks. Tops as a troop leader. He seemed to remain aloof from most of the conference, leaving the talking and details to Roosevelt. Roosevelt took right over, a bit nervous in manner at times, but entirely in control of the situation. They must have a fine division. Their talk and planning went along just like a maneuver. There was no doubt that the Division would accomplish everything, and in the exact manner they were planning.[iii]

The present plan contemplates having the entire Division land east of the Gela River with 16th Inf[antry] on the right, 26th Inf on the left. The 16th Inf is the outfit that will work with us. The town of Gela is to be tackled by a ranger battalion and two engineer battalions.

In the discussion of the technique to be employed in reducing the town Gen. Bradley outlined the SOP for handling snipers. All gave it the nod. In case of a sniper, everyone nearby is to be shot immediately and the building blown up.

They were very considerate of our probable lines of action, supply requirements, etc. We will work under them like any other regiment. They appear to expect a great deal of us and take for granted that we will turn in a good fight. I am sure

---

i   General Clark was very mindful of General Marshall's penchant for airborne forces and their use in the war. Clark saw Sicily as an opportunity to demonstrate his support for the concept.

ii   This was an issue for General Ridgway, who essentially had no job upon landing. Ultimately, he disregarded the command relationships and assumed command when he finally linked up with Gavin.

iii   The 1st Infantry Division had made its reputation in Operation *Torch* when it demonstrated it was one of the few competently led U.S. divisions. Allen and Roosevelt had a very loose style about themselves that bothered Bradley who preferred more traditional general officer leadership. Gavin quickly recognized their combat leadership qualities which were aligned with his own views.

that we will too, but there certainly must be reason for conjecture about exactly what will happen to us.

Yesterday I spent a great deal of time with the 52nd Wing.[i] It does not look as good as it appeared at a distance. Col. Clark is somewhat of a figurehead, with A-3 Maj. Crouch and his assistant Maj. Brown providing most of the decisions and command. The outlying groups are not pointing their training at what we will require and there is reason to believe that some of the CT will miss their DZs by a great deal.

In conference at the II Corps CP, we agreed on the formation to be flown, elements of three echeloned to the right rear, a formation consisting of nine ships. 1-1/2 minutes between formations. This will allow about ten minutes per reinforced battalion. There is to be a five-minute distance between battalions. The two third battalions are to jump at H-Hour.

The systematic bombing of the island continues daily. The lack of liaison between the air and ground elements is amazing. Endeavoring to establish air support channels for our operation is like the pursuit of the snark. The big picture people at the top are using, and no doubt planning on continuing to use, all aircraft under centralized control. The most simple request for air support must go all of the way to the top. There is no doubt about the strategic efficiency of such a scheme, but the tactical efficacy of it is zero. The little guy getting shot at gets nothing and can do nothing about it.[ii]

Gen. Andrew[s?] said that, if they would just quit bombing his own troops, he would not expect nor ask for anything else. Sad commentary.

Last night Gen. R had a party for Gen. Clark and staff. We are to put on a show for Gen. Nogues?, Gov. Gen. of Spanish Morocco, on June 3rd. I pointed out the lack of coordination between the various elements and consequently was made coordinator of the entire air show. I will never learn. The object is to impress Nogues as one political step in the direction of lining up Spain on our side. We will do all that we can. Gorham's battalion is going to jump it. He can do the job. Getting the cooperation and support of the different air elements will be a task.[iii]

---

i This was the C-47 troop transport element that would jump the troops. They supported the 505th PIR throughout the war due to their navigational skills as much as their commander's appreciation of the 82nd as a unit.

ii This was a period where there was no ground–air link with the deployed forces. This was eventually corrected when radio jeeps and ground control officers deployed to front lines and could call direct air support. In this case, Gavin is noting the growing pains of the Army Air Force as new elements arrive in theater.

iii Nogues was an ex-Vichy general who went over to the Allies. His support was crucial to ensure the U.S. rear area was undisturbed and in a position to block any potential Spanish-German incursion.

Oujda, June 1, 1943

Another month and it is to be a busy one. Saturday evening attended a party given by the officers of the 2nd Bn. They had about 15 nurses from the 95th Evac. present. It was a nice affair and an excellent affair. After officers sit around and glare at each other as long as we have, anything of this sort helps a lot. The chief nurse, one Miss Sigman of NY, and I exchanged assurances to each other that our broods would behave. Coy. [On this page of the manuscript the name Miss Sigman is circled, and, at the top of the page, there is written in pencil "later killed in Anzio."]

Yesterday had an interesting conference with Gen. Williams, CG of the African troop carrier command, regarding Husky-Bigot. Quoting Gen. Spaatz, he stated that no transport formations of greater than three ships were to be flown in the operation. We, of course, had already made complete plans with the 52nd Wing to fly nine-ship formations.

The conference went into several hours. Its background goes way back. The wing that is here now, and that has been the only one here during the past six months, and the only one with which the British have worked, is the 51st. They never have been capable of flying a nine-ship transport formation, even in daylight. Their fiasco with the 509th in the invasion operation was a fizzle. Everyone here is convinced that transports must be flown singly, each one a separate navigation problem. The results on the dropping end have never been short of disastrous, with patterns extending for miles. On the other hand, we have flown compact well-controlled formations for months and think that we can continue doing it despite hostile interference. It was finally agreed to let us try it in this show.

We go over in columns of threes, but close up into nine-ship flights at the DZs. There are many skeptics outside of the 505 and the 52nd Wing. If it doesn't work, there will be many I told you sos. If it does, we are all smarties. Sometimes on these unknowns we are right, but not always. The best we can hope for is to have a good percentage. No one is perfect, and anyone who insists on being perfect does nothing so that he will not make any mistakes.

On the matter of dropping with the crew-served weapons in bundles or on individuals, we have insisted on bundles and finally all of the people in this theatre have confirmed our ideas.[i]

I read an interesting definition of air-ground support. It is like marriage in that there must be complete cooperation. However, in one respect it differs from marriage. There is no moral, ethical nor legal reason why there should not be practice beforehand. As a matter of fact, there must be practice ad nauseum.

---

i   This refers to the nine Parapack containers carried under the C47. They carried the mortars and machine guns as well as additional ammunition, signal, medical, and food supplies. This system was developed by Gavin in Africa and used throughout the war.

Learned yesterday of the movement date forward to the take-off airdrome. We are to be terribly pushed for time. In all of this hurly burly and mad rush there is one thing that fortunately stands out as a blessing and a source of satisfaction. That is the anxiety of these people to get into a fight. They will, I haven't the slightest doubt, fight their heads off. They are going to be very tough for any enemy to handle. They are very anxious.

Bayonets have been sharpened. In their night work, which is daily, they habitually use Italian linguists and some German. Several people have been accidentally shot, but realism has been actually ever present in training.[i]

I told all battalion commanders last night that their priorities were as follows: 1st get every unit tactically intact on its DZ (time is not too important), 2nd get every unit tactically intact on Sicily, 3rd get every man on Sicily.

There will be no refusals. Dead or alive, every man will jump. There will be no ships returned unjumped. If no other choice is left, I expect them to jump on Sicily and fight to the last man and last round of ammunition. It will not come to priority three except perhaps in an isolated case or so. Some ships are sure to get lost, but no matter where they are they must and will fight.[ii]

I wish D-Day was not so far away. I like this stuff. All refusals either get a Purple Heart or a decent burial.

Had a malfunction Sunday morning in a free fall. Some fun.

Oujda, June 6, 1943

This goddam stuff is getting serious. The glamour seems to be fleeting out the window. Spent most of today with the 1st Div CG and staff. He issued his order for the attack. An enemy development in our sector changes our picture somewhat. The bastards are digging in a strongpoint between the present DZs of the 3rd Bn and the Regt(-). The problem arises whether to attack the strongpoint at night or continue on our present mission. I am inclined to continue on our present arrangement. There may be some tentative way to plan to attack the sp [strongpoint] sometime after reorganizing, say 4:00AM.

This is getting tougher. Talked to Bill Yarborough today. He asked me if I expected to get back to the States from this alive. Told him I didn't. I shouldn't do that. Optimism is a characteristic of any commander worth a damn. Still the picture looks

---

i   Gavin is describing the tough live-fire training he insisted upon as part of the train up. He understood that night operations and confidence in them was crucial to success.

ii   This is the concept of the LGOPs—Little Groups of Paratroops—a standard concept today. Regardless of where a troop is dropped, he begins his job of pursuing the war wherever he finds the enemy. This was especially effective in Normandy.

bad. As a matter of fact, I actually expect to live through it, probably—and very likely—wounded but not killed. I will have to be completely killed to be stopped.[i]

In many ways the show is going to be fun. In others it is going to be son of a bitch. Gen. Allen informed me today that he wants my regiment to be ready to move north in the attack in conjunction with the other regts of his division on D-Day. He is optimistic. I like the idea, however.

Gen. Patton talked to all of the officers the other day. Among other things he told them that "no son of a bitch ever won a battle by dying for his country, he won it by making those other sons of bitches die for their country."

Just this minute received orders for the June 11th reconnaissance over the DZs in Sicily. All parachute identifications are to be removed, etc. It should be OK.

Our operational planning is moving along OK. I feel that I am not getting the help from division that I should get. They do not understand our problems, however they do try to help, and I believe make every conscientious effort to be of assistance. It never ceases to amaze me how easy-going these higher headquarters are.

Had a prop blast Friday eve. About 30 of the nurses from the 95th Evac and the 52nd General were in attendance. It was a good thing and I believe that all of the officers enjoyed it. It left me convinced that my feelings are genuine.

We are in for one hell of a fight. I love the prospects but feel as scared as I did on my first jump. It is going to be exciting.

Oujda, June 9, 1943

Having our first night jumps of bundles, jumpmasters, etc. with units on DZs. During the past four days we have had two battalion jumps and one of Hqrs. Co. One battalion picked up 23 hospital cases, the other 53 cases, and Hqrs. Co. six cases and one fatality. With such losses the idea seems to be to jump as little as necessary and yet accomplish our training objectives in the coming weeks.[ii] Now would be no time to lose key technicians. I was loaded and all set to take off on the Hqrs. jump when the control tower called and said that Gen. Ridgway ordered me not to jump.

---

i   Major Yarborough was one of the original officers of the airborne cadre at Fort Benning. He designed the jump suit, the jump wings, the unit backgrounds to the jump wings, and was instrumental in getting the Corcoran jump boot. He was mis-dropped in the initial Operation *Torch* airborne assault and later transferred to the 504th PIR where Ridgway relieved him in Sicily for an incident that both regretted. Yarborough later commanded the 509th in Operation *Dragoon* in the South of France. He convinced President Kennedy that special forces should have a distinctive green beret and be better resourced for the developing war in Asia. He retired as a lieutenant general.

ii The issue of jump injuries in training was a constant challenge throughout the war. There was not a strong stream of qualified replacements, especially NCOs and with technical skills. Losses were not filled in many instances. Hence, jumps were minimized and truck insertions usually used.

Last night we were scheduled to jump the bundles, J/Ms, of Hqrs. but the ships could not get away from Guercif because of weather. All personnel walked out to the DZ combat loaded, complete with grenades and ammunition. It was a good idea. That is quite a load to carry, and everyone should find out about it as soon as possible. If I had it to do again, I would start doing this when the unit is activated.

We had an unusual thing happen yesterday. Four J/Ms jumped ten miles south of the DZ, away down in the hills below Oujda, because the leading J/M was color blind and jumped when the red light went on. Lack of color blindness should be a prerequisite to being a Parachute NCO.

We have been having trouble with night assembly. Lots of talk and not much accomplishment. The present practice of using bundle lights helps but is not the entire answer. Last night we had some luminous buttons out. They looked very good. We are also experimenting with metallic crickets. They seem very good. We are anxious to get luminous paint to mark bundles, and also luminous cloth of different colors to make streamers for bundles out of. This could also be used as armbands, etc. We had, and lost, about 20 rolls of luminous tape. It would have been very valuable, especially for aiming stakes, minefields, gaps in wire, CPs, etc. We have a long way to go on this type of training. If I have it to do again, I will do much more night training of the type that will do some good in combat. We did have a lot, but not enough of the right type.[i]

Just received word from CS that I am to leave tomorrow on a reconnaissance of our DZs in Sicily. We are to go to Malta and there take off with a low-level bomber attack on the 11th. I am looking forward to it. Appears now as though I will get to take along all Bn COs.

Oujda, June 13, 1943

Took off at 9:30 June 10th. Cols. Mitchell and Roberts of 52nd Wing, Majs. Kouns and Krause of the 82nd Div in the party. This included about all of the people who would benefit most from this reconnaissance. There were others, but other duties precluded their attendance. Particularly A-3 of the wing should have made the trip.

We arrived at Tunis about noon. A great deal of wreckage of German planes, especially Junker-52s, about. Our orders were to go to Hqrs. NAAF at Carthage, which we proceeded to do. They never heard of us. Our mission was of such an

---

i   This is the precursor to the development of pathfinders. No one knew how poor aircraft accuracy would be. Concurrently, recognition of units on the ground as well as the critical supply bundles would be continuous issues, especially at night. Today, with virtually 100 percent of jumpers having night vision aids, it is no longer an issue.

extremely secret nature that we could not explain to anyone just what in the hell we were doing, where we were going, or what we were trying to accomplish. Everyone looked upon us as dangerous characters.

We finally got a tip that sent us to Sousse, landing at Monastir airdrome at 4:00PM. After much palavering we chiseled a ride to Hqrs. at Sousse, arriving at 7:30PM. The British proved very difficult to converse with and more difficult to accomplish any business with. After a great deal of wandering about and guessing we contacted Col. Bagby of the TCC. This was about 10:00PM. At about 10:05 we were hit with an air raid of nice proportions, thus breaking a record of years' standing of never having heard a hostile shot.

The Eighth Army was all around Sousse and was exceptionally trim looking. They are splendid-looking soldiers—tough, tanned, clean, haircut, etc. I would be the last to say this of the British troops, but they are at this writing the best-looking troops that I have ever had the pleasure of seeing. With combat experience ours will look just as good or better.

The British attitude was very interesting and amusing. Compared to us they are like professionals and amateurs. We are sweating, tense, trying hard at everything we attempt. They are relaxed, appearing indifferent at times, no pressure, and everything seems to be getting done in tip-top shape.

On the way down to Sousse we passed over the final German positions on Cape Bon and the Mareth Line. Also took a good look at the Coliseum at El Djem. I would like to see it on the ground someday.

We slept in our ship at Monastir the night of the 10th and took off for an airdrome 20 miles south of Tripoli early the 11th. Here we got clearance and briefing for Malta. Tripoli is a fine place to stay out of. Very hot and dusty. My first view of a real desert. Nothing but scorching sand and occasional clumps of date palms. We are all glad that we are not going to fight down there.

The route to Malta was very precisely defined, going to a town about 60 miles east of Tripoli at 2000 and then turning directly to Malta. We arrived at Luqa, Malta at about 4:00. Went to see Air Comdr Trail, A-3, NAAF. No dice. Later developments indicated that he was at sea with Gen. Eisenhower and staff in the operation against Pantelleria. Pantelleria fell this date at 11:13AM.

Finally made arrangements to fly into our DZs the night of the 10th at 10:30PM, 600ft. Flew in one of the new mosquito bombers as navigator. Found DZs with no trouble shortly after leaving Malta. Flew over Lake Biviere, thence north, passing west of Niscemi. Around Niscemi and then south out over check point, the lake. Four searchlights tried to pick us up but fortunately missed. We were not fired on. Two of the Bn COs inadvertently flew over Ponte Olivo at 300 feet and had six guns working on them. No one hit.

We are all pleased with the results of our reconnaissance. The RAF strongly recommends against a repetition of this sort of thing in the interests of secrecy.

The DZs are OK, and we will hit them. We are going to do a good job. Flew directly back from Malta.

Oujda, June 18, 1943

A routine stretch. Pulled a problem, as the boys say. The ACTO operation, which was the dress rehearsal for the Husky-Bigot. The DZs were picked to give the pilots a problem similar to the actual show. This left the ground problem somewhat artificial, which is just what it was. The flying, considering everything, was not bad, but should have been much better. There were a few wild misses altogether. Continued practice with the 504, which follows us through the same problem, should go far to making the pilots do a better job.

The artillery did particularly well. The Second Battalion, commanded by Maj. Gray, did very poorly. Sooner or later, I will have to relieve him of his command. I would do it now if it were not for the imminence of combat. Maj. Krause is doing splendidly with his Bn. Norton, commanding H Co., is tops.

The fifteenth I went up to the 1st Div with Gen. Ridgway for their final order. Gen. Roosevelt present as acting CG. Looks like he will command that div, probably after this coming show. If those Italians are kind this show will bring many opportunities and promotions. We went over their plan with all of the staff and COs. Pretty well set except for minor points requiring coordination. Most interesting to attend such a conference with soldiers of such proven ability. I liked it very much. Everyone knew what they were talking about. They all respected each other's opinions and, although there were some differences of opinion, there were no arguments. They are all sure of themselves and each other. It is a pleasure to work with them.[i]

Sunday they are sending down a group of company commanders to see us work and to observe our uniforms and equipment. Some of their combat ideas, although unusual, seem good. For example, one battalion is going to have every man wear a burlap sack over their heads to blur the outline of the helmet and to dull the edge that is normally shiny from digging.[ii]

At this meeting it was decided to have the 505 jump groups that would seize and prepare for demolition the bridges over the Acate River. The present plan contemplates our jumping the first Bn at 2330B (Tunis) time. The 1st Div hits the surf at 2:45 same time. A bit longer than either of us planned, but it should work. It gives us the requisite hour of moonlight. Talking to Crouch today, we decided the entire drop could be completed in 36 minutes.

---

i   The 1st Division was a combat proven entity of the highest quality. Bradley and Patton both recognized this. However, Allen and Roosevelt were very hard to work with and kept the division aloof from everyone else. Ultimately, it led to the relief of both after Sicily.

ii This was a trick picked up from the British Airborne which had universal camouflaged helmets.

About a day ago the air support party reported for jump training, one officer and five enlisted men. Today two Navy ensigns reported for jump training in order to accompany us as naval gunnery liaison officers.[i]

This is getting to be an extremely interesting show. I love it. My command is increasing in size daily, the plan is getting closer to earth, and I am having lots of fun. Fortunately, my service as a line officer, and particularly as a plans and training officer, has fitted me well for what is here. I actually enjoy preparing and issuing orders and plans.[ii]

The troops are doing fine. Having withstood the rigor of the GIs [intestinal disorder], we are ready for anything. The African [service] ribbon, the saying goes, was awarded for the GIs. That is where the brown ends come in. It has been amusing to see these boys with the GIs. To travel 100 yards, removing a pair of coveralls en route, has come to be the measure of military attainment. Lacking the requisite skill and versatility becomes evident when one of the afflicted comes from a gallop to a dead stop, exuding strong unpleasant odors. It does happen. After one night of the stuff, I gave up atabrine. This is supposed to make me particularly vulnerable to malaria. Of the two, I would take malaria.[iii]

The 82nd continues to make plans for their participation in the coming show. I do not see how they are going to get into it. I would like to see the entire Div do well.[iv]

Learned from Gorham that Higgins' promotion was turned down. Haugen and Walsh got theirs. I will feel unhappy if I am passed over in this airborne effort. If they will wait for me I will prove in combat what I have already proven in garrison, that I can command.

Oujda, June 22, 1943

Days are fleeting and, in some ways, our big day is slipping up on us closely. This morning I bid goodbye to Col. Eaton, Chief of Staff, with a promise that we would

---

i   The 82nd set up an ad hoc jump school to familiarize attachments as well as non-airborne qualified division personnel. This was much shorter than the formal Fort Benning program and often just involved rigging the parachute, practicing falls, and making a jump.

ii This needs to be viewed within the conditions of the time. The vast expansion of the Army meant many officers and NCOs had no experience in writing plans or developing them. Gavin had a long history of it and was able to cover the staffing deficits.

iii Dysentery and malaria would plague the Army throughout the Mediterranean campaign. Field sanitation was rudimentary and malaria prevention with Atabrine was marginal. All the Africa veterans spoke of the horrible fly problem which brought dysentery. Items as simple as mosquito netting were largely unavailable. It was estimated that as much as 20 percent of the 82nd had malaria in various stages.

iv This highlights the existing distance between the Division HQ and its subordinate elements. Only time and combat as well as the personalities of Ridgway and Gavin would change that.

turn in a good fight, and I would see him on the beach. He and most of the Div staff are to ride the command ship. Gen. Taylor will remain in control at Kairouan.

Our movement to the forward areas has started with the movement of the advance parties. Trains and trucks move the 28th, and the troops move by plane the 1st and 2nd. There is little time to waste. These movements are time-consuming and take just about all training time.

I approved taking Cols. Ryder and Billingsly [Billingslea] with me as observers. I now understand that Gen. Clark has disapproved Billingsly's [sic] going. Ironic the 1st [sentence not completed].

This is getting to be a more unpredictable affair with every analysis. Air Gen. Student turned out a very excellent analysis of our probable use in Rome on June 10th. By some manner or means the British gave us a copy on the 20th. He is very sharp. I wish that many of our staff officers had his insight and appreciation of the capabilities of parachute troops. He has it all figured out. If the Italians pay strict attention to his study, it will be impossible for us to surprise them.[i] [Written in ink in the margin of this page in longhand: "This was a hoax perpetrated by Browning."]

I am not at all satisfied with our state of training. I do not suppose any commander ever is. I wish that I had it to do over again. My next outfit is going to be better trained. These men will fight well individually and in many cases as teams. I am not at all sure of our capabilities as a larger unit.

We have heard so little from higher headquarters. So many of the points that should be coordinated are left to me with little help from above. The 82nd figures I am fighting my fight OK and the 1st Div. figures that the 82nd is taking care of all of my needs. We are doing the best that we can. I am not getting excited and running around yelling about lack of cooperation or being sent to our certain deaths, but we lack a great deal that we would have if we were in a division fight.

I am determined that we will do well, and we will, but it is going to be a tussle. I am changing Norton to the 2nd Bn. Krause feels none too good about it. Gray was AWOL for a day or so early in the week. More bad judgment than AWOL. I should have replaced him in the States. That is one thing that I would most certainly do if I had it to do again, replace all poor officers without regard for their feelings in the matter or their probable ability to learn as they go along. That is the fatal viewpoint: "Oh, he works hard and means well and with just a bit more service he will be the best company commander in the regt." He never is or he would have been in the first place.

Gen. Student mentions tanks in Sicily. I have more respect for them than any other Italian weapon. They could create havoc with us if they catch us early enough.

Music, books, and a woman. Even shop saturates one after awhile.

---

i   Student was the father of German Airborne and led them at Eban Emael and Crete. Gavin read
     everything he wrote as a source of airborne lessons hard learned.

Improvised a simple panel code today. Obtained cork to blacken the faces. Metallic crickets and invasion armbands are on the way. Division ordered us to wear division insignia. We plan on covering it up with an OD patch. Issued new type M3 trench knives.

Sent 36 men to the 1st Div for familiarization purposes. Sending 16 to the 45th Div. Thursday for the same purpose.

The similarity between our uniforms and the Italian and German uniform will surely cost us lives.

A 1st Div Ln officer reported for jump training today. That makes one more, of which there are two Navy officers and one Air Corps officer.

If I have not done my job with this regiment before this it is little late now. There is nothing to get excited about, and what has been planned and prepared is done. The best we can be expected to do is to make the best of things as we find them. Nothing can be gained by excitement and swearing. We will or will not succeed or live, and who gives a damn which, except for success.

Oujda, June 26, 1943

Today, the 26th, all personal effects for the rear echelon are to be packed and stowed away. Tomorrow and the 28th trains leave for Kairouan, arriving about the 3rd. They will take forward all extra baggage over and above combat requirements. This includes extra Air Corps equipment required for maintenance. On July 1st and 2nd the combat echelon moves forward, arriving Kairouan the same day.

We are having combat load inspections right now. It is surprising at this late moment how many men are short items of combat equipment—helmets, dog tags, entrenching tools. If I had it to do again, I would certainly require every officer and enlisted man to pay for every lost item in the first weeks of their training until I was certain that they were watching the property as though it were their very own. ARs notwithstanding. We have been too generous in giving out property. Now, on the eve of combat, we find that some officers and men cannot hold on to even the most essential piece of combat equipment.

Last night our luminous tape and cloth came in, just under the wire. We will need it. We are still missing ammunition bags M2 and a few small items.[i]

This last-minute filling out of unit's equipment is caused basically by the above. Zaj is splendid as an S-4. Having combat load inspections early in their training would tend to eliminate much of this last-minute rush also. It should be done.

The Bn COs are going ahead with their planning. Gorham at this writing appears to be the most steady. Krause will no doubt get results. At this point he is so wrapped up in getting results, despite any orders or anyone, that he is somewhat of

i   An automatic carbine with folding stocks for airborne troops.

a problem. His type is frequently uncooperative. He is endowed with high initiative and intense ambition. He is difficult for other unit commanders to get along with. The payoff matters little so long as he accomplishes his battle mission, but at the moment he is troublesome.[i]

We are taking a total of 2,200 Hawkins mines now, 300 per Bn and 1,000 for the Engineer Company.[ii] This promises to be an interesting fight. I would like to survive, although that is not the most important thing. Charlie told me at breakfast that there are to be two new Divs formed in July and August. I would like to start out training one of them. I was thinking of that last night. Perhaps I would prefer to stay with the 82nd. It is a good division and after its first fight it will be hard to beat.

Since all my personal effects are to be packed today, I am going to seal this and put it away. I do not expect to see it again until after the fight. I wish I had it to do over again. Even this past week we have been complacent. I will not be with my next outfit.

[A handwritten inscription on the bottom of this page]: Our Air Corps supply has been worked to death turning out the following—4000 M1 ammo pockets for pistol belt. 200-star identification panels. Geneva [?] brassards. 50-505 [sic] medical kits. Carrying harness for Altus lamps. Carrying harness for MG ammo boxes. Padding for 511s. White panels, [++], large.[iii]

Oujda, June 30, 1943

This is my last day here. Tomorrow, starting at 5:30AM, the CT starts moving to the Kairouan area. These past few days have been full. Conducted an inspection daily of each battalion with its combat loads, individual and unit. Generally, they were satisfactory except for Kouns. I am not so sure of him. He has had his own way with Tucker too long. Now, when he is told to prepare a type load, he does something else that he thinks is better.[iv]

We received luminous tape and cloth, both of which look very good for our purpose. Gorham is having every man wear a piece of tape around the wrist, covered by the cuff of the jump suit. In the attack at night, they are going to roll up their

---

i   Krause was highly energetic and emotional at virtually all times, hence the troop nick name for him "Cannonball." Gavin had a mixed view of him after Sicily, but he commanded the battalion through Normandy and was re-assigned as Executive Officer of the 505th PIR for Operation *Market Garden* and the Battle of the Bulge.

ii This is an anti-tank mine with a tilt rod fuse. A troop would jump one as part of his combat load.

iii These were canvas items manufactured on an ad hoc basis in lieu of unavailable manufactured products.

iv Then Major Kouns commanded 3-504th for Colonel Tucker.

sleeves. We also received some blinking lights. They look fine for many uses but are too visible for us.

Sunday night I went up to the beach at Port Say. This seems to be the thing to do here. Somewhat of a disappointment. Certainly, made me miss N.

All set to take two observers with me, Billingslea and Ryder. Gen. Clarke turned Billingslea down, so it does not look as though he will go. I understand a Jack Thompson, columnist of the *Chicago Tribune*, wants to come along. OK if he will jump.[i]

The CT staff is just about complete with two Naval ensigns to adjust gun fire, two interrogators from Div, and one from the 1st Div.

I am glad to leave this place. It is getting very hot and dusty. We are having some of our usual troubles. Yesterday several parachutists beat up a couple of French officers because they objected to accosting one of their wives. It is quite serious and could become an international incident. I talked to all of the NCOs and Officers last night. The NCOs were more interesting. They are set. I expect a lot of them, and I am sure they will come through. They are, I believe, just about right, not too confident, yet sure of their individual and collective ability. They know, and I know, that we are going to have casualties, but we are both resolved to take them in order to do our job.[ii]

I wind up this year's training convinced of the merits of tests. Competitions bring out the best in a unit and an individual. Mortar tests are very important. Sniper tests also. Be ruthless in weeding out misfit "leaders," commissioned and enlisted. Be realistic and practical in night training. Property responsibility must be cultivated. Use the chain of command. I am requiring all officers to carry escape kits, hidden files, and compasses. There will be no air resupply.[iii]

Last night I picked up some kind of a throat and nose infection. Do not feel too good today. I will have to be about dead and be carried to the dispensary to fall out now. This is all a wonderful experience.

Bivouac 20 mi N Kairouan, 10 mi S Enfidaville, July 6, 1943

Time is flying. Closed in here without incident. Quite an understatement. The move was accomplished by train, truck and air transport. The Bns are scattered over an area 40 miles across. We all realize now that it would have been much more convenient

---

i   This is Beaver Thompson of the *Chicago Tribune*. He and Gavin became fast friends and Thompson's articles greatly increased Gavin's exposure to the public.

ii Throughout his career, Gavin emphasized the necessity of the NCO corps as essential for combat success, a truism that exists today.

iii These are classic points in how to make a high-performing unit and are part of basic Infantry training programs.

and efficient to have bivouacked all troops of the CT together, then move them to the takeoff airdromes in time for the move.

Two days ago, I went up to Algiers to a final conference with the 1st Div. Algiers is quite a town. Accompanied by Jack Thompson of the *Chicago Tribune*.

Made all final arrangements. This should work, provided we hit our beaches and they hit their DZs, or vice versa. The 82nd appears to be working into the picture more and more. They very likely will get into the show, a bit late perhaps, but nevertheless in.[i]

This is quite a place. A lot of the debris of the recent fracas still about. The loneliest sight in the world is to come across a lone grave in the desert marked only with a simple wooden cross and a rusty helmet. Most of the bodies are assembled by now in larger plots. A soldier suggested yesterday that that would be a good job for the strikers back in the States. It appears as though a lot of fighting was done around here. Many mines and booby traps still about.

Ryder and Billingslea arrived yesterday. Glad to have them. Final conference with all Bn COs yesterday. I have a feeling that the troops are not in the condition that they should be in. Bn COs do not push enough. If I had it etc., would supervise more closely the training of the Bn COs, especially in these last few weeks. They are inclined to take things too easy.

July in Sicily is going to be hotter than hell. Our work following being relieved by the 16th Inf is going to be difficult, both as a march and as a fight. Altus lights are being jumped on individuals in the lead of each flight, different colors for each Bn. They are to be used later to bring in the 504 and 325.[ii]

This plan of being under the 1st Div and 82nd Div is not going to be too good. Let's hope the thing works out OK. The rations have been very poor. Believe that everyone is losing weight. Morale is high. Found a man in the 2nd Bn yesterday with a rifle across his knees and a Bible in his hands, intent to commit suicide. Said he was going to be killed anyway. So it goes.

A conference with all unit COs of the command serial this AM. Del units and chutes to field at 8:00AM D-1. PM troops bathe and clean up. Troops at field at 1900. Take off 2121. Formation leave field 2141. Kuriat Islands 2200, etc. How does CO feel at this time? Butterflies? Yes. I know something is going to happen. It is a bit like the hunter trials and athletic competitions of my younger days. That is why those things are good for a youngster. You learn to experience and cope with this "impending fight" feeling. If I am ever to appear confident, calm and deliberate, now is the time. Every ship is to jump, even if on a second pass. There

---

i   Note the studied displacement he holds between himself and the division.

ii   These are Aldis lamps with colored filters. They would be used to identify the DZ for follow-on flights. All were a precursor to the pathfinder teams.

will be no refusals. It is going to be some affair. I will be ready to retire to a life of quiet and peace.

Same base, farther from Kairouan, July 7, 1943

Two days to go. Yesterday was organization day. Officers Club bought ten young bulls and several sheep to be barbecued for the troops. Also 4,000 litres of beer. The beer was great, although not quite enough. The beef was particularly welcome. Most of us are having trouble with receding gums from a continued canned soft food diet.[i]

In the Regt CP area we had Col. Clark, Col. McCawley, etc. in for some vino before the barbecue. It worked fine. After supper I assembled the group at the Hq & Serv. Co. mess tent and spoke to them for a few minutes. It was very satisfactory. They are enthusiastic and keen. Lots of yelling and cheering. Makes one feel good.

This morning went around to see the First and Second Battalions. I believe that they are right. If anything, may be getting stale from waiting. Talked to a newspaperman yesterday who was inclined to believe that we did not have as much confidence as he expected to find. We do have, I am glad to see, a healthy respect for our opponents. It will be a real fight. I would like to go into their next one with them.[1]

All units should by all means bring radios and bicycles with them.

First contact with the sirocco yesterday. Temperature 142, a shock.[ii]

Note

1 At some point shortly before entering combat the 82nd Airborne Division held a final review. Colonel John McNally later described it in his book *As Ever, John*, p. 37. "It was in Africa that our division held its last review before combat. For us, there will never be another review quite like it. We knew instinctively that it was to be our great day." "The line of generals receiving the review stood motionless—Eisenhower, Patton, Giraud, DeGaulle, Ridgway." "There was no cheering crowd, no waving handkerchiefs—just the Division, almost lost in the empty expanse. It was our greatest moment. Sometimes I think the men who marched there for the last time that day are the real winners, with this, their brief, bittersweet moment of glory."

---

i Hot prepared A rations were a luxury in the 82nd. Most meals were field rations or B rations (dehydrated).

ii The Sirocco was a phenomenon of Africa. Very windy, hanging, almost impenetrable, dust with greatly increased temperatures. Nothing could move and it just had to be waited out.

CHAPTER 2

Sicily

5 Mi West of Trapani, Sicily, July 31, 1943

This is the second attempt at this since landing, the first having been lost in the confusion of recent weeks. A separate report has been made on the jump and subsequent action. This is evidently now being investigated.[i]

After the jump on July 10th in which parachute groups captured Nato, Vittoria, Santa Croce Camerina, and numerous smaller towns, they moved to a common objective, generally speaking in the vicinity of Gela.

It was while in this process that most of the 3rd Bn, with Regt Hqrs Co and a Btry of the 456, became involved in the fight on Biazza Ridge with the Herman Goering Division.[ii] This fight took place on Sunday, July 11th.[1]

Following that we moved to a bivouac area north of Gela several miles, where a reorganization took place. We were still having men come in. They still are. The CT remained there for about three days, when we moved up the southwest coast in division reserve.

The Div had the mission of advancing beyond Licata towards Marsala. They were on the Seventh Army's left. The usual action of the Italians was to fire a few shots, rifle and MG, cause the AG to deploy, and then surrender as soon as pressure was brought to bear on them. It made for treacherous action. Even the white flag could not be trusted.

There was always the possibility that Germans would be strengthening their defense. Some Germans were captured. During this advance, extending over three days and stopping just short of Menfi, the 504 lost 2/3rds of its effective strength

---

i   He is referring to the "friendly" shoot down of more than 20 aircraft carrying the 504th as well as the gross navigational errors and mis-drops of the 505th.

ii   Biazza Ridge was the penultimate engagement of the 505th in Sicily. The Hermann Goering Armored Division strove to take it and press to the beach. Gavin and Krause and a mixed bag of troopers held by a breath. Both Gavin and Krause were awarded a Distinguished Service Cross for their efforts.

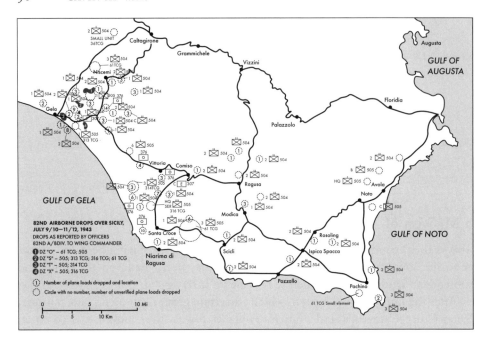

from stragglers.[i] I have never seen anything like it. This thing must be licked. All of us were ashamed of them. All along the roads they were bumming under trees, around houses, and in fields. On the march officers and men alike would leave ranks to pick grapes, melons, and get water.

Probably one of the greatest sources of losses was in "capturing" vehicles. Every wreck and abandoned vehicle that had not the slightest chance of ever operating again was the center of a group of from three to six parachutists who, upon being questioned, said that they were getting it ready to run to use for the regt. This had the sanction of the regt in its desperation to get transportation.

Our experience was that even the good serviceable vehicles soon broke down and became much more of an automotive liability than asset. Orders were accordingly issued forbidding troops from leaving ranks to capture vehicles. This is important and must be provided for in orders. You cannot expect to get any good enemy vehicles without some cost. If they are not booby-trapped, they are not serviceable. They may run for an hour or so, but then more time is spent endeavoring to improvise repairs or towing or pushing them than they are worth. Bring mechanics on the jump and

---

i   After the disastrous airborne assault where much of the 504th was shot down, the bulk of the regiment was landed by sea at Gela and moved inland to join the 505th and a small division HQ with Ridgway.

arrange for a D-Day convoy of essential motor vehicles. That is the answer.[i]

Upon the relief of the 504th at Menfi the 505[2] was given the mission of occupying the line of the Belice River north of San Margerita [Santa Margherita]. The 2nd Bn was given the AG and had to move on foot. Starting from Sciacca at 1:00AM they reached their objective at 3:00PM. No food nor water was available during the march. Some water could be obtained at wells at regular halts. A 20 min halt was taken at 11:00AM. The remainder of the regt was brought up on trucks by shuttling. The 2nd Bn had no stragglers until the last mile, when the objective

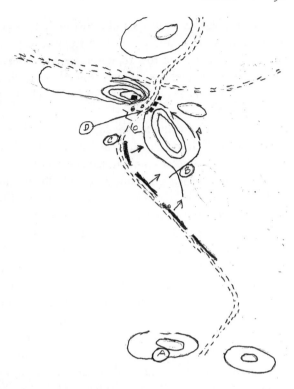

was in sight, and it was evident that there would be no fighting. They were all disappointed because they did not get to fight. We did come up on a fight involving the 2nd Bn 504, an account of which follows.

It was an unfortunate affair. The 2nd Bn 504 was moving on a road crossing and Mt pass four miles south of S. Marg as a march objective. They had been marching all night. They were very tired, hungry and thirsty. Upon reaching a point about ½ mile short of D they called in their point and AG because "it was moving too fast."

I arrived at A [as indicated on the sketch map] in a jeep with a staff officer about 6:00AM. The 2nd was following on foot at about 8 mi. At A we were fired at by a single Arty piece or AT gun. The jeep was put in defilade, and we went to the crest to see what the shooting was about. The 2nd Bn 504 was streaming off the road to the hills to the right. They appeared to be under fire. Their MGs and rifles were firing at enemy evidently in the vicinity of D. A group worked around via the pass at B and the enemy, amounting to about 200, mostly arty, surrendered. They had a dozen assorted casualties.

---

i   This issue was never resolved. The troops made use of whatever they could find with support from the leadership who needed the transport for logistics throughout the war.

The 504 had six fatalities and 20 wounded. They stated that, upon reaching the point C, they were fired on by an arty piece at point blank range. They were very lucky. The Italians said that they were debating whether or not to surrender and an enlisted man opened fire. This is probably untrue. They fired on me on the hill at least a dozen times and registered in very well right on the road, within 50 yards of our group.

We were most fortunate. The fight was not a breeze. It lasted about an hour or an hour and a half. It looked particularly bad for awhile. Bill Yarborough commanded the 504 Bn. Alexander commanded the 505 Bn.

Gen. Ridgway arrived about 8:30 or 9:00 and directed me to take command of both Bns, get them reorganized, and push on with the mission to the Belice. As usual, the reorganization was a hell of a mess. It always is much worse than fighting. Most of the 504 had taken off their coats and were getting water, disregarding the possibility of an Italian counterattack. About this time, I was informed that a tank was around the hill to the north. Some fun. It turned out to be an abandoned Italian tank ditched beside the road, but it took some time to find that out. Around 10:00 the 2nd Bn 505 passed through and continued on towards S. Margerita, where they were greeted with flowers and cheers at around 12:30PM. They reached their objective at about three o'clock. It is particularly [important] to note that in this, as in other affairs, that the Italians do not "all around" defend.

The line of the Belice was held for about three days. During this time the probability of a move, either to the Catania front or to occupy Palermo or Trapani, was outlined. An alert plan was published, and the necessary physical attachments made to all Bns, just in case. Early the morning of June 23rd the CT was ordered to seize Trapani. Enemy information none. CT to be motorized. First units hit the IP at 11:30.

It was a most interesting affair on which a separate report has been made. The Admiral surrendered at about 8:30. Capt. Ireland, S-1, representing the 505, was present. I have his [the Admiral's] sword and one of the Italian garrison flags.

The next day the 2nd Bn reinforced was ordered to seize Cape [San] Vito, which it accomplished with no opposition. Then followed the usual throes of reorganization. July 28th we were given a four-day reconnaissance and salvage task extending from Cape [San] Vito to Calatafimi to Marsala. The included territory was assigned to the 505 for military police, salvage, and supervision. Four days were allowed to completely go over the job. Today, August 1st, is the final day. We have captured several hundred additional prisoners and piles of arms, ammunition, tents, etc. Our losses since Biazza Ridge have been negligible (wow).[i]

---

i   Biazza Ridge was the greatest and most critical battle the 505th fought and largely raised the visibility, later fame, of the 505th and Jim Gavin, in particular, with both the Army and the general public. It was fought against the Hermann Goering Armored Division and against great odds, beat off the Germans from gaining the Gela beach head. Gavin was awarded the Distinguished Service Cross for personally leading the effort.

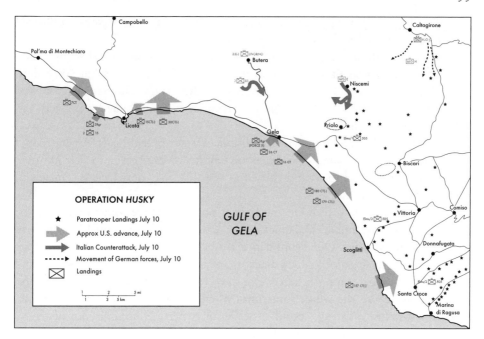

Today I received an alert from Gen. Ridgway to return the CT to Africa without delay to prepare for another fight. It may come in a month. It may or may not be parachute. With our present scarcity of effective AT weapons and no better pilots or planes, I am not anxious to jump into another snafu fight. Every man in the CT loves a good fight, but an even chance to live through it doesn't appear to be asking too much. But they will do it, and do it well, no matter what it is.[i]

I am to get a Purple Heart, for which I am very grateful. I wanted it more than any other. Gen. Ridgway has also recommended me for a DSC and my BG star, which all helps.

We have learned many lessons in the past few weeks, foremost of which is the basic fact that there is no substitute for discipline. It must be iron. The troops themselves, once having been in combat, want it, but it must be exacted from them.

Parachute troops are extremely courageous and love to fight. They will take on odds gladly. The Germans are good fighters, but can be beaten badly, especially if outsmarted and attacked when they least expect it. Surprise is costly to them always,

---

i   The issue of anti-tank weapons plagued the division throughout the war. Gavin ordered that all German Panzerfausts be kept by the regiment for later use. The 2.75" bazooka was virtually worthless against German armor. Later, at Normandy, the division integrated the British 57mm AT gun to good effect.

whereas a paratrooper will fight anytime. [Two following lines have been blacked out on the manuscript, presumably by Gavin himself.]

American marksmanship is far superior to any foreign. In fact, the impression most of us get is that other troops do not shoot accurately for a kill every shot. Instead, they appear to fire area fire, even with their rifles. The best defense is to attack. Pillboxes can always be taken by determined men and they are at a very bad disadvantage in any fight.

All men must be able to march long distances with combat loads. A paratrooper needs a weapon immediately available upon landing. We are going to start jumping with the M1 rifle assembled and carried at the side. We must have AT means in order to do anything.

Loud-talking, certain to be in the fight, troop leaders are sometimes the most unstable officers in combat. The quiet types are frequently more valuable because of their emotional stability. Quiet confidence, deliberate orders, and quick decisions are necessary, even in situations where defeat is apparently certain. Troops respond and reflect it in their behavior. An officer can show caution, but not fear. Even caution should be tossed to the winds sometimes when the moment appears opportune. Troops will follow a daring, confident leader anywhere. Nine times out of ten all that they need is someone to say, "Let's go."[i]

East of Trapani, Sicily, August 2, 1943

Gen. Ridgway returned from Africa yesterday. Next show all set. We are evidently to be in the Fifth Army, probably as an amphibious force. Very short time to train. Italy or any of her possessions are ripe for invasion now with Mussolini out. The Sicilians seem glad, without exception, to see him go.[ii]

The Sicilians, like all Italians, are not to be trusted. Went up to Erice yesterday. Very old, B.C., and looks it. Italians could have held out there for months. I have never seen a better natural defensive position.

Artillery CO who opposed us in the capture of Trapani says that our Inf advanced so rapidly, despite his artillery fire, that he could never go into fire for effect, which is just about what happened after a certain point. The Germans will not let us get such a start.

All men received a wine ration last night, ½ or better cup full per man. Also had some fresh beef, the first since arriving on the island. Don't know if they can chew it. Doubt if I could.

---

i   The division, with the example of Gavin and Ridgway, evolved into the model Gavin describes. The chain of command was noted for its calm, confident up-front leaders. Vandervoort was noted for being extraordinarily competent and never raising his voice. Likewise, the seniors were quick to weed out incompetents.

ii   This is the background to the Salerno invasion by Clark that was nearly defeated.

August 3, 1943

It now appears as though we are to be here for awhile, at least a week. Mail is scheduled to arrive at Palermo today. Mail, next to ammunition and rations, is most important.[i]

Checked all Bns in their final areas after their reconnaissance. They are in good shape. Opened the recreation building. Rates 25 lira per piece. Three girls last night. About 325 pros administered. Had the Bn COs talk to their men about it today to be certain that they understood that they were not expected to patronize the place. It is not required.[ii]

Continue to collect salvage. Italian small arms, arty, food, flares, ammo, etc. Met Bill Yarborough on the streets of Trapani this AM. He was strolling along rather moodily. Told me that the Div was putting the axe on him. It hurt to talk to him about it. That is a shame, and it is not entirely his fault. The Div erred in placing him as much as he erred in performing his duty. I went to the chief of staff about it, but could not catch him in. I will do all that I can. It seems but yesterday that we were both on Gen. Lee's staff at Bragg planning big things for the airborne units of the army. While many people were standing around, not even interested in how the thing would make out, people like Bill Y were risking their necks and staking their careers on a chimerical probability.[iii]

Loyalty has got to work down as well as up. If the officers of the div ever begin to feel that the top has only a cold selfish interest in them it will do us a lot of harm.

I went to the G-1 and asked him to let me know if Gen. R's recommendation on my BG was bounced back for any reason. If it does not go through, I am going to look for a new home. I have organized, trained and fought this regiment over a period of a year and a quarter. It is a satisfying accomplishment in itself. Continued carrying on in this same spot only means that I am blocking the advancement of deserving officers in the regiment, and I am becoming stalemated myself.

August 7, 1943

With the capture of Catania and the continued withdrawal of the Germans, the complete control by our forces appears to be a matter of a short time. Gen. Patton estimates August 15th, I hear.

---

i   As a field infantryman, Gavin recognized the internal value system that makes troops fight and was always mindful that they be fulfilled whenever possible.

ii   This refers to an "official" brothel. While frowned on by the very senior leadership, it was condoned as a means to control venereal disease which was a continuous problem.

iii   This refers to Yarborough's relief of command by Ridgway during the fight across Sicily. As Gavin states, the conditions were unfortunate and later regretted by Ridgway.

Jack Thompson came in for a few days, leaving today. He is a likable chap, not the traditional type of newspaper man, serious, all business, and quite capable. Our continued association may be to our mutual gain.[i]

Area assigned to the combat team enlarged to include all of the area formerly held by the 2d Armd. The 2nd Bn was accordingly moved to the vicinity of Alcamo. A bags [sic] brought over from Africa arrived yesterday. Mail came several days ago. That is an enormous morale problem. Order of priority should be ammunition, food, mail. The GI house continues to enjoy an excellent patronage.[ii]

We hunt for mines and recalcitrant natives hoarding firearms. Visited Erice with Jack Thompson the other day and talked to the American Civil Authority, Maj. Sheean. These AMGOT people are doing OK.[iii]

Rumors reach us that the 325 is taking amphibious training. Horrors. I have not yet told anyone that that is the dope and that we will probably enter Italy amphibiously, and damn soon at that. It should be a good show. The morale is excellent. Mail and news clippings from home help tremendously.

Recommended "Design for Conquest" to Jack T and he may take a lick at it. He is in the process of working up a book on paratroops.

I am again getting soft and fat. Need a return to the field. This present task does not permit much getting out and walking. I will get lots of it when we hit training in Africa.

August 10, 1943

Routine reconnaissance of the assigned area. Little activity. Civilians pleased with the paroles granted all Sicilian soldiers. Had a pillbox demonstration put on by the 1st Bn. They really know how to knock them out. It is a pleasure to watch them work now. A taste of combat makes different soldiers of them.

Received my DSC per GO 11, Seventh Army, yesterday. Everyone very nice about it. I feel that many of the fine boys now buried on Biazza Ridge are much more entitled to decorations than I am. It will nevertheless be nice to have and [be] of considerable help professionally. I have many battles ahead of me and, before I am through, I fully expect to be wounded. So, the medals may or may not be of much help after the war.

---

i   Gavin was mindful that Thompson's praise of him in the Stateside papers increased his visibility as a combat leader, which it did to a great degree. This was also a source of friction with Ridgway who got little credit outside the senior leadership.

ii   This is a reference to the bordello.

iii   He is referring to the civil affairs teams that followed the fight and re-established control and management of towns and villages.

There is only one way to fight a battle or a war, I am more than ever convinced. Fight intensely, smartly, and tough. Take chances personally and in matters of decision. Nothing ventured, nothing gained never was more applicable.

Most people become somewhat mesmerized by the holocaust and the danger to be promptly and energetically aggressive in a fight. That moment, the initial moment of indecision, should be made the most of. Hit them quick and hit them hard. Keep the initiative, even on the defensive. Most men do not think, they merely do as they are trained. That is OK. If they thought, chances are they would do nothing or spend all of their time figuring out fancy plans. The leader should think, and he will if he is battle trained and has any guts at all. Having decide what to do, the machine starts instantly to put his thoughts and plan into execution. Close with them and kill them. Clausewitz says "overcome their will to fight." Perhaps that is better.[i]

Trapani, Sicily, Friday, August 13, 1943

Trouble with this system is one forgets what was said four days ago. Yesterday went to Palermo and there met Lt. Col. Yardley and Col. Clark and Maj. Brown. They were in town to confer on an airborne show on the north coast. Plan is to put the 509 Bn in at dusk and then reinforce it with an amphibious regt at dawn or just before. A hell of a good idea. The Germans and Italians are streaming back to Messina and the road is jammed. Jumping back of them should cook their goose. An ideal use.

Air Corps objected to flying the mission, that is the 52nd TC Wing objected. Said that it was going to be too costly for the probable results. In a way they are right, it will be a costly mission, but hell you can't expect to win a war without losses. Anyway, the parachutists are ready to not only fly but to jump and fight and die if necessary. The present plan calls for July 15/16 [sic: August?] or thereabouts provided the front does not collapse too rapidly. Maj. Gen. Keyes, the Prov Corps commander, presided. Gen. Ridgway present, plus many brass hats.

There was much small talk among the intelligentsia about the reassignment of Gens. Allen and Roosevelt. I'll bet that they are getting promoted. They are both excellent. The attitude of brass hats, all of them totally devoid of combat experience, in cases such as the relief of combat officers is annoying and disturbing. Many of them neither desire nor are capable of handling troop command, yet like shrews at a knitting circle they gossip and always imagine the worst about relieved troop leaders.[ii]

---

i   This is the heart of the Gavin leadership by example ethos. He demanded the same model from his subordinate leaders. This is a large part of why he was so revered by his troops. In sum, he did not order, he led.

ii   Gavin is referring to the relief of Allen and Roosevelt in the 1st Infantry Division. Bradley, the corps commander, thought—with some evidence—that the division had too much of an autonomous attitude and was lax in basic discipline. All engendered by the top leadership. He replaced Allen with Major General Huebner, a known strict disciplinarian and by-the-book commander.

Yesterday I let three lieutenants and one captain go. Inability to adjust themselves to combat conditions. One actually withdrew in the face of heavy enemy fire while other paratroopers were going forward. Another fell out on a march and did not show up for several days.[i]

I talked to Yardley about his plan, and it looks pretty good. If he hits Italians who are not too anxious to fight, he will be OK. If he hits Germans, he will take a shellacking and lose heavily. I would like to be going with him. It is going to be an intensely interesting fight, losses heavy but lots of fun and excitement. He appeared a bit worried and not quite sure how it would all work out. Well, he might. You never can tell.

Amphibious landings have been made the past three nights on the north coast and the front seems to be folding rapidly. Mines and booby traps are the biggest obstacles.[ii]

"Fighting men are not to be fashioned out of textbooks and old men's tales." Fight we must. *Rivers of Glory* by F. van Wyck Mason 1942.

Trapani, Sicily, August 14, 1943

Well, here we go again. First discussion and orientation this morning on Avalanche, the invasion of Italy. Just remembered today of the bazooka vs. MkVI incident when we received the War Dept Intel. Bul. about Aug 1st informing us that the bazooka would not penetrate the front armor plate of the MkVI.

We of course had trained under the premise that the bazooka would penetrate anything. At least we knew of nothing that it would not penetrate. What it actually would penetrate in inches was a secret. Well, I saw at least two or three men of the 505 brought into the burial plot with large sections of bazookas wrapped in their arms and innards. And I saw one MkVI in front of the position that we finally had stopped that had three bazooka hits on it that did not penetrate. This all in a large measure due to slow distribution of intelligence.[iii]

To get back to the invasion of Italy, our sector is a mountain pass about five miles southeast of Pompeii. Mission is to hold two mountain passes until the arrival of the amphibious forces consisting of an American and a British corps. This critical period may last 24 hours. There is a great possibility that the British may yet put on the show with their A/B troops. Our gliders expect to participate.

---

i   Gavin recognized that once an officer lost credibility with the men he could never lead them.

ii   These are the famous Patton end runs attempting to outflank the Germans defending the final stretch to Messina. Gavin clearly favored audacity over conventional tactics.

iii   The inability of the bazooka to destroy German armor was a great initial shock to the troops and leadership. Gavin then ordered the men to collect and integrate the Panzerfaust which was a far superior weapon. This was not well received by the more senior leadership other than Ridgway, who fully endorsed the idea.

The 52nd Wing does not seem to want any part of it. Afraid of the mountains, for one thing. And, I believe, afraid to get into a fight for another. They wanted to drop us in the open on a plain about three miles from our defensive positions. I argued against that in favor of dropping us right on our defensive positions. We may lose rather heavily from jump injuries, but at least those who survive will be together where they can fight with some promise of accomplishing their mission and living thru the fight.[i]

Accomplishing the mission is the big thing, but living is a big part of this. A dead soldier cannot accomplish much of a mission. Since the drop is recommended for the mountain pass itself, the point arose about jumping at such altitude as to permit the entrance, maneuver, and exit of the planes from the pass. From the map study of the pass there appears to be no reason why they couldn't drop us at any desired altitude. However, I specified 1,000 ft as the minimum above ground. Actually, I told Gen. Ridgway that I would sooner jump at 1,500 or a bit more and take the consequent scattering of the men and still jump in the pass rather than jumping away from the pass where we would have to fight to get to it. Gen. Ridgway a bit under the weather with a fever, possibly malaria. There is a great deal of it.

Our first white bread today. Some treat. The U ration is very good.

"I have never yet served under a real general who ain't sometime lost a battle. Only the real soldiers can survive a setback." *Rivers of Glory*, p. 145[ii]

Trapani, Sicily, Aug. 17, 1943

Word received today that Messina fell to the 3rd Div yesterday. That cleans this place up. Now for the next show. Can't be too soon for most of us.

The 509 jump was called off because of the rapid advance of the ground troops. That is the stated reason. Actually, I feel that the show would have gone if the TC and the A/B had evidenced any ability to put on a quick show successfully. As it was the TC bellyached about having to do the job and the A/B appeared dubious about the success of the mission if they didn't have radios, photos, and all sorts of special arrangements. We will never get anywhere until we are able to say "Sure, we can do it" upon being given a mission. Now we still act like we were special problem children who need detailed orders, very particular instructions, etc.

Just received an alert for return to the Kairouan area. Glad to move. Africa may be much hotter and not quite as comfortable as here, but a change is good for the morale. They have a feeling they are going somewhere, and the war is moving along.

---

i He is referring to Avellina Pass. It was eventually tasked to the 509th which took significant casualties and was all but wiped out.

ii This is an example of Gavin's constant reading of military history to re-learn the lessons of the past. He had a library throughout the war and encouraged his officers to constantly read about previous warfare experiences.

By now they think of how nice it would be to get back to the States and home. After a man's first fight, if his interests are at all diversified, he looks to other fields. There is obviously nothing to be gained by continued participation in the sort of rat race this last show of ours was. For a first time, yes. But after one or two good fights you have a hell of a good idea of what it's all about.[3]

Notes

1   Later Gavin would write of the difficulties involved in this mission, which was to assist invading amphibious forces by blocking the movement of the Germans toward the beaches. First was a 35-mile-an-hour wind that scattered the parachute battalions about five miles apart. Then the 1st and 3rd Battalions encountered the Hermann Goering Panzer Division, positioned to attack the amphibious landings. The Germans threw the equivalent of a reinforced combat team at each of the 505th Infantry battalions. Per Gavin: "A struggle ensued, as the historians say, and at battle's end troopers of the 82nd Division and the amphibious forces were in control of all of the southwest coast of Sicily."

2   During this action Gavin commanded what was designated the 505th Parachute Combat Team (Reinforced). In his book *Airborne Warfare* (p. 2) he recalled the constituent elements: "505th Parachute Infantry Regiment; 3rd Battalion, 504th Parachute Infantry; 456th Parachute Field Artillery Battalion; Company B, 307th Airborne Engineer Battalion; and Signal, Medical, Air Support, and Naval Support detachments. The force totalled 3,405 troopers, requiring 227 C-47s for transport."

3   After the battle of Sicily Gavin wrote this in a letter to his daughter Barbara: "When this war ends, I think I would like to be a curate in an out-of-the-way pastorate with nothing to do but care for the flowers and meditate on the wickedness of the world. I have had more than enough excitement and danger to do for a lifetime."

CHAPTER 3

Africa

30 mi N of Kairouan, August 28, 1943

At this stage things are in one hell of a mess. We have been here for about ten days preparing for the next show. We are to have organized an airborne task force consisting of the 505 (less 1 bn), 504, 320 gl FA bn, two Cos Engrs, two Btrys 57mm AT. Mission: To seize and destroy the crossings over the Volturno River from Capua to the sea and prevent enemy troops from moving south across the Volturno.[i] The nearest friendly landings are to be made in Salerno Bay. They estimate contact on D+3. Therein lies the rub. We could be in for a very rough time. We must have air supply, particularly ammunition. I have paid a visit to the British 46th Div, which is on the allied right flank.

A great deal in this operation depends upon whether or not, and how much, the Italians will fight. Their ack ack and fighters continue to be effective. The feeling of the British is that their ground troops will not fight. This is a hell of a big question. If they really get tough and fight as well as they are able, they will annihilate us. At least they will kill most of us. They will get one hell of a good fight anyway.

If the Italians do not fight there is the next possibility, that the Germans will. They will of course fight. The unknown is where will they be and what will their reaction be. If they are north of the Volturno we may be able to hold them there until relieved. If they are east, towards Foggia, they may attack across the mountains and get between us and the British. Our present plans contemplate a withdrawal along the spurs of the mountains until contact with the British is gained. That is if we are forced to withdraw. If we are not attacked by the Italians and are without pressure along the river, we may occupy Naples. D-Day will be about Sept 9th or 10th, our H-Hour about 9:15PM. The DZs do not look bad. At best, however, a lot of us are not coming back from this show.

---

i   This was the primary German reinforcement route to counter the Salerno landings.

30 mi N of Kairouan, Sept 4, 1943

This has been a hectic time. On Aug 31st a conference was held at the Hqrs of Gen. Clark at Mostaganem. Everyone of importance in Avalanche was present. Gen. Eisenhower, Admiral Hall, Air Marshal Tedder, all British and American corps comdrs and the concerned div comdrs.

Gen. Ridgway allowed me three minutes to talk on the Volturno River plan. To come to the point, after many hours of discussion it was decided by Gen. Eisenhower, on ordered [sic] by Gen. Clark, that the Volturno plan would not go on. Instead, only the Capua area and bridges would be taken and held with five days' supplies. It at last became evident that they knew that the Italians were not, definitely, going to fight.

This new one was a two-battalion mission, so Gen. Ridgway decided to give it to the 504. Appropriate orders were issued. The 505 was alerted to be prepared for any orders, airborne or amphibious, for D-1 on. I was told that a dock landing at Naples or an air landing at Rome was possible.[i]

A lot that had been going on in the past few days was now becoming understandable. The afternoon of Sept. 2nd I was called to Div Hqrs and told to board a plane for La Marsa to go to a conference at Gen. Spaatz's Hqrs with the Div Staff. We arrived uneventfully and, after a brief conference with Gen. R, we were hustled into a plane and took off for Sicily. We landed at Syracuse, Hqrs 15th Army Grp. Gen. Alexander and the tops again went into a huddle. An open discussion was inaugurated at about 8:00PM. At that time, I was informed that the present Italian government was negotiating with Gen. Alexander for the prompt occupation of Italy by American troops. The Italians promised to turn about and fight the Germans. It was particularly desired that the American troops occupy Rome to prevent its capture and destruction by the Germans.

Several plans were accordingly made for the movement of an airborne task force the night of Sept 8-9 to the vicinity of Rome. The airdromes are to be occupied initially by parachutists. These are to be followed by air landing troops, and these are to be reinforced by more air landing troops and amphibious troops. At last, these airborne planners are getting on the beam. It's a fascinating mission.

Castelvetrano, Sicily, Sept. 11, 1943

Arrived in Sicily as per plan Sept. 5, 1943. The 504 was to jump on Furbara and Cerveteri airports, 20 miles west of Rome, at 2115 on Sept. 8, 1943. All plans and negotiations with the Italian representatives of Marshal Badoglio were evidently

---

i   Unknown to Gavin were the frantic efforts by Eisenhower and his staff to orchestrate an Italian surrender. This would, potentially, allow the Allies to occupy Rome and cut off the bulk of the German forces on the peninsula.

completed. Gen. Taylor went to Rome on the 6th with the understanding that he would radio if the expected assistance from the Italian army would not be forthcoming.

There was one hell of a rush getting the 504 ready. Gen. Ridgway designated me as the coordinator for the entire airborne lift. Div was spread over 11 airfields with no communications. All communications had to be worked through the TCC. Sooner or later, we will come under the command of the TCC if we don't soon learn to take care of ourselves.

Noon Sept. 8th the Italian government notified Gen. Alexander that they were incapable of meeting the commitments that they had made in the preliminary armistice conferences. Specifically, they were unable to oppose the present German troops with enough force to be effective and therefore we could expect heavy AA and ground opposition if we attempted an airborne invasion. Gen. Taylor confirmed this later in the day. Just before takeoff the entire mission was called off.[i]

On schedule the Italian government announced the unconditional surrender of their armed forces. Germany, in anticipation of this move, had already heavily reinforced the German garrisons in and around the city of Rome. It was well that we did not jump, particularly since we were only sending in two infantry battalions the first night. Any airborne effort made beyond fighter support is impossible with our present air transports. They are clay pigeons.

Early the morning of the 9th Avalanche went in on schedule. It will be interesting to watch its progress, since our relief along the Volturno depended on the British 46th Div getting to us in a hurry. It appears now as though the Germans will attempt to hold a line generally thru Spezia, including the Po valley in the defensive area. It would be a good idea for us to get the Po, but beyond that I do not think it is worth the lives it would cost. We can use Italy for support air bases and then make the close infantry contact from another direction. I would think that we could get up through the Balkans.

For several days, until the return of Gen. Taylor, I operated from division somewhat in the capacity of assistant division CG. I felt very much like a fifth wheel and got the hell out of there as soon as I could. There is so damn much to be done. It hurts to see it go undone, yet every suggestion, and it can't be more than that, is looked at with askance and a "and just who the hell do you think you are?" look. Until the BG commission gets here my best bet is to take care of my own regiment. Then the sparks will fly and there will be much bitching, but this infantry is going to get to the standard it should be if it kills me.

---

i   Taylor, the 82nd Artillery Commander, was secretly inserted into Rome to meet with Marshall Badoglio and determine if a drop by the 82nd was feasible. He reported a strong "no" by radio, cancelling the drop.

Yesterday, while checking on my own units around here, I ran into signs from the 3rd Bn, 7th Inf, so I stopped in to talk over old times. As it turned out, Johnny Heintges was the Bn CO, so I was quite surprised. Didn't talk to him about his marital difficulties, only mart[++].[i]

At present we are sitting tight waiting for a mission from Gen. Clark and the Fifth Army. It will probably come, but very likely not to the entire division. At present the 504 is on priority for the next mission, so I would not be surprised if we had a layoff for some time. We can certainly use all of the training time that we can get. We had planned on using a pathfinder unit, eureka, on the Rome mission. Now that it has fallen through, we are going to train a pathfinder platoon for each battalion. We learned from the Sicilian show that you can do many things on the ground immediately after jumping that we did not think possible. The defenders are twice as scared as the jumpers, and besides they cannot cover all over, even if they could see the jumpers.

---

i   John Heintges was a friend from USMA and battalion commander in the 3rd Infantry Division. He later retired as a lieutenant general.

CHAPTER 4

Italy

Naples, Italy, Oct. 19, 1943

A great deal of water has gone over the dam in the past two months. After considerable planning to jump on the Volturno line, then Capua only, then Rome, and finally to be ready for anything, the regiment jumped at Paestum, Italy.[1] The right flank of the Fifth Army became endangered by the German units withdrawing from the front of the Eighth Army. It was a good use of parachute troops. It is regrettable that glider troops did not get into the affair by air.

After some fighting by B and C Companies at Altavilla in which they sustained light casualties, the division went into army reserve. Thence to the peninsula north of Maiori. Troops were rapidly moved to Agerola for an attack on Germans entrenched in the vicinity of Castellammare-Gragnano. When the thing was finally set up the Germans withdrew and Castell' was occupied without a hostile shot.

After several days in Castell' the 505 was attached to the 23rd Armd Brig (British) for the advance on Naples. It was to relieve the 1st Bn 143rd of the 36th Div. With some small piddling around and a few casualties Naples was taken on, I believe, Oct. 1st. The 505 was the first unit in the city after the British Recon.

Within the city our troubles started. There were still Germans fighting about in spots, but worse the Italians were fighting each other, accusing friends and foes alike of being fascists or tedeschi, and the shooting started. In about 24 hrs the picture cleared up and billets were occupied. After the usual round of police jobs the 23rd again called for the 505 and it went north to Qualiano, from where it made a night attack on German-held Villa Literno. With some losses the place was captured. The advance was continued to the Volturno. It was characterized by the typical British attack methods.

There are many things about their technique that I admire, but their attack tactics are not among them. Their employment of armor was a great disappointment. They are reluctant to take losses, but when they do lose, they die well.[i]

---

i   Gavin was always concerned that the British did not use infantry and armor together as the U.S. did. Rather, they tended to send armor in by itself where it took severe casualties. The relative ponderous slowness of the force was also a concern, particularly later at *Market Garden* where speed was of the essence.

About the time of the arrival of the 505 at Qualiano I was designated as Asst CG of the Div. Sunday Oct 10th word was received by radio of my promotion and so, at a formation in front of Div Hqrs, the stars were pinned on.[2] I do not believe I wear them particularly well. I may in time.[i]

Div headquarters is in the Questra Bldg. Since many of the buildings were mined by the Germans, with charges actuated by 21-day clocks, we are all sweating out the 21st day. Another 24 hrs should clear up all of them. One went off this morning. Two British soldiers and a few civilians lost. Sunday the 10th a heavy charge went off in the 307th Engr barracks, killing 45 men and injuring about 40.[ii]

The best available rumor at the moment is that we will go to England next month for employment on the northern front. We all like that very much.

I realize now that it is particularly important for me to keep a personal record of all conferences and planning activities in connection with our operations. Div G-3 is now endeavoring to get together a report on the Sicilian show and the Italian jump. It is surprising how much in the way of accurate records that we do not have in Division.[iii]

This morning the experimental airborne test group, under the command of Capt. Norton, was sent to Comiso, Sicily, for the purpose of conducting tests of radar and similar navigational aids. It is hoped to find the answer to the many questions regarding the correct use of radar equipment and combined parachute-glider employment.

The Sessa operation has been definitely called off for the 82nd Airborne Div. A group of transports arrived at Pomigliano for permanent station. To date I have nothing more than rumor regarding our move to UK. Gen. Ridgway talked to me a short while re my relations with Col. Lewis. Finished the board report on the explosion in the engineer barracks. Evidently a German time bomb, helped along by TNT stored by our own troops.[iv]

Naples, Thursday, Oct 21, [1943], 1700

Gen. Clark came in for a conference on the combined training and experiment that we are about to conduct in Sicily. He agreed to the plan as now arranged. Came

i   Gavin became the deputy CG and Herb Batchchellar his replacement as CO, 505th PIR.
ii The Germans had hidden large bombs or charges with delay timers in many of the public buildings, knowing they would likely be occupied by Allied forces. These created considerable casualties and morale issues.
iii This was to be a continuous problem throughout the war. The division was notorious for bad record keeping, which was particularly hurtful for many men given impact valor awards who later had no documentation to prove it. Both Gavin and Ridgway employed Captain Bob Piper as the perpetual HQ Commander as they knew he kept a meticulous journal. After Normandy, his journal was virtually the only document that approximated personnel records.
iv Lewis was the commander of the 325th GIR. He was over age, deliberate, and viewed as unengaged. The 325th had a poor record and Gavin wanted to add some airborne energy. It can be assumed that Gavin was lobbying Ridgway for a change of commander. On June 9 in Normandy, Lewis had a heart attack and was evacuated.

to lunch and dinner with us at the villa. Gen. Guenther [Gruenther?] and Gen. Pence also came to dinner. Col. Hume of the AMGOT also there. Considerable talk about the local civic situation. Guggenheims discussed and saw an interesting G-2 report on one of them. Gen. Guenther talked of the efforts being made by Col. ? Butcher, aide to Gen. Eisenhower, to find suitable quarters for him. The villa seemed to Guenther to offer as much as any place in the city, so it was decided to offer it to him, contingent upon the departure of the 82nd from the city.[i]

Finished the investigation of the explosion that occurred in the engineer barracks on Sunday, Oct. 10th. Went to a 325 party at the Orange Gardens from five until six.

Naples, Friday, Oct 22, [1943], 0730

Investigated the shooting of Lt. Col. Dolman at the Capodichino airport by a sentinel from the 504. Particularly looked into the negligence on the part of the OD aspects of the case. Completed the investigation of the engineer demolition affair.

In the late afternoon Col. Jones, A-3 TCC, arrived from Palermo. Discussed the pathfinder training. He invited Gen. R and myself to come over to Palermo and Comiso this coming Sunday to witness the employment of some new equipment. This will also give us an opportunity to inspect the training of our special group over there.

Went to the villa to dinner at 1730. Col. Blakely of the AGF there. First Jerry air raid since our arrival came over at about 1900. The heaviest that I have been into date. They scored a direct hit on a British battery about 100 yards from the villa. Broke a lot of the windows, frames, etc. Cut up Col. Blakely a bit. Estimated 25 Jerries over, none seen going down, none of the docks or ships hit. Don't know why they picked last night for the show unless it was because Gen. Eisenhower was in the city. He arrived at about noon. About 1800 Col. Jones came down from Fifth Army with a plan for a drop in about a week well north of Massaco. The operation looks fine, but at present is not to order for us. Tomorrow we start our training out north of the city.

Naples, Saturday, Oct 23, [1943], 0650

Finished the investigation of the shooting of Lt. Col. Doman [sic] and completely exonerated Lt. Keep, the OD, of negligence. Visited all Regtl CPs to check the damage of the air raid. One killed and about 40 wounded, mostly falling flak. Informed all unit COs that hereafter they would send a runner to Div during such raids if the phone goes out. Had lunch with the 505. Wrote an estimate of the airborne

i Grunther was Clark's Chief of Staff and everyone's desired bridge partner. Butcher was a news-paperman and confidante of Eisenhower and became his companion/aide/factotum.

situation on the present front, especially near Spigno. In it made a case for the use of a parachute battalion. This was the particular wish of Gen. R since he does not want us to have to leave a larger unit here when we go to UK. Yesterday Gen. Eisenhower suggested leaving at least a battalion.[i] Went to a 2nd Bn 505 affair in the evening. Dragged Springer, all ambition to get to the Air Evacs.

Naples, Sunday, Oct. 24, [1943], 0730

Assisted Gen. R in preparing his report to AFHQ on the planning for the Italian jump. Interesting to read his notes on the conferences with the Italian representatives of the Badoglio government on Sept 3rd and 4th, when it was planned to jump on Rome.

A conference with Gen. Brann, G-3 Fifth Army, and Gen. R at 1315 regarding the Spigno jump. His analysis of the German setup interesting. From his agents and contacts with the former Italian G-3 he estimates that the best defensive position on the boot is coming up along the Mt. Massaco line. They are in artillery range of it now. In order to crack it he wants to use parachute troops and amphibious troops for an end run.

Went out to the training area in the afternoon. Krause, 3rd Bn 505, having a problem. Problem must be so laid out as to be free of combat artificialities necessitated by peacetime safety restrictions. If someone gets hurt, OK.[ii]

In the evening dinner at the villa with Batcheller of the 505, Dick Tregaskis, Lang and Corman, all newspapermen. Interrupted by a Jerry raid. He came closer to the harbor this time, and in fact hit a dock. Seemed like a strong raid. Lasted about 25 minutes.[iii]

Naples, Monday, Oct 25, [1943], 0730

Due to the rush of office business Gen. R postponed the planned trip to Sicily for 24 hrs. Attended mass at the cathedral at 1030. Lt. Sigman attended lunch at the villa. Visited the training area at 1400, observed and critiqued a problem, checked 504 bivouac (2nd Bn Maj. Danielson), returned at 1730. Visited Pimisentos piano,

---

i   This became the entire 504th PIR which was heavily engaged and could not extract. This created a significant issue later in the UK when its unavailability meant no PIR other than the 505th was combat tested. Both the 507th and 508th were independent PIRs in the UK assigned to augment the 82nd.

ii This is another reference for Gavin's consistent requirement for tough live-fire exercises to maintain proficiency at the small-unit level—a technique that the rangers and airborne still use.

iii Richard Tregaskis, of *Time* magazine, was a first-rate combat reporter, later writing *Invasion Sicily* in which he praised Gavin profusely.

Italian lessons, etc. During the day assisted Gen. R in compiling his report on the Italian campaign. Wrote P, some letter. No air raid for a change.

Comiso, Sicily, Tuesday, Oct 26, [1943]

Left Pomigliano with Gen. R, Turner G-3, and aide Capt. Faith. Flew via Vesuvius, Aeolian Islands, Messina, and Syracuse. Arrived Comiso 1100. Met by Gen. Hal Clark. Noon meal at AC mess. There joined by Gen. Paul Williams, Lt. Gens. Patton and Spaatz.

After lunch inspected jump loads of individuals participating in afternoon show. Went to Ponte Olivo and there witnessed drop of radar equipment, flight of gliders, landing of gliders with and without parachute arrestors. Arrestor appeared to be of definite value, some gliders landing within 50 yards.

Parachutists jumped from glider tugs about one minute after gliders were released. In the interim the tug ropes were dropped. Upon release the gliders turned aside, the glider LZs being off the line of flight and about 1,200 yards short of the DZ. It was a good show and served the purpose, at least, of piquing Spaatz's and Patton's interest. We knew, however, that we could do those things. What we want now is to do them at night.

Returned to Comiso at 1630, inspected all division troop areas, messes, etc. Conference with all experimental group heads at 1830. Gave them instructions to work on the scheme of dropping parachutists from tugs after the glider is released and the rope dropped. Conference with Norton, who is sick in bed with jaundice, at 2000. To bed at 2100.[i]

En route from Comiso to Pomigliano, Aeolian Islands, Oct. 27, [1943]

Grounded by weather. Visited area of drop and first flight in AM. Biazza Ridge in afternoon. Our mistakes become more clear with each return trip. A number of bones still around the vacant graves. Dinner with the 505. Doc Cibelle prepared his favorite recipe for spragetti [sic]. Nice to be with the boys again.

Present at take-off and landing of gliders in total darkness, no moon. Used Comiso strip. Regular lights were turned off and pathfinder marking lights (delta) were used. Worked very well, but there are still many problems to overcome. An infrared light visible only to personnel wearing special goggles would help. Parking gliders appears to be a particularly difficult problem. At 2000 conferred with experimental group and pilots, all keen on their work. To bed early at 2115.

---

i   Both Gavin and Ridgway concluded that a joint airborne/glider drop would cause excessive casualties and was not worth the price. From then on, they planned for separate drop times and, in some cases, separate locations. The British usually mixed both forces.

Naples, Friday, Oct 29, [1943]

Returned uneventfully Wednesday. In afternoon went out to the training area north of the city. There joined the 2nd Bn 325 for its night problem. It was disappointing as those things go. Non-parachute troops are not as keen, nor as responsive, as paratroopers.[i] Problem ended at 0730 yesterday, Thursday.

Went up to the front to visit the 504, which has just gone up. It left Naples Wednesday. Stopped by the VI Corps CP. Talked to Col. "Dutch" Kaiser, new CofS I believe. Dawley was apparently relieved after the Salerno fight. Too bad, but those things seem to happen, perhaps too often. It makes a commander super-cautious and afraid to take a chance.[ii] As we go along in this war a bit longer, we will probably appreciate the fact that everything does not automatically go perfectly in every engagement, regardless of the excellent planning and leadership given it by the CG. Mistakes will be made. Only this way do we learn. We will never progress in the tactical evolution that must be taking place without making mistakes. Mistakes are part and parcel of progress. He who does not make a mistake does not make progress, or if he does it is so goddamn slow you cannot recognize it as such.[iii]

Went up to the 504 CP at Alife. Expect to move to Gallo tomorrow and then attack in the direction of Macchia. They are to protect the right flank of the VI Corps and Fifth Army. They are being supplied with pack mules and packers today.[iv] Enemy opposition at this point appears to be little except for mines and booby traps, but it might develop. The 26th and 29th Panzer Divs are on this front.

Fifth Army currently is basing their belief in enemy capabilities on stories coming from prisoners, all to the effect that the Germans are not going to defend in strength for some time and are merely delaying at present. It is evident that if Rommel wanted to, he could counterattack and drive the Fifth Army one hell of a long way back. They are very tired and have no fresh troops in sight. The number of divisions present are barely enough to cover the front, leaving wide gaps between units.[v]

If the German counterattacked in force at any one point, he could really roll them up. It would be difficult for him to concentrate a large enough force for such

---

i   The glider troops were draftees, not volunteers, and lacked the elan of their airborne counterparts, especially in Gavin's mind.

ii This is another example of Gavin's belief that combat requires leaders willing to take risks, which ultimately saves lives.

iii He is referring to the problem of risk aversion at the top which turns operations into slow, ponderous exercises that fail to take advantage of evolving conditions.

iv The 504th was operating in very steep, rocky hills. Resupply was only possible by man-packing or mules. The mules had very recently been imported by General Clark as a combat necessity in the terrain.

v   The Italian campaign was always short of resources and would remain so throughout the war. The U.S. was focused on resourcing for the invasion and the British simply did not have anything more to give.

an attack without it being picked up by our air. We have complete mastery of the air on the entire front.

Returned to the city and spent the night at the villa for a change.

Saturday Oct 30, 1943, 0700

Gen. R left for Algiers at 0800 to get some information on our proposed move to UK. I hope that we can get away very soon, in the next few weeks. If Raff or Shinberger have anything to do with planning our next operation it is most imperative that we get up there. Gen. Marshall evidently handling this one in person.[i]

Worked around the office in the AM, out to the training area in the afternoon. Winton's Bn out there. Talked to Ireland for quite awhile. A good officer. To the villa at an early hour after a rather futile attempt to get Springer lined up for tonight, Halloween. During dinner the discussion drifted around to Dawley's relief. Everyone feels about the same. Lee would have been relieved in '61 if our present system were in effect. Capt. Faith was of the conviction that Terry Allen of the First Div. and BG Roosevelt were relieved for cause. Dropped $6.00 at poker.

Sunday Oct 31, [1943], 1030

Left to visit the 504 near Gallo at 0730, arrived 1100, returned to Naples at 1500. Talked to Tucker and Billingslea about their administrative troubles.[3] They are having them. Tucker does not realize, or if he does, he has at last gotten fed up with the pressure, but his situation is critical. Gen. R thinks that I will be his hatchet man if the necessity arises and, as much as I would hate to harm Tucker, I will be it if it is necessary. The foremost consideration is that this division be at its maximum combat effectiveness when it goes into its next fight. The question is, is Tucker the officer to get the best out of the regt. Judging on his performance so far, no.[ii]

An affair at the villa last night. Later went to the 505, escorted Springer. Gen. R, who had spent the day at Algiers, returned at 1800. When everything broke up this AM, about 0100, he talked to Doc and myself about coming events. He has recommended me to go to the UK as advisor on airborne matters for the coming show. It is to be a job on Gen. Marshall's staff. Upon arrival of the division, I am to

---

i   This is a referral to Colonel Edson Raff, whom Gavin and Ridgway disliked. Eventually, in the UK, Raff became the "spare colonel" bringing in the sea tail relief force to the 82nd. When Colonel Millett of the 507th was captured, Raff became the de facto commander.

ii   Colonel Reuben Tucker, commander of the 504th PIR, was recognized as an exceptional combat commander but a terrible administrator. This meant his logistics were poor and his personnel administration non-existent. This was a period where Tucker commanded in combat for an extended period. He would later be the best field combat commander of all the PIRs. However, Ridgway was clear that he was not General Officer material when the issue arose.

return to it. This is opportunity with a capital O. I am going to work hard. There is yet a chance that Gen. Marshall may not order me up. I believe that he would prefer a more junior officer. Gen. R was nice enough to tell me that ultimately, he wants me to get the division. I am a bit young for it.[i]

Monday, Nov. 1, [1943], 0705

To the office early to get plans started on the coming move to UK. Conference with all unit COs re the turning of the electricity today, Monday. The city is to be vacated of all civilians, a large section of it. Military personnel move at the discretion of the unit CO. We are doing nothing more than vacating excess personnel to the streets, increasing patrols, having firefighting standing by. The first fears were for booby traps and mines. Currently the fear is more for fires started by damaged wiring, etc. At the unit commanders conference, they were given our sailing date and approximately our schedule.

Language and piano lessons in the evening.

En route from Naples to Palermo, Sicily, Thur Nov. 4, [1943]

This is a new experience, but if I do not get this done now it will never get done. Monday afternoon Gen. R, Col. Lewis, Col. Boyd, Col. Turner, aides, and I took off for Comiso at 1300. Arrived 1500 there, were met by Col. Smyly, and proceeded to inspect the navigational equipment that the board had devised and procured for their training and tests. Saw the RE equipment, 5G tests, Aldis and Delta lamps. Went to Agrigento strip to witness the demonstration prepared by the EG of night pathfinder drop and glider landing. The pathfinder equipment came in in excellent shape at 1745. It was followed by the first troop-loaded gliders (8) at 1800. They too came in and landed as per plan, uneventfully.

Twenty minutes later a group of 12 gliders from another unit attempted to come in as per their prearranged plan. It was a miserable performance. Despite the lights marking the entire strip, which was 5,000 ft. long, they all landed at the end of the strip, endeavoring to come to a stop at the end of the strip where everyone else had already parked or were trying to park. One completely overshot and landed a mile beyond in the hills.

---

i   Ridgway and Gavin had an excellent working relationship. Ridgway understood that Gavin was the best man to undertake the initial airborne assault while he managed the overall division in support. While there was some friction related to Gavin's belief that Ridgway was overly ambitious, this was put aside for the greater needs of combat effectiveness. General Marshall was very keen on using the airborne forces in the coming invasion and had picked Col Raff and LTG Brereton to be part of the COSSAC planning staff. Both Gavin and Ridgway saw it as crucial that Gavin become involved and ensure proper use of the division.

Miraculously, we had no fatalities. There were some injuries, but from a tactical or operational planning viewpoint it was a very, very poor performance.

At this point it is clear that any night glider operation on a large scale is certain to end in disaster. I still believe that it can be done, and it will be done. Training and proper equipment are our pressing requirements.[i]

Everyone stayed at Hqrs 52nd Wing overnight. The following day had a flight in the PPI ship to Pantelleria, Trapani, Comiso. Very promising. Landforms show up on a screen. It is a step in the right direction.[ii]

Gave Col. Smyly an OK to continue his work until Friday. Returned Naples, arriving about 1500. Immediately grabbed a blanket and went up to Gallo via VI Corps CP. Ar[rived] Gallo 2230. 504 rear CP and supply dumps there. Left Gallo 0700 Wednesday, travelling by foot, and reached 504 front 0900. Talked to staff, CO, and some of the troops. Returned via 319th FA positions, arriving at Gallo at 1230. Little activity other than patrolling. Germans all around, but regt and corps confident that everything is OK. British on left flank dangerously far behind.[iii] 34th Div on left a mile or two behind. Tucker and Billingslea doing a good job. VI Corps very pleased.

Returned to Naples via VI Corps, arriving in Naples at 1630. Left orders with Tucker to send back elements of the Div Med Co now with him. Informed him of location and strength of D Btry 319. Dinner at the villa, Lts. Springer, Sigman, and Perdu there, not so good. Went to the Div Arty dance later.

En route from Palermo to Naples, Friday Nov. 5, 1943

Took off from Pomigliano at 0930, arrived in Palermo at 1100. Went directly to Hqrs TCC there. Conferred with Gen. Williams re Gen. Ridgway's letter. He felt, and I believe properly so, that it was a bit too emphatic, however well intended the motive. It disparaged the TCC effort. Admittedly they have made many mistakes and their combat performance has been very poor. They feel that, everything considered, they have done as well or better than could be expected under the circumstances.[iv]

Working with a new weapon, as we are, we are certain to make mistakes, and many of them. When the time comes in this airborne effort that we are not making mistakes, then the time has come when we are ceasing to improve and grow. We should always be overreaching and extending, probing into the future, groping into

i   In Normandy, the division glider landings were all done in daylight. Even so, there were considerable casualties.

ii   This refers to an early radar system intended to be the flight lead on airborne operations.

iii   The 504th was very aggressive and took ground well ahead of the flank British units, creating significant gaps. The Germans did not take advantage of this.

iv   This is a reference to the poor performance of the air transport elements to maintain formation and hit the right drop zones.

the black uncertain beyond. Only so do we grow. Mistakes are to be our lot despite every effort to avoid them. Soon, I suppose, we will have newcomers in our ranks who will be satisfied with things as they are, content to polish our present technique and to hell with the future. Then it should be time to look to greener fields.[i]

After conferring with Gen. Williams, he showed me a newsreel shot of the Lae drop. Mostly MacArthur. MacA watches the preparations, MacA says goodbye, MacA watches the drop, MacA congratulates the victors, and so it goes. He sure plays his public relations chips very cagily and well. The drop looked OK, although some of the shots were faked.[ii]

I believe that Gen. W felt a bit hoodwinked or outsmarted by the publicity blurb the TCC in Australia, whereas his Sicilian show was throughout the press a snafu affair.

Left Palermo at 1330, arrived Agrigento about 1500. Called Gen. Clark and left draft of Gen. R's letter at operations for him. Left for Comiso, arriving there about 1530. Conferred with Lt. Col. Smyly re the coming move. He had orders to move everything to Syracuse and was starting the move today, Friday the 5th. If any part of the total troop move is cancelled, he will have a most difficult time withdrawing part of the property.

Left after a short stay, arriving at Agrigento at 1730. Spent the night at the 52nd Wing hotel at Agrigento with Gen. Clark. He felt much the same as Gen. Williams about Gen. R's letter. Talked of bombing winning the war. Seems to have good possibilities.

Naples, Italy, Saturday, Nov. 6, 1943

Took off Agrigento 0830. Palermo 1000. Arrived Pomigliano 11:30. Spent afternoon at office going over papers, etc., and redrafting Gen. R's letter to OPD. Gen. R sent letter to AG WD recommending that both general officers of the division be selected regardless of branch, one not of necessity being an artilleryman.[iii] Left office about 1800. En route to the villa an air raid started, a good size one. It made big waves in the bathtub. Col. Lovell (tt?) WD G-2 Section in for dinner.

Naples, Italy, Sunday, Nov. 7, 1943

Polished off a lot of office business. Letters, etc. Getting ready for the UK move. Visited ?nd Bn 505 in training area in afternoon. Excellent exercise in locating enemy weapons. In evening went to 1st Bn 505 party at Orange Gardens. Really not much accomplished.

---

i   This is another musing over the necessity for risk taking as a means to grow both the leadership and the unit.

ii   This refers to the 503rd Airborne drop on Lae, New Guinea.

iii   At this point in the war, each U.S. division had a brigadier general commanding the artillery. Brigadier General Maxwell Taylor was the 82nd Division artillery commander.

505 officer told me of incident in Sicily when they left a wounded Italian officer or NCO who said he couldn't walk. A grenade with the pin pulled was placed under him. They had hardly left him when the grenade went off. He had gotten up already. Another incident, where a parachutist shoved a bayonet thru the throat of a complaining wounded Italian. There was bad blood in that fight. The stories will never be told in full. Talked to Hagen about his part in the Biazza Ridge fight.

Naples, Italy, Nov. 8, 1943

Sunday was more quiet than usual. Close to the office in the morning. Some conferences re the coming training period. Gen. R told me that 27 U.S. divisions are to be in UK. He is recommending that we train during the winter with the 52nd Wing in the vicinity of Casablanca, Rabat, Morocco, Africa.

Visited the 2nd Bn 505 in its training area during the afternoon. Visited Yarborough and talked to him re his planning for a coming drop for the Fifth Army. An unusual show but sounds OK. This theatre offers little in the way of opportunity for an airborne effort. The SW Pacific is the place. It is about time we went into the Balkans.

Naples, Italy, Nov. 9, 1943

Accompanied Gen. R and Col. Turner to the 505 to talk to men who had carried and fired the bazooka in combat. Heard some very interesting tales. Almost all agreed that they preferred to carry a pistol with the bazooka, but that in combat they preferred to have a rifle handy. Preferred the two-man team. Talked to Falen re machine gunnery. A keen promising officer.

Visited Batcheller in the PM to talk over his troubles with the colored troops. That situation potentially bad. His troops resent the colored troops associating with their girls or trying to anyway. They consequently keep them out of the Regt area.

Out to the test of the 2nd Bn 505, Vandervort commanding, at 1500.[i] Back in time for dinner. Maj. Gen. Gerow, CG V Corps; Maj. Gen. Gerhart, CG 29th Div; BG Larkin, SOS; BG Pence; BG Stewart; BG Ford present. Ford, DCS NATOUSA, told me that my orders had come through ordering me to Gen. Marshall's staff in London. I am looking forward to the trip and service. I am going to work hard and try to do the best job I can. Gen. R still feels that there is a possibility that I may leave the division if I get entangled in Bolero.[ii]

---

i   Major Vandervoort was Gavin's S3 in Sicily. He proved to be the most able battalion commander in the division.

ii   *Bolero* was the build-up of forces in the UK.

Naples, Italy, Wednesday, Nov. 10, 1943

Up at four AM and out to the division test problem for the 2nd Bn 505. Enthusiasm and interest of the participants particularly gratifying. CG inquired about Alexander's qualifications as a regimental commander, and I recommended him.

Back to the office by 1000. Conferred with Norton on the results of the experimental group tests in Sicily. Above all else they pointed the way to much vitally essential training. Conferred with CG on the results of the tests. Shuffled papers. Gens. Clark and Williams in for a conference with CG Fifth Army on a coming show for the 509. Threatening German counterattack necessitated committing 509 on the front yesterday, so the airborne show is off. I have frequently wondered why the German has not made a strong—division or two—counterattack. It would do more to slow up the allied attack than anything he could do. Naples would be in a bedlam. Gerow, Gerhart, Henion, Clark, Williams all to dinner at the villa. We are all anxious to get out of here.

Naples, Italy, Thursday, Nov. 11, 1943

Air raid at 0320, over at 04020 [sic]. No damage. Missed city widely. Some conferring about hqrs. Norton re the tests of the pathfinder equipment. Talked to Gen. Williams and Clark about remedying the tug rope release to make it positive.[i]

Out to witness a problem of the Div Recon plat. In afternoon went down to the docks to see the skipper etc. of the *Monterey*, which had just come in. A most pleasant visit. They gave us each a Coke, which is the first we have had since we got off her six months ago, to the day, in Casablanca. She brought a Canadian unit in that had been in England for 3½ years, God forbid. Later attended a review for the awarding of several Legions of Merit and some Silver Stars. L/M for Col. Lewis, Weinecke, Schellhammer, etc.

Naples, Italy, Nov. 12, 1943

Off for the front at 0700. Proceeded via Macchia, arriving at a blown bridge ½ mile west of Colli at 1000. No one in sight. Last infantry seen gave me a puzzled look, down the road mile or two. Crossed the river, waist deep and colder than hell, and walked into Colli. Made a careful approach because the situation looked screwy. Saw some parachutists finally and, upon entering the town, found out that 80 men of the 504 were there. They had been held up by a minefield and enemy patrol action the night before, having lost four men wounded and one killed. Talked to them

---

i   This refers to the tow rope for gliders and who did the releasing, the glider or the tug. Ultimately, it was decided the tug would release.

for awhile and then walked back to Fornelli, where the regimental CP was located. There talked to Col. Billingslea and said my goodbyes.

Returned to Naples, arriving at 1630, wet and frozen. Found out in the 504 CP that there was a gap between their left flank and the right of the 34th Div of a mile or two. They must have figured out that I was one of them crazy paratroopers going into the German lines in a jeep.

Naples, Italy, Nov. 13, 1943

A day at the office catching up with papers that accumulated during the previous day's visit to the front. We continue to have trouble with colored troops. To be certain of avoiding a race riot we now have the white troops backing up in every questionable situation. Every white officer realizes that it is his career if trouble starts, and his troops are involved. Nov. 9th a group of armed, firing negroes from a QM Port Bn took several drunken colored soldiers from a lieut. of the 505 when he was returning them to their organization in that state after curfew. They refused to get their CO or to tell where he could be found.

An AC officer was beaten up when he attempted to give succor to two white girls who were being molested by colored soldiers. Expressions such as "This is a race war, and we know what to do about it" are being bantered about too freely. I will be glad to see the division get off this powder keg.[i]

Col. Tucker came in to say his goodbyes. Doing well on his front. Parachute troops are making a name for themselves with the Germans. 504 captured five Germans from a seven-man patrol the other day. They had killed the other two. One of the Germans told the 504 that their company commander had gathered the company together and asked for volunteers. He told them that the troops to their front were special troops and barbarians. This boy was one of those who volunteered. The 504 picked up the patrol working its way up the mountain. They surrounded it, killed two and captured five. They did the same thing to an eight-man patrol the next day. Lt. Gorham, Regt S-2, says that if he does not go out and plead with the men, he does not get any prisoners.[ii]

The Germans are using a wooden-encased S-mine and doing well with it. The 504 is on the 34th Division objective and working across to the front of the 45th Div. Two 504 people who were taken by a German sergeant the other day

---

i   The issue of black and white soldiers fighting over women and unsegregated bars was continuous. The Europeans did not understand the U.S. segregation ethic and freely associated with black soldiers, enraging white troops. This was a major problem in the UK and resulted in numerous fights during the Normandy train-up period.

ii The 82nd troops were more inclined to kill than capture, as they didn't want the burden of processing prisoners. In time, the troops learned the value of POW intelligence to a degree.

jumped him and killed him. They were given hell because they shot up his Zeiss glasses.[i]

Naples, Italy, Nov. 14, 1943

A day spent mostly around the office. Visited the 505 in the AM. Lieut. Gen Courtney Hodges, CG Third Army, came in in the afternoon and stayed for dinner at the villa. Talked of his experiences with his army, now numbering 450,000 men and 21 divisions. Very interesting and instructive.

Orders came in the afternoon sending me to ETOUSA. Expect to leave tomorrow Nov. 15th. Will try to go via Palermo, Gibraltar.

Notes

1   In the late afternoon of September 29, Gavin met with General Ridgway on the top of a mountain near the Amalfi–Gragnano road. About ten miles north they could see Naples partly in flames. Ridgway directed Gavin to capture the city the next day. They moved out just before daylight, expecting to meet German resistance, but their only obstacles were blown bridges and, for some unfathomable reason, tons of chestnuts strewn over the road. By about noon on October 1 they had control of the city.

2   Later Gavin wrote of the run-up to his promotion. After getting replacements and being refitted, he noted, the parachute regiments of the 82nd landed in Salerno Bay on the night of September 13/14, 1943. Compared to Sicily it was "a piece of cake," as there was no opposition on the drop zones. The 504th Parachute Infantry, he recalled, "did a splendid job of clearing the Germans from key observation towns," and he mentioned Altavilla and Albanella, "thus assuring the success of the amphibious landing and the survival of the beachhead."

3   Gavin recalled an interesting occurrence when the 505th Parachute Infantry Regiment was given the job of policing the city. That included supervising the water lines that formed each morning at fireplugs and other water outlets. The Neapolitan housewives would line up to get water, carrying their pails and buckets. In a short time they would be flailing away at each other, yelling in Italian, as they sought to improve their position or settle some old family feud. The troopers, who were there to maintain order, did so, but the housewives didn't like it. Finally an English-speaking Italian explained to the paratroopers, "Look, this is their social hour. They are having fun. Leave them alone. They won't hurt each other." The troopers took that good advice, left the ladies alone, and all went well.

---

i   Zeiss binoculars were highly prized.

CHAPTER 5

London

Wednesday, Nov. 17, 1943

Received orders Saturday. Packed Sunday. Attempted to leave Monday but held up by weather. Departed Pomigliano 0830 the 16th. Arrived in Palermo 1000. Lunch with Gen. Williams at Hqrs TCC. He gave me a ship to Algiers that I could keep and fly into Marrakech if necessary.

Left Palermo at 1330. Arrived Algiers 1730 Tuesday. Attempted to arrange flight from Marrakech to UK, but no success. Stopped at Aylete Hotel. Walked down to Maison Agricole to see Jack Thompson, but he was not in. Algiers rather well lighted up, the brightest place I have seen in six months.

Early AM of today, the 17th, attempted to arrange onward and encountered considerable red tape. Finally, after visiting MATS G-1 ETOUSA, AGO NATOUSA, MATS in that order, all was fixed.

Took off at 1030 for Marrakech in plane provided by TCC. Uneconomical as hell. Started reading John P. Marquand's *So Little Time* and am enjoying it immensely.

Before my departure Gen. R warned me of the machinations of Maj. Gen. Browning, stating that he was intelligent, charming, and very close to Mr. Churchill. Further that he was unprincipled and ruthless in his efforts to align every operation and every piece of equipment to the complete benefit of the British Empire at our expense. Worse still, he had completely taken in Gen. Lee, who thought his word was law. This is just about entirely true, and Browning must be handled cautiously but firmly.

I am aware, however, that he is thinking beyond this war to the creation and maintenance of an international airborne force. I am especially interested in it and I believe he will head it. This is not the time to alienate his friendship. The officers of the army tomorrow must be international-minded. I have 30 years of service ahead of me. I must see beyond the next battle, whether I get clipped in it or not.[i]

---

i   This is an indication of the breadth of Gavin's vision going well beyond the tactical issues and relating to future needs.

London, Friday, Nov. 19, [1943]

Arrived Marrakech 1630 Nov. 17th, took off 2230 for Prestwick, Scotland. Arrived 1100 Nov. 18th. Left for London 1400. Arrived in London 1600. Reported to ETOUSA. No one seems to know just what in the hell I am supposed to be doing here except that I am on the COSSAC staff.[1]

Called on Gen. Barker, Deputy C/S, this AM. Called on Gen. Bradley this AM. Talked with him for about an hour on the coming operation. He has some sound ideas. It is wonderful to see people here with whom I have served in combat. Saw Ralph Doty, now of the embassy. Driver most pulchritudinous. Called on Col. Eyster, G-3 ETOUSA.

London, Saturday, Nov. 20, [1943]

7:15 breakfast, followed by a long walk. Met Col. Raff in Hyde Park. Talked over the coming show.[i] Shinberger is now a LnO with the TCC. Called on Gen. Bull at 1000.[ii] He took me in to see Gen. Morgan, there met Gen. Browning. Talked to him for quite awhile. He is as smooth as ever and quite generally distrusted by American high commanders. Afterward General Barker said, referring to him, "Oh, yes, he is an empire builder." I still think a lot of Browning. We can go a long way together.

Gen. Bull told me to contact 9th Air Force, TCC, 101st Div, and then come in and see him before going to see the 21st Army Group. He explained that the 21st Army Group was a British command set up to do all of the tactical planning and ordering after receiving the decisions of SAC. The First Army (Bradley) would take over upon landing. Later the American 1st Army Group would be formed. A screwy setup.[iii]

Went to G-3 ETOUSA in connection with A/B training doctrine, Gen. R's probable arrival, and how to get to the 9th Air Force. Left at 1300 for Sunnyhills and there reported to Gen. Brereton, CG 9th AF, and talked to him and his chief of staff for about an hour. His attitude and plans make the picture look very, very black.

He has one TCC group now, another closing next month, and a third by Jan. 1st. Beyond that he is afraid to predict. They are quite green and untrained, know nothing of night operations, and haven't begun to get realistic combat training.

---

i   Colonel Edson Raff was sent to England as an airborne expert. His personality grated on both Ridgway and Gavin. He was later commander of the seaborne relief force of the 82nd for the invasion and the acting commander of the 507th in Normandy when Colonel Millett was captured.

ii Bull was British Major General Bull, the G3 of COSSAC. He would be highly regarded by Gavin and Ridgway serving as Eisenhower's G3.

iii This refers to the initial organization for the invasion where all personnel would be under 21st Army Group commanded by Montgomery.

I told him that we were endeavoring to arrange the transfer of the 52nd Wing up here. He was lukewarm, or even resentful, of the scheme. Said it should have been coordinated through Eisenhower and the War Dept. in the first place. Then he said that, if it did come up here, he would probably transfer a lot of their personnel around to other inexperienced groups in order to raise their experience level. I argued against that, to no avail I am certain. He appeared to be a most difficult man to deal with.[i]

Returned to London at 1630. Arranged with ATC to get Lt. Oakley to Belfast tomorrow. Reached a decision to go to see Gen. Lee and the 101st Div. as soon as possible tomorrow. Gen. Brereton told me that the group that were to arrive later were in training in the States. That is a joke. Even the training of the TCC units here is absurd by combat standards. I hate to be associated with an effort that has such little prospects of success as this. Their ideas of what they can do are so remote from what combat has shown they can do as to be fantastic.

London, Nov. 23, [1943]

Sunday went to the 101st. Arrived about 1100. Conferred with Gen. Lee, Col. Higgins, Col. Stewart (Div AO) and BG McAuliff. Gen. Lee outlined his most pressing problems, principally getting a statement of A/B policy from COSSAC. Despite letters written by his headquarters, they have been ignored. Getting gliders unpacked in time for Jan. 1st Opn Plan commitment, lack of cooperation from TCC, particularly TCC Exec, who was Borum's Exec. I promised to do all that I could. Returned to London 2100.

London, Nov. 24, [1943]

Attended a conference with Higgins and Pratt of the 101st at the Grosvenor House re the new TO and TE. All in agreement with no difficulties.

A conference at G-3 ETOUSA with Gen. Noce, Cols. Holmes, Eyster, A39th AF, re changing the billet area of the 82nd Div from North Ireland to the area occupied by the TCC north of London. Gen. R said that an area 10 miles by marching or 60 miles by motor from the TCC fields would be OK. He also stated that 100 2½-ton trucks would suffice to move troops from their billets to their training areas. Gen. Noce is having the area resurveyed and the answer is due today, the 24th.[ii]

---

i   Brererton commanded all troop transport aircraft and eventually the Allied Airborne Army, though he never involved himself in actual ground operations. He resented the 52nd coming from Italy as they were not part of his initial transport force and were clearly aligned with the 82nd. He was unfamiliar with the issues in Italy regarding airborne operations and did not "buy in" to Gavin's techniques for accurate troop drops.

ii This refers to selection of training and billet areas in the UK for the division near to the air transport fields. This would require a move from Quorn, Leicestershire, to Leicester.

Arranged with G-3 ETOUSA to have an inquiry sent to NATOUSA re the date the 504th can be expected to arrive. Gen. R followed up on this later with a memo to Gen. Barr. Gen. R had a conference with Gen. Bull re probable commitment plans for A/B units. The situation looks auspicious. A copy of a radiogram received indicates that Gen. Williams with the XII TCC may come up here, as well as the 52nd Wing. Called on Gen. Bradley in the evening. Dinner at mess. Gen. Devers sharp, alert, relaxed, all good qualities in a man with his responsibilities.[i]

London, Nov. 25, [1943]

Arrived at the office early and accomplished little. Called on General Noce. In his absence talked to Col. Eyster and Col. Holmes re our billets. Everything remains as is until about 60 days prior to the coming operation, at which time we will be moved to the vicinity of the departure airdromes.

This decision was made by Gen. Bradley, so Eyster says. Talked to Noce by phone later and he stated essentially the same thing. A short conference with Brig. McLean at which time he emphasized the difficulties of a cross channel operation because of the following:

1. There are only four or five days during a month when the tidal and related meteorological conditions are satisfactory for an amphibious effort.

2. The airborne troops particularly desire favorable moon conditions.

3. The probabilities of combining points 1 and 2 to stage a successful attack in complete conformity with everyone's wishes have been calculated at 100 to 1 against such a thing occurring.

I told him that I had no comment to make either way on it.[ii]

Sunday, Dec. 12, 1943

Conference with Gen. Bull at which he pointed out the undesirable portions of Memo EA/BT. I have never seen such a command as this. A. M. Leigh-Mallory thought that the 38th RAF Group was ½ inch too low on a schematic chart. General Bull thinks 21st Army Group is an inch too low. A. M. Leigh-Mallory will say that they are not on the same level. Before an order is published everyone must be queried on their attitude toward its publication. It makes for an intolerable situation since in some measure, large or small, depending on the circumstances, squabbling, jealousies,

---

i   Devers was responsible for managing *Bolero* within the UK which was a huge logistics and housing exercise. He later commanded 6th Army Group in France.

ii   These conditions became requirements which limited the dates available for invasion planning—roughly two three-day periods a month.

politics and self-aggrandizement are rampant. Go[o]d to get back to soldiers. This, however, is an education.

Conferred with Gen. McLean on the same memo. Conferred with RAF Wing Commander MacPherson on the minutes of the last meeting. Lunch with Oldfield.

Afternoon conference with Gen. Bull, at which time I obtained permission to visit Northern Ireland on Monday. Called Col. Eaton regarding the situation in the Division. Conferred with Capt. Strauss, Operations USN, on the memo EA/BT. Gen. Bull is doing a splendid job under most difficult conditions. This situation feels intolerable at times. Dinner at Ciro's. Upstairs afterward for brandy.

Wednesday, Dec. 15, 1943

Sunday a quiet day. To Div CP at Castle Dawson early Monday. Visited almost entire area. Conferred with some of staff and C/S. Returned Tuesday. Arranged for Capt. Ireland to go to TCC as Ln O from Amer A/B troops. Div did not look good. Appearance of individuals was not up to par. Attitude sloppy. Div Hqrs area not so good. Coal situation very serious.[i]

Thursday, Dec. 16, 1943

Worked on new draft of EA/BT most of the day. Visited Gen. Browning's CP in afternoon. Could not contact him. Planning at 21 Army Group well underway evidently. Arranged to see him today, Thursday. Conference with Brig. McLean in afternoon, also with WC MacPherson.

Dinner at Bentley Priory in honor of the 9th AF. Told Gen. Lee that I would get a naval officer and go down to see him Friday. Cablegram from Gen. Ridgway indicating that he would be in Sunday. [Handwritten penciled addition follows.] Conference with Raff re org. of [corporate?].

Friday, Dec. 17, 1943

Prepared to a finish a new draft of EA/BT. Turned it over to Brig. McLean, who is to refer it to the high-powered A/B committee under A. M. Leigh-Mallory. If they feel that it serves any purpose, they will return it for publication with, of course, recommended changes. In its present general form, there is absolutely no need for it. WD Cir 113 fully meets our needs. However, a specific interpretation of it is badly needed for this theatre. But specifically interpreting anything around this

---

i   This refers to the shortage of coal for heating billets etc. There was a coal strike in the UK that was a major issue for everyone.

headquarters is asking for trouble. Everyone, everything, is keen. Keep the upper hand is the watchword.

I believe that Lt. Gen. Morgan is double-crossing me. He sympathizes with Barker when Barker calls me in re the Browning scheme and then, I believe, he goes to Browning.[i]

Browning was promoted to Lt. Gen. yesterday. He now commands our airborne troops, whether we like it or not.

When Gen. Ridgway gets here we will be able to straighten it out.

Attended a meeting yesterday with the general planning committee from 21st AG. Later in the day attended a meeting at Gen. Browning's Hqrs. (notes attached). Gen. Ridgway's arrival delayed until Monday. Col. Jack came through yesterday on way from First Army to Div.[ii]

Sunday, Dec. 19, [1943]

Conferences with MacPherson re EA/BT memo. Gave him a dozen copies of the latest draft. He favors the earlier draft that specifically mentions units and responsibilities. He will take it up at the meeting of the A/B committee. Called Higgins re return of Gen. R. Also promised him some help in his pathfinder school and mine school. Moved office. Arranged transportation to Glasgow. Promised Jerry to visit the 101st next week. Dinner at Quags.

Tuesday, Dec. 21, 1943

Gen. Ridgway's arrival changed to Monday. Left London on night train Sunday night, arriving in Glasgow 0800 Monday. Met Gen. R. To Prestwick by car. To London by plane, arriving 1600. Little accomplished outside of conferring.

The situation regarding Browning looks particularly bad. There is no doubt that he is doing some long-range planning, planning that will ultimately encompass the entire allied airborne effort well into the peace beyond this war.

If there is a British SAC appointed, his position will become very solid, and I am not sure what we can do about it. He is still endeavoring to get control of the entire allied A/B lift. I suspect now that A. M. Leigh-Mallory's disapproval of his consolidation plan was all prearranged and staged for my benefit and Brereton's. They actually figure on taking it over in a more painless way later when the tactical plan makes it a necessity.

There is growing now a plan to use all of the A/B lift for the British. They are endeavoring to make it appear tactically and strategically necessary. I am also

i British Lieutenant General Morgan was in charge of COSSAC until it became SHAEF.
ii Whitfield Jack who would serve as the division G2 for the remainder of the war.

convinced that Gen. Morgan, Deputy C/S COSSAC, is playing both ends against the middle. He goes to the Americans tch-tch-ing when the British make an empire-building move and having sympathized with them, gotten their reaction and damned his own people, he goes to them and tells them of the American reaction to their latest move. I am quite sure that this is the technique. As a result of it I am at the moment persona non grata with Gen. Browning. It is hard to know whom to trust and it is a bit difficult to sense who has been taken in by the British.

If, on the other hand, the British begin to feel that one of us is not, definitely not, playing ball their way, they undermine your position even with your own people. This place is rife with indolence and politics. This morning I had a most interesting talk with Gen. Devers. He has a hell of a good idea of what is going on and has a good view of the airborne situation. He said that there are too many people in COSSAC who are fighting next year and the year after instead of fighting the present battle. This is so true. It is well that the troops in the front combat units do not know what goes on. Gen. R is as anti-British as ever and feels that Mr. Churchill has Mr. Roosevelt under his thumb. The army finds itself in an awkward position.[i]

London, Sunday, Dec. 26, 1943

The past several days spent escorting Gen. Ridgway around to the different Hqrs with which he was concerned. The most important question, that of appointing an American airborne corps commander, was discussed with Devers, Lee, Bradley, etc. The answer as arrived at is to recommend the creation of a large airborne staff section in the hqrs of the American 1st Army Group. This group will very likely be commanded by Gen. Devers. If Ridgway heads it I will get the division, provided Taylor does not return. This may be the final outcome.[ii]

A radiogram was sent to Marshall requesting the assignment of Swing to ETOUSA to take over the job, but there is a possibility that Swing will not be available for the job.[iii] I am at last getting along very well with the British and all planning hqrs. It is with a much better feeling of satisfaction that I get about. It takes quite a while to work one's way into a hqrs like this, particularly when the British are to be worked with. They are difficult to get close enough to to feel that you have their confidence, which in this business is vital.

---

i   The issue as to "who is in charge" was a continuous battle. It was eventually resolved simply by numbers, as the U.S. forces far exceeded the British and they lost the ability to control events. This is a harbinger of the contemporary joint and combined operations issues.

ii   The final outcome was there would be no Airborne Corps commander for Normandy. Taylor would become commander of the 101st when Major General Lee had a heart attack and Devers would be sent to the Mediterranean.

iii Major General Joe Swing was sent to the Pacific Theater to command the 11th Airborne Division.

Xmas day was spent at Val Porter's rather quietly. Oldfield, Ireland, and Oakley, all of the 505, were in for a drink Xmas afternoon. Dinner at Val's in the evening. She is swell. Her family is a nuisance. God help the man who marries into that family.[i]

Xmas Eve dinner at Ciro's. Check a bit over 17 pounds, champagne at 135s per qt. Wow. It is a good thing that the past six months were spent in Kairouan and environs.

Monday, Dec. 29, 1943

Daily conferences on the employment of the A/B units in the Overlord operation. Basically, we are in total agreement with the British. There are difficulties on such points as the hour of the first drop. We all want to make it about three or four hours before H-Hour. The amphibious people are against that and the TCC people are not equal to it except in limited numbers. The British lift is dwindling away to practically nothing. They of course are holding out for pooling the ships and insist on placing a recommendation to that effect in our paper. Bayouex [sic: Bayeux?] stands out as being the priority one mission. With further study it is becoming clear [sentence not completed].

London, The Norfolk House, Saturday, Jan. 29, 1944

Operations again resumed on what appears at this time to be a much more promising basis than the past efforts. A not too busy day by most standards. Went to Hqrs 21st Army Group (BR) and talked air support to Col. Cole, A-3 IX AF. The time is opportune for us to get in our plan before the current thinking on Overlord air support matters becomes crystallized.

Several conferences during the morning with SAC staff members on airborne and troop carrier problems. With one week to go on this particular assignment my feelings upon imminent relief are mixed. Definitely mixed. This is a most difficult place unless one is committed to a staff career. A troop officer feels frustrated with the evident dearth of accomplishment, despite the lengthy and profound conferences that take place.

I like some aspects of it, however. It has been particularly gratifying to get along so well with the British officers and at the same time accomplish so much. They have many fine professionally well-qualified officers in their high commands.

Had a long talk with Oldfield yesterday.[ii] First, we want to build up some publicity for the TCC pilots. We have got to convince them that they are tough people,

---

i   Val was an English lady who would be a serious romance for him throughout his stay in England.
ii Oldfield was a journalist and raconteur and became the 82nd Public Affairs Officer. He was very flamboyant and well connected.

then maybe they will be. He told me of a movement afoot to write up a story for *Collier's* on me. Wm. Courtney is to do the job. He is excellent. I am rather skeptical, however, of the merit of being written up as a jumping general, a glamour boy. In the long run it may do harm. Looking, however, to the days of peace to follow it may do little harm and much good to be well known. Return to a captaincy is not very promising for the next ten years.

First news releases this morning on the Japanese treatment of the survivors of Bataan. It is interesting to conjecture why the War Dept. saw fit to release this information at this time. It is certain to stir up a wave of anti-Jap feeling that might well upset the War Dept. plans to finish off Hitler first. For that reason, particularly since Mr. Eden released the news to the British simultaneously, it may be part of a well-laid plan to solidly line up the British behind us in the Asiatic theatre after the end of this European mess. Seems a bit premature for that, yet why would it be released now? I do believe that the British will be behind us in Asia, perhaps not as intensely as for this local affair, but that is entirely understandable.

I wish to hell that tomorrow were D-Day. It is the waiting that is bothersome, not the fight itself.

London, Monday, Jan. 31, 1944

Gen. Lee came up for lunch. This was followed by a conference with Col. Edwards at ETOUSA re the reorganization of the A/B units. The 507 is to be broken up, the 501st to the 101st, and the 508 to the 82nd.[i]

Had a long talk with Gen. Lee re his plan for the Carentan operation. Sounded to me as though he was dissipating his division before ever getting it organized after landing. He has a difficult job ahead, really one that takes more experienced troops and troop leaders than he will have in the 101st. He is to come up today and we are to confer with G-3, First U.S. Army, at 1000. His mission at present does appear rather extensive.[ii]

Talked to Gen. Ridgway and Col. Eaton several times during the day. Hagan and Roy to come to London on Gen. R's staff. Appears as though Norton may go to Div. as G-3. About time. This is more and more becoming a parachute show despite our most intense efforts to get the gliders in.[iii]

Called Gen. Giles re packing buildings in the Grantham area. Having difficulties.

---

i   This refers to the plan to augment each division with several of the independent PIRs in theater. The 101st would have the 501st and 502nd while the 82nd would receive the 508th. When it became apparent that the 504th could not participate, the 507th was assigned to the 82nd. This gave each division three parachute infantry regiments and one glider infantry regiment.

ii   The 101st had no combat experience.

iii   The key issue was lack of transport aircraft to have both elements land together.

Went to Ciro's Saturday evening with Val. Yesterday noon took her and her mother to lunch at Barclay's.

London, Tuesday, Feb. 1, 1944

Conference with Gen. Bradley and Gen. Lee in Gen. Bradley's office at 1000. Gen. Lee concerned with the difficulties of his mission. Talked to him quite a bit about it. Didn't realize before how ideas from the last war carried into this one can be confusing. He is thinking in terms of a coordinated broad scale attack against an extremely vague German coastal position, whereas nowadays the system in such a case is patrolling in force and then going thru the holes and mopping up. His mission is not an easy one, perhaps too difficult for his division as green as it is.

Gen. Bradley is a good soldier. He knows the details of organization and equipment that only can be acquired through long familiarity with them. I know of no enemies that he may have in the service. A most interesting case study.

Conference in afternoon with Bagby on air support, troop carrier training standards, etc. Conference with Schellhammer late in afternoon on reorganization. It appears to be more difficult of accomplishment on further study.[i]

Dinner at the Empire.

London, Wednesday, Feb. 2, 1944

Several interesting but unimportant conferences in the AM on Overlord. Matter of terrain models was inquired about by SHAEF staff. Called 101st and they said that they were going to send their own man to school and, after training him, make their own.

Lunch at Chas. Lytle's, 24 Park Lane. Stag. Some very nice civilians there, including the Chief of Scotland Yard, now W. C. Horwell, RAF.

Conference on training at 1430. Arrived at a rather general but, I believe, satisfactory solution.

Understand that the memorandum on "The Employment of Airborne Forces" is not being too well received. Same rehash of Cir 113 etc. etc.

Dinner at Ciro's. Didn't sleep well. Worried about lack of tangible accomplishment in office. I waste too much time. For many reasons it will be the thing for me to get back to the Div.

Prime Minister had a conference yesterday at which the matter of more airlift for Overlord was discussed. It shows the fine hand of Browning. Montgomery is back of him, or he had better be. It appears possible that more ships may be obtained

---

i   This refers to the integration of the independent parachute infantry regiments with the two airborne divisions.

and that the size of the American lift may be lessened to increase the British lift. I do hope that the 82nd gets in, or that I get in.

London, Thursday, Feb. 3, 1944

Conference with Bagby, McIntyre and MacPherson on the training program and SOP. Cleaned up a number of personal chores about the city in view of my coming relief. Called ETOUSA. Orders should be in today. Business here is slowing down. When enough officers are present to permit travelling to units to check on training it should pick up. Maj. Roy reported in. He is to be the glider expert in the new section.

London, Friday, Feb. 4, 1944

Maj. Roy to duty in AM. I left for CP 101st at 1000. Arrived at 1200 in time for lunch. After lunch had a long conference with Gen. Lee and Higgins. He is concerned about his mission, and well he might be. It is difficult to see how it can be worked out to the satisfaction of everyone with the means he will have. The probability of an increase in the British lift at the expense of the American lift becomes increasingly greater.

Returned to Norfolk House in PM. Maj. Hagan for duty. Dinner at 82. Called Jack Thompson, who has just returned from Algiers. Lunch date for tomorrow.

London, Sunday, Feb. 6, 1944

A very busy day what with getting Hagan and Roy started and getting cleared myself. Conference with Gen. Bull and said goodbyes. SOP and training conferences to complete final drafts. This all finished. Called Gen. Ridgway. He OKed my Sunday departure. This may be impossible, however.

Dinner at Ciro's with Jack Thompson, Eil and Val. I am anxious to get back to the division, although this has been an education.

Note

1   Later Gavin wrote that his assignment in London was to be Senior Airborne Advisor on the COSSAC (Chief of Staff, Supreme Allied Command) staff. "My final responsibility," he recalled, "was to make recommendations to General Bradley on the employment of our airborne forces in the anticipated Normandy battle." By February 1944 that work was complete and Gavin returned to the 82nd Airborne Division, then in Leicester, England.

CHAPTER 6

Back to the 82nd

Leicester, England, Friday, Feb. 11, 1944

Sunday evening, referred to above, I received a call from Division directing me to go over as soon as possible. Difficulties of some sort in the 505. Left Heston Field 0900 and arrived Langford Lodge 1300. Met Gen. Taylor at the Ballyscullion House. He had just returned from Italy. The 505 troubles were AWOL, 60 in the regt, of which 32 were in Vandervort's battalion, the 2nd.

Gen. Ridgway was particularly concerned because an inspection by the Div IG showed that there was apparently unfair treatment, and that the situation could easily get entirely out of hand if it was not already so. Allegedly Vandervort was a martinet, the officers aloof and unapproachable, the men overworked, and punished for the offenses of others. Van was using his favorite mass punishment technique.[i]

I spent a day and a half around the regt. Had several meals. Quite clearly it rests on Batcheller. Inadequate and unforceful supervision of the regiment. Gen. Ridgway holds me closely responsible for the behavior of the regt, since he feels that I brought it up and know it well.

Batcheller is a headache. He can do the job, but it will take effort. Commanding a parachute regiment is quite a job. It never just happens. It must be commanded.[ii]

Wednesday morning left for England. Stopped by Half Penny Field at Kidderminster and called on CG of the VIII Corps, Gen. Reinhart. We are attached to that corps upon arrival in England. Had lunch with him and his staff.

Arrived in London at 1500. Sent letter to AEAF on packing shed requirements of U.S. airborne troops and took Gen. Ridgway to call on Gen. Browning at British AB Hqrs. Signed out and cleared flat at 2000.

---

i   Vandervoort went on to become the finest combat commander in theater as judged by Ridgway.
ii Batcheller, actually a favorite of both Ridgway and Gavin, was self-indulgent and lax in training and discipline. He was replaced by Colonel Ekman (a new arrival from the States) and assumed command of a battalion in the 508th, a highly unusual situation.

These are the only surviving photos of Gavin as a young boy, in sailor suit at maybe age five and first communion perhaps seven. Born James Ryan in Brooklyn to an Irish mother, he spent his first two years in a Catholic orphanage, then was placed with foster parents Martin and Mary Gavin, taking their name. (Gavin family collection)

Gavin as a corporal in Panama, 1924–25. Gavin's foster parents, both illiterate, were not interested in education. At the end of eighth grade, they took him out of school and put him to work to help support the family. Desperate for more learning and a better quality of life, he ran away from home on his 17th birthday. In New York City he managed to enlist in the Army. He had found his calling. (Gavin family collection)

As an Army enlisted man stationed in the Panama Canal Zone, Gavin was encouraged by his first sergeant to compete for an appointment to West Point. He entered with the Class of 1929 and, at graduation, stood 185 of 299 on the Order of Merit List, a truly spectacular performance for someone whose previous formal academic experience had ended with the eighth grade. (*The Howitzer*, 1929)

In early September 1929 Gavin married Irma Baulsir in Washington, D.C. (Gavin family collection)

Tactical Department instructors, West Point, 1941. Gavin is in the second row, second from the right. (*The Howitzer*, 1941)

Gavin with *Chicago Tribune* correspondent Jack Thompson in Sicily in 1943. (U.S. Army)

Gavin sent this photo of himself, taken in England in March 1944, to his daughter Barbara to use if anyone asked for one. They did. (Gavin family collection)

Painting of Gavin at La Fiere. (Gavin family collection)

A conspicuously youthful Gavin strapping on his gear for the September 1944 jump into Holland, the fourth combat jump in which he was the first man out the door. (U.S. Army Signal Corps photo)

Gavin and Dempsey in Holland in September or October 1944. (Courtesy of Keith Nightingale)

Gavin with King George VI in Holland, talking with Gavin's regimental commanders. "There are no finer regimental commanders in the Army," Gavin wrote to his daughter Barbara, "rough, tough, and all of them good paratroopers and ready for anything." (Gavin family collection)

In this iconic photo, taken in Belgium during the Battle of the Bulge, Gavin is shown with an M-1 rifle, the weapon of the basic infantryman, rather than the carbine or pistol most officers would carry. He used it, too, fighting right alongside his troopers while earning two Distinguished Service Crosses and two Silver Stars. (U.S. Army photograph)

Gavin during the Battle of the Bulge, January 28, 1945, using a field telephone to direct rot-line troops near Herresbach, Belgium. (U.S. Army Signal Corps photograph; Cpl P. J. Petrony)

Gavin with General Matthew Ridgway in Belgium during the Battle of the Bulge. Gavin succeeded Ridgway in command of the 82nd Airborne Division when Ridgway was promoted to command the XVIII Airborne Corps. To Gavin Ridgway was a superior, a mentor, and then a rival, but always much admired. (U.S. Army photo)

Gavin and General Dwight D. Eisenhower at Tempelhof Airfield in Berlin sometime in 1945. In both his wartime diary and, more harshly, in his later writings, Gavin was highly critical of Ike's leadership during the drive across Europe. (Gavin Papers, Army Heritage and Education Center)

As the war in Europe came to a close, Gavin and his units met the Russians. Here he is at a party hosting the Russians at Ludwigslust, Germany, in May 1945. Of course, the Russians reciprocated, leading to a series of marathon sessions requiring stamina rivaling that needed for combat. (Gavin Papers, Army Heritage and Education Center)

Members of the 505 Parachute Infantry Regiment who survived all four combat jumps. The 505 is the only Regiment that made all four jumps. One thousand men jumped into Sicily in 1943, but by 1945 only 23 had survived in the Division to make all four combat jumps, including James Gavin.

(Above) Gavin shaking hands with the mayor of Nijmegen, Holland, during celebrations to mark the first anniversary of the town's liberation, in September 1945. (Gavin Papers, Army Heritage and Education Center)

(Left) Stained-glass window in the church of Sainte-Mère-Église depicting paratroopers landing in the early hours of 6 June 1944. (Istock, Joaquin Ossorio-Castillo)

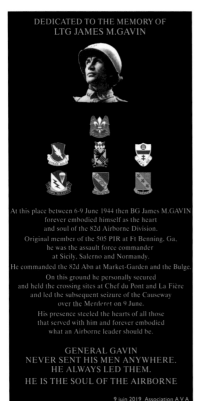

Statue of Gavin at La Fiere. (Wikimedia Commons)

Had dinner at Val's flat and departed London at 0030 Thursday. Arrived in Leicester at 0430 and, after considerable searching, found the 82nd CP area at Braunston Park at 0500. Slept until 0700 and then to work. There was much to do. Turner, G-3, left permanently for the hospital with ulcers.

After a lot of preliminary conferring, started around on a reconnaissance at 1100, visiting Stoughton, Scraptoft, Quarndon, Nottingham, and returning to the Div at 1600. There was more conferring until 2000, at which time I was ready for some sleep.

There is a great deal to be done if the division is to get in here with a minimum of confusion and get started on its training program. Training is the most serious problem, both the extent of it and the magnitude of the problems, and it is the one least solved, particularly because of Turner's denouement. The future shows promise of being very, very busy, many headaches and much worry, lots of dissatisfaction. I hope our difficulties are appreciated by the higher ups. There will be many, and we are starting late.

Leicester, Feb. 12, 1944[1]

Accompanied by Col. Pettit went over the 325 area to determine whether or not alternate billeting would be necessary in the case of that regiment. Decided not. Actually, all of these units will be very well off compared to many of the camps that I have wintered in.[i]

Went to Cottesmore to check the interior construction in the division packing shed, an excellent hangar for that purpose. They are assembling, the RAF, Hamilcars [gliders] in adjoining hangars now or we could easily get another hangar for brigade. Went to Grantham to Hqrs IX TCC.

Had lunch with Gen. Brereton and Giles. Brereton had just dropped in to apparently look things over. Talked to me and Col. Crouch a short while on pathfinder training. He is an unusual chap. Evidently quite smart, but with it rather pompous and opinionated. It is difficult to obtain anything definite in the way of training plans from them at this time in view of Gen. Giles' impending relief.

It is clear, however, that training, even on the regimental scale, must be coordinated with the Navy, RAF fighters, and Land Procurement people.

Returned to the Div CP about 1700. Col. Weinicke came in from Ireland. He is to be the Div G-3. A good choice, although I would prefer to have someone with some practical parachute experience.

---

i   Finding sufficient land for billets, training, and live fire was difficult given that so many elements were involved in the approval process.

Leicester, Sunday, Feb. 13, 1944

Spent the morning visiting the billets and camps of the artillery and engineers. Some of the homes that the British have turned over to us for occupancy are lovely and have seen days of prosperity and gaiety. I wonder if they were not actually bankrupt, or approaching that state, when they turned them over to the government. Actually, they are castles of a size and inefficient arrangement that would preclude their economic maintenance.

Back to camp by noon. Met Gen. Ridgway, who had just come in from London. It was good to see him and talk to him of our problems. I need an expression of confidence from him occasionally. It is, after all, his Div. He has positive and definite ways of running it. It is his staff, so despite my best of intentions and industry I feel at times that a word from him helps.

He told me that Gen. Taylor would probably replace Gen. Lee, who has been taken seriously ill. Since his replacement would very likely be junior to me, I would at last feel like and actually be the Assistant CG. Sorry to lose Taylor. His presence in the Division was some guaranty of Gen. Ridgway's availability for promotion to a corps. I may be considered a bit young to take the Division by some people, although I would give anything to get it.

Spent the afternoon taking Gen. Ridgway around to the different billets. He seems pleased with them. At the suggestion of the G-1 spent the night at the Grand Hotel in town.

Called Val. Makes one feel good. Aren't we fighting for blueberry pie?

Leicester, Feb. 14, 1944

A late start. Breakfast at the Grand. Out to camp by 9:00. Visited the 325 camp to check its readiness, it being the camp of most concern. All set. Talked training with G-3 in the afternoon. Drafted a swell schedule. All bns to get a parachute actual lift proficiency test. I hope it works out. Each Prcht regt to get a CT lift in early April.

G-3 agreed that the ideal A/B division at present would consist of three parachute regiments, with four glider arty bns, an AT and an AA Bn plus services. No glider infantry. Until we devise a better way to carry glider infantry, they are not worth much to us airborne.[i]

It appears that I am in for a very busy three months, with little time to visit London.

---

i   This is the continuing issue regarding the efficiency and quality of the GIRs as a combat force.

Leicester, Feb. 15, 1944

Checked the 505 and 325 camps. Both are coming along in excellent shape, especially the 505th. G-3 returned in the evening from IX TCC. Richards, the TCC A-3, is at times most difficult to work with. I presume that in any test of knowledge he would rate very high. He appears to be smart and quite competent as a boss. But as a staff officer he is headstrong, opinionated and disloyal. Gen. Williams, who is to take over the IX TCC, is due in any day now. He may change things around a bit. Anyway, it appears as though we should be able to accomplish some excellent training.

Lately I have felt a bit lost. What it is I want, or whether I am just simply tired of all of this, I don't know. It has been the attitude of the British to say, when we say anything about being tired of being away from our normal way of life so long, "Well, we have been at war for four years." Being here with them now I realize that, to them, being at war is like being on WPA in uniform, except for the overseas armies. Even those they grant leaves and furlos to whenever possible.

The people of ours that must get fed up at times are the 45th and 3rd Divisions. They are in the Nettuno beachhead now. A young man doesn't give a damn. He has his whole life ahead of him, and maybe opportunity lies right where he is. Who knows? A middle-aged man must have a home, family, and something to fight for besides himself. He realizes that there is little opportunity except for death or injury in his present vocation. An old man is out of place and, if he is there at all, it is because he knows nothing else and has no other choice and probably has followed the profession of arms all his life.

Leicester, Feb. 15, 1944, 1945

This is no time to write this, but it is as good a time as any. It is now 7:45. I have just come from the mess, having eaten in splendid solitude. Not an officer present. Not an office open. The Division closed in its billets and by now not a call has come in notifying Hqrs of their arrival.

Yesterday had a conference with McRoberts and Wilkins to the TCC (LnO). They are ready to go ahead on our training, however the TCC A-3 declines to permit his unit to start planning until formal orders are received.

Later in the day made a reconnaissance of the probable Bn test areas with G-3. It took all afternoon. Returned to the CP at 5:30 and there found Gen. R waiting to find out why A-3 of the TCC is putting us out of the necessary office and billet space at Cottesmore. After some sparks and phone calls we got nowhere and repaired to the Glebe House for dinner.

I hate, actually hate, being treated as an incompetent. Despite the time and effort put into this job there is an unmistakable lack of trust, especially at times when it is most needed. This fast-growing habit of officers putting their troops in tents and then getting themselves a fine house in a nearby village burns me up. At present every Regimental CO has himself a house, while his troops are under canvas. Then we wonder about accusations of officers being aloof, unapproachable and unsympathetic. I don't like the mud and rain any more than anyone else, but neither do the troops. Someone is losing their sense of values, maybe its perspective.[i]

Leicester, Feb. 16, 1944

Visited the 505th, 325th and Engrs in their new billets. Everyone doing very well. Actually, the billets are excellent. Pyramidal tents with stoves and board floors. Nissen huts for offices and the dispensary. Kitchens and messes in large Nissen hut-type buildings. Lights in the offices and messes. Six men to a pyramidal tent.

Walked home from the office for dinner, accompanied by Gen. Ridgway. About 5¼ miles. Walked it in exactly one hour. Gen. R in a good humor. Had a feeling that he would not have been displeased to find me faltering at his pace. He takes considerable pride in having walked many people off their feet. It is unfortunate in some respects, and well in others, that we are so goddamn much alike.

Discussed training after dinner. Much to be done. He definitely arranged packing sheds at Cottesmore.

Leicester, Saturday, Feb. 19, 1944, 9:30PM

Thursday the 17th visited the area in the vicinity of Nottingham and picked what I am sure will be an excellent area for an A/B exercise. Called on Col. Chappel at Bottesford. He is CG of the 50th TC Wing and at the moment somewhat lost. Gen. Williams is needed very badly to get the IX TCC in hand.

Returned to Div Hqrs at noon to lunch with Gen. Ridgway and Maj. Gen. Harter, local district commander, British. Being an old soldier, he had some interesting tales to tell. After lunch accompanied him around on an inspection of some of his British units. Stopped by the CP of the British 4th A/B Brigade. Brigadier Harper commands it.

Gen. Ridgway told me that I had to get to London without delay to attend a meeting at Bentley Priory early Friday morning. Left at 5:15 and arrived at Val's at 8:00. She had a date with Carl Hausauer. Called on her later, 2:00 to be exact.

Attended the meeting at Hqrs AEAF conducted by AVM Leigh-Mallory at 11:00. He wanted to discuss airborne operations with people who have had practical combat

---

i   This is a specific indicator of one of Gavin's key requirements—officers must share the same conditions as their men.

experience. He is to have a conference with Gen. Montgomery Monday, and he wanted to be well fortified.

It appears as though the entire A/B picture is to be revamped. There is some talk of an exclusive A/B show on the Brest peninsula. I am for that. Generally speaking, there is a feeling that the proposed plans for employment of the A/B troops in the coming operations lack vision and boldness. As Gen. Butler put it, it is like having Michelangelo paint a barn. AVM [Leigh-Mallory] made no decisions nor commitments, merely discussed all aspects and encouraged arguments. The meeting ended at 1:00, at which time he took everyone to an excellent lunch in the same area.

Upon returning to the CP, Gen. Ridgway told me that I would have to stay for another meeting Saturday morning. Went to Ciro's with Val. Attended a meeting, again at Bentley Priory, on the subject of establishing a combined TCC-A/B operations room in the vicinity of Uxbridge.

During the night had a good air raid, the best for me in London to date. Sixty planes came over, dropped mostly incendiaries.

Discussed the appointment of an A/B officer to the SHAEF staff with Gen. Ridgway. He is having a difficult time filling all of the requirements for high-ranking A/B officers. I was glad that SHAEF wanted me, and more glad that Gen. R refused. My future is with the division. Higgins may get the job.[i]

I feel much better about the whole picture. For a change I feel like working hard and bucking. It has been a long layoff. Gen. Taylor's status still in doubt.

Leicester, Sunday, Feb. 20, [1944]

To work early this morning. A conference with G-3 on the training program, followed by a conference with Gen. R. Gen. R now has authority to qualify parachutists for the division staff, which will help both personally and help the division. The situation is a most interesting one. Many of them would like to get the pay, and many of them have talked each other into how good the idea of being a parachutist is. The consensus of feeling is that we should have two categories, 1st regular qualified active parachutists and 2nd qualified parachutists except for pay. The latter would only take such instruction as would be necessary to permit them to enter combat with some chance of making it.

This afternoon made a reconnaissance with G-3 of the training areas. Snowing, and snow and ice on the ground. The first drops are going to be frightfully uncomfortable, but I must participate in the first ones of the Bns and Regts.

---

i   Brigadier General Higgins would be the commander of the 82nd sea tail landing at Utah late on D-Day.

Leicester, Monday, Feb. 21, [1944]

Out on a training reconnaissance after a good night's sleep. Colder than hell, food for thought about the coming training. A hell of a time to spend nights in a foxhole.

Awakened by the returning bombers. Quite a few over last night. Quite a few were over London also. Was calling Val when the alarm sounded.

Picked an excellent area for the bn tests and the division CPX and FX. The DZs are not too large and have a canal nearby, but I hope all works out well. We have a terrific training program outlined.

Visited the 505th in the afternoon. Always enjoy seeing those kids again. They are beginning to look rather good. A few months of good training and they should be ready, or as ready as they can get.

Dinner at the house with Col. Grubbs this evening. He is in charge of all colored AC troops in UK. Some job. We had trouble with them downtown last night. Everyone is scared to death of the riot potentialities of the situation. Our troops are touchy about the problem after Naples, and tough enough to do something about it if anything starts, a bad combination.

Leicester, Tuesday, Feb. 22, [1944]

Several near riots in town last night. English people, especially the lower classes, do not discriminate in any way. In fact, they prefer the company of colored troops. The colored troops have been in this community for almost a year, and they are well entrenched. Many are living with local English women. With the advent of the white troops, frays and minor unpleasant encounters have occurred in the local pubs and dance halls. American whites resent very much seeing a white woman in the company of a colored soldier. Here they almost see them in bed with them.

Last night the 505th had its officer patrols armed. The negroes resented this, alleging that the white officers intended to get them. A group of negroes broke into an arms storeroom, secured arms, stole a truck, and headed for town. They were intercepted on the way by one of their own officers and taken back to camp, thus avoiding what might have been a disastrous situation.

Today I had conferences with the EBS PM, local SOS PM, SAF PM, plus anyone else interested. Placed Leicester off limits until further orders. Had all unit COs make a shakedown for weapons and talk to their men personally. Now is no time to settle our racial problem. The attitude of the British is in many respects difficult to understand. Their treatment of colonials is deplorable, yet they entirely mishandle the colored problem. They inflame it and run, yelling all the while. This is no way to do things in a democracy.

Visited our packing sheds in Cottesmore. They will have chutes ready for the Bn tests and the jump school.

The colored problem took most of the damn day.[i]
Received several Xmas packages.

Leicester, Feb. 23, 1944

Presented the local-colored situation to General Ridgway. He went to work on it this morning. Little can be done at the moment but talk and let the situation simmer down.

Took Norton and Batcheller to the problem area and showed them the DZs. They were rather enthusiastic in their approval. Looks like an excellent exercise, and damn good test problems for the Bns.

This afternoon visited the 325 training. Coming along OK. A steady-appearing regiment. Probably never will fight with the elan and dash of the parachute regiments but can be counted upon for a steady fight.

Conferred with Gen. R for a few minutes on the present state of the operational planning. He attended a conference yesterday at which Gen. Bradley and the British army commander outlined their requirements for the use of airborne troops to Gen. Montgomery.

Air Marshal Leigh-Mallory dissented, recommending another use. Montgomery backed the army commanders and firmly set the mission for the 101st.

The British are to get 200 C-47s, which they estimate will be enough to lift one of their brigades. Next the 82nd was told that its mission on the western side of the peninsula was being firmly set and that very likely that would be it. We are to plan accordingly. Gen. R hopes to get in all four regiments. I am afraid that further study will indicate the impossibility of getting in that many gliders. It will be an interesting mission and a hell of a tough one. Any kraut, no matter how dumb he is, surely realizes the importance of that bottleneck.

The present count of divisions in western France is 53. Last month it was 24. That shows, better than anything else, what is happening on the Russian front. To an unbiased observer it must appear at this moment as though the Germans are preparing to invade UK rather than the reverse. They even have an A/B division at

---

i   General Gavin, despite the inference, was an advocate for integration throughout his service. He integrated the all-black 555 Independent Airborne Battalion, relegated to Stateside duty in WWII, into the 82d in 1947—a full year ahead of the formal end to segregation in the military. This unit became the 3-505 Abn Inf Bn.

  During the Battle of the Bulge when black soldiers were allowed to join white units as fillers, Gavin posed no objection to receiving them. Other division commanders did. Priorities placed them elsewhere.

  Gavin and Ridgway understood the dynamics behind the fights and knew that "sharing" pubs etc. was not feasible. Hence, working with the businesses, separate facilities were identified to reduce fighting.

Rheims. Some day we are going to get kicked off a beachhead. Let's hope that it is not this time. That would be disastrous for the A/B troops.

Val is a problem, but grand.

Leicester, Feb. 24, 1944

Up at 4:30 and out to see the 3rd Bn 505th perform. Wrong coordinates, so much time was lost. Returned at 10:00. Several conferences on training with G-3, Gen. R, Gen. Howell. Gen. R said this evening that he was going to keep the brigade intact and employ it as a brigade in combat. This certainly was a surprise. He still hopes to get four regiments in. He said that, if there were a mission for 2 para regts, he would send the brigade. A bit of a change and a screwy setup.[i]

Contacted IX TCC and 50th Wing and 438th Group re training. Things are shaping up. The Brigade is finding reasons already why they cannot take the training tests.

Ran home in 49 min. tonight. Ran and walked. Getting back on the beam. It's about time. Lewis suspects that I will inherit the division and he is becoming quite ornery. It will work out.

Leicester, Feb. 25, 1944

A conference at Langar Field with Col. Chappel, CG 50th Wing, and Lt. Col. Donaldson, CO 438th Grp. They will not be able to meet our training schedule starting Mar 1st. Instead, they hope to be ready to drop at night by Mar 5th. Even this is optimistic, I believe.[ii]

Gen. Hal Clark of the 52nd Wing here for lunch. Had a nice talk with him. Our units have a great deal of confidence in each other. Personal friendship of officers goes a long way to establishing confidence among units.

A staff meeting at which the initial directive for "Curveball" was put out.

I suspect that I have never properly appreciated the donor of the books and sweater that came today.

It is so good that I am busy. The minute that things slow down I become introspective, restless and unhappy as hell.

---

i   The brigade concept was that a brigadier general and small staff would control two PIRs.

ii   The troop transport elements were plagued with a flood of incoming pilots and planes with no
     training experience for airborne operations. The 52nd was the only experienced carrier and it was
     tagged to fly the 505th PIR.

Leicester, Feb. 26, 1944

Called Val. A bit like old times in London. Worried some and awakened at 5:30. Couldn't sleep.

Up to Langar Field to the 438th Grp for a reconnaissance of the DZs. Looked satisfactory. Millett and Lindquist in for an inspection of their Nottingham areas. Good to see them again. Sounds as though Lindquist has a good regiment. There will be lots of bad feeling if Millett must be relieved. I wish that someone had the moral courage to relieve him before he had come this far.[i] They came by the house for dinner.

Snowing tonight. I have felt very much alone the past few days. A general officer in one of our divisions is a lonely person. The juniors can all frequent the local pubs, meet people, have some fun, but not the generals. It gets to be a tough proposition at times. Val is a lifesaver.

Taylor went to London today to take over the AB section in SHAEF. It is expected that he will shortly get the 101st, Gen. Lee's division. A long time ago I had figured out that the place for me at this stage of the game was on higher staff. That may have appeared correct at that time, but it seems as clear as can be that the place for me now is with this division. I am certain that Bradley will give Ridgway a corps soon. I may be fortunate enough to get the Division, although I will certainly be rather young and there will be lots of clamoring for it. I do not ever want to jump and fight the division for anyone else. I am getting tired of the prospects of an A/B general, certainly for someone more.

Leicester, Feb. 27, 1944

Called at 1:30 and all was superwell. So pleased could hardly go back to sleep.

A conference with Gen. Ridgway in the war room, the first. Our mission is becoming increasingly firm. For the first time today, he said that I would go in with the parachute mission. So here we go again. I feel really like I would like to raise hell for the next couple of months until target date.

This A/B general is like nothing else in the service. You have all the hell and dangers of any paratrooper, yet you cannot raise hell and get the worry out of your system.

The mission does not look too bad. The German continues to build up, taking from the Russian front. Since we are depending on the 101st for relief, I am not expecting too much. I wish that it were an older outfit. We may be cut off for four or five days. That will be a long nasty hard fight. That is my present job, to get

---

i   Colonel Millett was a lax trainer and disciplinarian despite admonishments by both Gavin and Ridgway. Mis-dropped in Normandy, he was captured for the duration. He was replaced by Colonel Raff.

ready for it. Training is coming along, but not well enough. The next week or so will show a lot.[i]

Leicester, Feb. 28, 1944

Accompanied Gen. R to Hqrs IX TCC at Grantham. About an inch of snow here, at least a foot at Grantham. Countryside beautiful. Now I know where they get those superbeautiful pictures for calendars, etc. Quaint buildings, church spires, snow-laden evergreens, clusters of brick houses.

From Grantham went to Cottesmore to call on Gen. Clark, CG 52nd Wing. A very nice visit. As a result of both calls, we reached a good understanding of our mutual problems. Gen. Williams will of course do everything in his power to help us. We need A/B training badly. His groups are not ready to fly nine-ship group formations yet.

Studied the operational area some more. I like the looks of our mission in many respects. We should not, with a bit of luck, meet too much resistance upon landing. We can accomplish our mission for a day or two, that is a certainty. My only worry is when we will be relieved. With only two divisions hitting the beaches, one to be exact, and only one A/B, I hardly see where they can come to our rescue soon.

Fortunately, we have Gen. Bradley in command. I am sure that he would not sacrifice us. Anyway, someone has got to do that job. I hope in some respects that this is the last of this type for some time. We should pick better spots. Resistance upon landing and intensely thereafter is curtains for many.

Leicester, March 1, 1944 [Entry misdated by Gavin. Actually February 29]

Trip to the 505th to check training. 8 inches of snow has hindered them considerably. Several conferences on training. Drew up an outline defense for the combat area. With a bit of luck that should be a good mission. I am sweating out a bit going into it. The likelihood of encountering hostile resistance during the landing and reorganization phase is greater there than it should be. Still, if we get away with it we know that it will probably be our worst.

Had an idea, so went into London for dinner. Forgot that it was Feb. 29th. Dinner at Josef's. Left here 5:15PM, returned 4:00AM.

---

i   The invasion plan was solidifying. The 82nd would seize the ground west of Sainte-Mère-Église and the 101st the high ground above Utah Beach and Carentan. Ridgway directed Gavin to lead the assault element of three PIRs.

Leicester, March 1, 1944

Went up to Langar to confer with Lt. Col. Donaldson, CO 438th Group. He will be able to fly us Sunday night, or evening rather. He does not feel equal to a night drop yet.

Back to division. Accomplished little, actually. I will be happy as hell when this show finally comes off. The waiting is worse than the fighting. The cold weather does not help things much. Batcheller and Alexander received word today that they were to receive the British DSO for their work from Naples to the Volturno with the 505th. I am very glad to see them get it.

Leicester, March 2, 1944

An extra full night's sleep and off to a busy day. A trip to East Leicester Airfield to call on Group Capt. Venter, CO, then out on the field to observe the Horsa glider activities. Went aloft for a ride, my first glider ride, and enjoyed it very much.

Called on Col. Kingston, local British District CO. Not in his office. Had a meeting of all Infantry unit COs at 1400 hours. Outlined the training program for the coming two months and discussed some of the training points to be emphasized in order to point our training towards our combat mission. This is the most interesting phase of training. We are beginning to see what the future holds for us. The men take their training more seriously. We are endeavoring to lay particular stress on defense against German armor. Now is the time to drive home the proper techniques. Also, AA and A/B defense. The decisive A/B battle is fought on the ground of the A/B commander's selection. There are no retrograde movements.[i]

Leicester, March 4, 1944

Out to observe a battalion problem staged by the 2nd Bn 505. Back at 9:00. Gen. Ridgway's birthday. Sherry and coffee with cake in the office, quite nice. He was leaving for London, so things had to be done that way.

Inspected 3rd Bn 505 in the afternoon in connection with its proficiency test. Many shortages. Strange thing, and one that most of us have long since learned, and that is that a unit commander will repeatedly profess complete equipment and weapons status for his unit, yet a showdown will show up many, many deficiencies. There is no substitute for a combat load showdown and proficiency test. The competition and pressure always bring out the real stuff.

---

i   Gavin caused the training to be specific to the known intelligence of what would be encountered. It was not the traditional unit exercise but more along the team concept designed for specific tasks e.g., defend a crossroad, seize a bridge, ambush etc. This is a technique still very much in use today in both the airborne and ranger units.

The British have an Ordnance Corps School in Leicester. Last evening, they had Gen. Taylor, Col. Weinicke, and myself to dinner.

Leicester, March 5, 1944

Val called at 1:30AM. That helps. Up at 1:45, left at 2:30 for Langar with Gen. Ridgway. Arrangements at the takeoff field ran smoothly. Stations at 5:10, takeoff 5:45, drop 7:00. One of the best drops that I have seen. An interesting experience to drop in snow. I still wonder what in the hell I am doing in this business.

Krause is handling his battalion much better. Could be gotten ready in very short order. He is still a most interesting case. I do not believe that he could stand up long in sustained combat. He still appears to be very emotionally unstable at times.

Returned at 11:30. Chow and off to Cottesmore to a meeting with Gen. Clark and staff re the 507–508 drops. Appears to be shaping up satisfactorily. These weekends are hard on me. Little work is done, but I am invariably tied up. I would really like to get away for a day or two.

Leicester, March 7, 1944

Most of the day spent close to the office. Visited the 325 on the range. Continued to investigate the malfunction in Sunday's drop. Static line broke.[i] At this point it appears as though the government has been sold inferior materials for static lines. Pushing the investigation this morning.

Last evening had the first staff conference on Overlord. G-2 and G-3 presented their estimates. We are all in agreement on what ground we will attempt to hold. It will include St. Sauver le Vicomte, extending to the west to include all of the woods five miles west of the town. Efforts will be made to block the neck of the corridor by advancing from our base.[ii] Provided the German is not occupying the area in force it will be a grand mission. If he is there waiting it will be a hell of a fight from the time the first feet hit the ground. If we can only have an hour or so to get organized everything will be OK.

Val called at 9:00, been trying since 7:00, to tell me that I am to be promoted to Maj. Gen. Said that she had heard it and that Johnny Richards had seen a cablegram. Her dope allegedly came directly from Gen. Bradley. Couldn't convince her that she was in error. She was going to Ciro's. Was to call when she returned but didn't.

---

i   This refers to the cotton webbing used to pull the parachute out of the pack as the soldier descends. If it breaks, the jumper is doomed. This problem was fixed internally by sewing a canvas sleeve around the webbing until new material arrived.

ii Less than two weeks before the jump, imagery showed that Saint-Saveur was heavily reinforced, causing the division to move its drop zones directly west of Sainte-Mère-Église.

That would really be an impossible situation. I should realize it, even though bias [sentence not completed].

Leicester, March 7, 1944, 2100

A lazy day about the office. Checked the annexes for the Div. Field Exercise. Inspected the 1st Bn 505th. Maj. Kellam, although definitely under a cloud, is doing a fine job. It is of course impossible to tell just how well he will do in combat, but he is trying like hell and getting results now. Under the circumstances it is impossible to reclassify him. That is what Gen. R wants.[i]

Ran home in 43½ minutes. Not good enough. Olson ran along. Gen. R was very badly stove up after our last jaunt. Sometimes it is difficult for a formerly active man to realize that he is aging. I expect to have the same difficulty myself.

Leicester, March 9, 1944, 0800

Over to the 325 for a talk with Lewis in the AM. The way he bounces about since Gen. Ridgway talked to him is embarrassing, well almost. He dislikes the Horsa glider. Still expects to have his Regt go into combat. I don't know who will tell him that it can't.[ii]

Attended a P/JM conference in the afternoon. Then over to Nottingham to the 507 camp at Tollerton and the 508 camp at Wollaton. They are lovely sites, formerly castle grounds of some of the local rather small-bore royalty.

In the evening went to a division officers dance. Had a very nice time, although made no connections. The general's rank is awkward at an affair like that. You can never tell when people are being nice because of your grade or really because they like you and have some interest in you.

The division is now directly under VII Corps for supply, all planning, etc. Looks like the finish of the A/B section in London. Just as well.[iii]

Leicester, March 10, 1944, 0745

Went to Bradgate Park to a British battle course. 325 firing. Too much exposure over open ground to be reasonable. Problem jump last night had to be called off. Fog and limited visibility. We will stage it tonight.

---

i   Kellam would be killed bringing bazooka rockets to his teams defending La Fiére Bridge.

ii   This was a transport issue. It was later decided that the GIR would come in later in the day with returned aircraft. The 101st GIR, the 327th, landed intact at Utah Beach while the 325th took almost 35 percent casualties due to accidents. Apparently, Ridgway had admonished Lewis for the unit lack of tactical proficiency.

iii   This would be Major General Lawton Collins as the corps commander, a close friend of Ridgway.

Gen. Taylor back from London. His assignment to command the 101st is evidently set. It will be interesting to see how it works out. He is smart and capable, but better suited to one of the many war commissions being formed.

Looks like I will not see V Saturday afternoon. There is no one who can cause me such damn concern and discomfort at the moment. This must be corrected.

Leicester, March 11, 1944, 0815

A rough 24 hours. A dilemma. What in the hell is the answer?

Checked in at Langar and had lunch with the 1st Bn 505th. Kellam looks not too good, yet it is difficult to put your finger on what his trouble is. He just does not appear sure of himself. The battalion looks good. The morale and attitude of the 505th is at its best. Had to call off the drop of Kellam's battalion on account of the weather. Most unfortunate.

Just arranged with Gen. R to go to London today.

Leicester, March 13, 1944

Left at 1:30, arrived 82 Portland Place 4:00. Visited U.S. A/B Hqrs and talked to Ireland and Michealis [sic: Michaelis?].[i] Procured my liquor ration.

Met Val at Park West at 6:00. Went to Ciro's for dinner. Brunch at 11:00 Sunday and off for Leicester at 1:30. A perfect weekend. I sincerely hope and pray that we can work this out and, what is most important, that after working it out we get along well and Val is not unhappy away from her home, friends, way of life and standard of living. This latter is the most serious problem.

Leicester, March 14, 1944, 0815

A 325 exercise, bn proficiency test in the AM and PM off. A 40-mph wind in the evening, so the 505 test had to be called off. A very busy day. Gen. Taylor's orders to the 101st came in in the morning. Sorry to lose him in many ways, although it gives me an opportunity that I hope to be able to make the most of. A cocktail party for him at the Glebe Mt. House at 5:30. [Following sentence blacked out in the manuscript, presumably by Gavin himself.]

Everything looks so good now, this training and waiting period that I so disliked doesn't look so bad. I feel now that I will get through the next fight. I certainly want to.

---

i   Ireland would be the division G1 at *Market Garden* and Michaelis a battalion commander in the 101st.

Leicester, March 16, 1944, 0745

Val called. Out on a trip for four or five days. Called last night from Bristol.

The test of the 2nd Bn 505th was held on the 14th. Drop and A/B planning OK. Execution of the ground phase unsatisfactory. I am ready to recommend the relief of Col. Batcheller. We cannot take him into combat in command of a regiment. I still remember his action at Biazza Ridge and the day prior thereto. Now the regiment is going definitely sour. Morale is slipping and the attitude of the officers, especially the higher-ranking ones, is not what it should be.[i]

Inspected the 507 and 508 Bns taking the test yesterday. Their new equipment looks wonderful. I forgot that there was such nice new stuff. If they fight as well as they are equipped, we have nothing to worry about.

There are times when I have enough [of?] this eager newness on newly arrived noncombatants. They all want to get shot at, and many of them will be much the worse for having been shot at I am afraid.[ii]

Leicester, March 16, 1944 [Second note with this date]

Visited the Bns at Cottesmore and Barkston Heath. They are taking the tests. Both looked good. The 507 and 508 look better to all appearances right now than the 505th. I spoke to General Ridgway this evening about relieving Batcheller. Recommended Ekman to take his place. That is a tough spot to step into for Ekman, but I am sure he can handle it. It would be disastrous to continue counting on Batcheller. I have never told anyone of his behavior in Sicily, neither on D-Day nor at Biazza. I had hoped that he could do the job when put on his own. [Following line and a half blacked out in the manuscript, presumably by Gavin himself.]

Leicester, March 18, 1944, 0800

It hardly seemed like St. Patrick's Day. Nary a drunk nor a speck of green. The Irish are rather unpopular at the moment. Went up to Grantham, where we laid on the 8-group lift. It should be a big show. Checked the CPX in the afternoon. Not working too well. Weinicke's greatest trouble has always been that he is inclined to do all his G-3ing in the office.

Went to Cottesmore at 11:00PM. Jump called off on account of weather. Ground fog. Too bad. Will make it today, in daylight if necessary.

---

i   Batcheller was having an off-post affair known to the troops and did not oversee training despite counselling from Gavin and Ridgway. He was shortly relieved by replacement Lieutenant Colonel Bill Ekman who commanded the 505th for the remainder of the war.

ii   The 82nd and 101st conducted their own jump schools to get replacements qualified. Many volunteered for airborne duty but were shipped overseas without qualifications.

Called Val at 10:00. Not in. Supposedly out to Widewing.[i] [Next three lines blacked out in manuscript, presumably by Gavin himself.] I do feel that it has its compensations.

Spent some time in the war room. That, coupled with a talk that I had with the A-3 of the 9th TCC, just about convinces me that we are making our main effort in the wrong place. Surely the high command will shift. Here he is making his main effort where the kraut is strongest. It is so basic and obvious. The Balkans is the place. I would not be a bit surprised if we went there. If we do, this big build-up for a second front into France is being done very well. For my money it is being overdone. That is why I am becoming suspicious of it. The German now has 56 divisions in there, one the 243rd in our landing areas. It should be a rat race to end all rat races.

Leicester, March 19, 1944, 0900

Bns of the 507th and 508th jumped Operation Curveball at 1600 yesterday. Called the thing off at 2130 and 2200. A well-carried-out exercise. It is refreshing to work with troops fresh from America, enthusiastic and anxious. They listen and hang on to every word and, as far as I could observe, try to do exactly as they are told.

The battle-hardened veterans of the 505th are by now a bit calloused. The 507 and 508 appear to lack the technical proficiency of the 505th, but what they lack they more than make up for in their zeal and interest in doing the correct thing. They will do all right.

Called Val at 10:30PM. She was just calling me. Will try to get down for her mother's birthday. [Following three and a half lines blacked out in the manuscript, presumably by Gavin himself.]

Critiques at 1000 and 1100 this AM. Looks like a busy Sunday. We need more busy days.

Leicester, March 20, 1944, 1100

Critiques at the 507 and 508 in AM. Conference with Gen. R on Overlord at 1300. He is getting firm ideas on how he wants to carry out our mission. Still looks like a hell of a mess, but if it must be done it will be done. The current favorite idea is to drop the parachutists of both divisions during the night of D-1 and reinforce them

---

i   Widewing (also known as Bushey Park) was the HQ of the Army Air Force and later Eisenhower's HQ for D-Day planning.

with glider essentials at dawn. Neither division would get [sentence and paragraph end there].[i]

Leicester, March 21, 1944, 1000

A much brighter day today. Went to London Sunday evening. On the return somewhere an hour and a half out of London the car chugged and came to a dead stop. Out of gas. What a mess. Finally begged, for a pound, two gallons from a civilian truck driver. That got as far as Lutterworth. Here we found two U.S. sailors asleep in a GI truck and they gave us enough to get us to Leicester by 0500.

To work at 0700 and so it was a full day. Conference on the subject of refusals at Brig Hqrs at nine. Gen. R stated that each refusal would be handled on its own merits, that old recurrent injuries that subjected an old-timer to jumping jitters would be grounds for transfer to a quieter unit, non-jumping, and that obvious refusals to avoid hazardous combat duty would be tried by general CM and the maximum punishment meted out to them. Cases from Africa were cited wherein the sentences ranged from 6 to 20 years.

Returned to Brig to inspect their test Bns at 1:30PM. Met Gen. R in the war room at 5:00 for further conferences on the coming operation. At this second it does not look too bad. He drew up a plan that was again read at Glebe House at 2100. So, all in all it was a full day.

Conferred with Col. Hunt of a Lt Tnk Bn at 1100. He is going to bring us some Lt Tanks for training in April.

Endeavored to arrange accommodations at one of the nicer local hotels for the 505th Prop Blast. Impossible to find any.

A very nice birthday party for Mrs. Came. Gen. Lewis and Lovett were there. A nice family, although at times the old lady is painful. She likes to play up the girls and draw them out in front of company, a natural state of affairs of a proud mother, I suppose.

This is the first day of spring. One would never know it from observing the local conditions of weather. It is improving a bit, still damp and at times colder than hell. Wish that we were either fighting or going. Complicates matters to stick around one place or community for too long. Either home or at war. The combination is pleasant, but hardly satisfactory.

---

i   Gavin may well have been intended to write "sufficient airlift to have a simultaneous airborne and glider assault." The concept Gavin mentions is, in fact, what occurred.

Leicester, March 22, 1944, 0745

Stayed close to the office all day and cleaned up some problems and letters. Drew up the FO for Operation Sidecar. It looks like a good show. Scheduled for the 1st–2nd and will involve 3 Prcht Regts, not to mention Gen. Bradley, Air Marshal Leigh-Mallory, etc. It follows very closely the A/B plan for Overlord.

As a result of a conference that Gen. R had in London yesterday, it appears as though we might go in the night of D-1. I like that. I am getting anxious as we get closer. Things are shaping up in definite form. I fully expected a big change or two in our planning by now. I'll find myself going out the door over Cherbourg muttering, "I'm sure we are going to the Balkans."

Called Val and definitely arranged for a billet at The Flying Horse in Nottingham for the Prop Blast.

Leicester, March 23, 1944

A phone call from Val at 0830. Cocktails by the Division staff at the Glebe Mt. House at 6:45 and a nice dinner at 7:00PM. Went out to the 507 and 508 night drop at 9:30PM. They hit on schedule and hit their DZs. Despite this unusual good fortune, by daylight they had not yet organized their defense nor dug their men and weapons in. Neither Regt CO appeared all day. Called the exercise at 2:00 this afternoon.

It worries me. They are not ready to take on the combat mission that Gen. R is lining up for them. He believes that they are. There is so much to be done. The officers are dogging. Col. Timmes' Bn in the 507 has the worst attitude that I have encountered in many a day. What to do? More and tougher training. Chop off the worst heads. Put the heat on where it will do the most good. Our combat commitment with these people is a worry.[i]

Leicester, March 24, [1944], 1145

A long talk with Gen. [Ridgway, presumably] re the state of training of the two regiments. He will quite probably reclassify Millett before we are through. Lazy, soft, indolent, lacking leadership necessary for combat. Kellam is to go now. All good changes if we are to be combat effective.

---

i   Lieutenant Colonel Timmes, commander of 3-507th, would be an outstanding commander. Isolated on D-Day, he held an Alamo position until finally relieved on 9 June. There is a permanent monument to Timmes' Orchard on the site.

Talked to Capa of *Life* this morning. He is to take a jump course and go in with us. I am very glad. Excellent for the morale for the troops to know that they are to get press coverage, especially parachute troops. They are glory hunters.[i]

Looking forward to the visit of Val.

Leicester, March 26, 1944, 0900

Val arrived 1500 Friday afternoon. Went to the 505th Prop Blast Saturday evening. It was frightful. I was a bit ashamed of the entire performance. Nothing was organized. The prop blast ceremony was slighted, if not overlooked. They forgot the toast to the former members whom we have left buried in foreign soil. There was no food worthy of the name. The girls were terrible, with few exceptions, and the drunken condition of some of the officers and their dates was deplorable. I was very sorry that Val was present. It was certainly not a party worthy of being a regimental affair. Val was wonderful about it all.

Planned a drop last night. Had to call it off on account of the weather and bombing missions to Berlin.

Leicester, March 27, 1944, 0800

A conference with Gen. R re the probability of our mission being called off because of German occupation in strength of the area we plan to land in. This, if it happens, may make it necessary for us to drop nearer the 101st or not drop at all.

Lunch with Val and in the afternoon walked in Abbey Park. A very lovely afternoon.

Left for the DZs at 2000 and returned at 2300. Exercise called off on account of ground fog.

This is it, the first reason I have had to return from the war.

Leicester, March 28, 1944, 0800

A conference at Cottesmore with Gen. Clark re the conditions of weather necessary for flying. We are getting farther and farther behind in our training. Jumped the Bns of the 507 and 508 at 1500. Not what we wanted, but the best that we could get. Killed one lad in the 507. Appeared as though he may have made a faulty exit. In addition, unfortunately, he had placed a wooden paddle in his chute, evidently home-made for tucking in the flaps, and it got caught in the chute. After falling

---

i   Ultimately, Capa went on the First Wave with the 1st ID at Omaha Beach and captured the iconic photos of that event.

with the main about ¼ of the way out for 100 feet he pulled his reserve. It went right up into the main and didn't open out, so he came in. Regrettable.[i]

The Bns taking the test looked much better yesterday. It is surprising what a little heat applied in the right places will do. Human beings never change. We all need a little checking up on every now and then. I wish sometimes that there was someone checking up on me a bit more closely.

Leicester, March 29, 1944, 0800

Attended the 507 and 508 critiques yesterday. Millett bitching as usual about anything he can find to bitch about. [Following five lines blacked out in the manuscript, presumably by Gavin himself.]

Yesterday I had some heated words with the IX TCC staff re the coming Operation Sidecar. They say that they [sic: we?] occasionally put out orders arbitrarily, stating what we will do or where we will land, and their too frequent condescending attitude makes me wonder of the future.

It is definite in their minds that there will be a separate air force after the war. I am in agreement with them that there should be. They also are of the opinion that the airborne troops should be part of the air force and not the ground forces, and in this I am in agreement with them.

Right now, it is clear that our place may be in the ground forces, but with the development that is certain to come in both the airborne forces and the air force it is clearly the proper thing to do, i.e. look ahead and put the airborne troops and the Troop Carrier in the same organization and command.[ii]

Considering all of this, I wonder then of our future role. Certainly, in peacetime it should not be doing guard duty, KP, boards, court martials, PX Off., and all the nasty administrative jobs for the Air Corps. If the airborne troops are to be the stepchildren of the air forces, I want no part of it, nor does any other parachutist. We are not built that way.

But the question arises. Is the best and most promising future in the airborne troops, even if they are in the air force, or the ground forces? Everyone knows the answer, but I can foresee a life of struggle and dissatisfaction. I'll never be a hind tit for anyone, nor will any parachutist.

---

i   This was a time where every jumper packed his own chute.

ii Ultimately, this is exactly what was done after Normandy with Lieutenant General Brererton commanding all troop transport and airborne forces which were under Browning and Ridgway's command.

Leicester, March 30, 1944

Day spent around Hqrs getting the details of Sidecar arranged. Gen. Williams and Col. Crouch came over in the afternoon to talk TCC organization to fit our organization for both Sidecar and Overlord. Gen. Ridgway has an axe over them. I am uncertain of what it is, but they have a great deal of respect for his wants. I believe that his action in the Gen. Dunn case in Africa put the fear of God into them.

Gen. R told me that I would command the Prcht Task Force of the 82nd in Overlord.

Leicester, March 31, 1944, 1000

A day of final reconnaissance of the Sidecar DZs. Looks rather good from the DZs. Just found out that I am to jump in it, so I hope that they are OK. I would certainly hate to crack an ankle at this stage of the game.

Weinicke doing a very poor job at G-3 for the moment. He has an odd and most unusual faculty for shirking work and at the same time polishing the CG's apple enough to lead him to believe that he is doing everything. I am ashamed of the tactics of this coming affair. I hope that the administrative aspects of it work out. We could have serious trouble.[i]

Leicester, April 1, 1944, 0745

April Fool's Day. Twenty years in the army today. It seems like a long time. As soon as the war is ended, I should take a four months' vacation, wear civvies, get a civilian job, and get away from it all. Would like to go to West Africa.

The show for tonight is all set. I am not to jump now unless Gen. Ridgway decides not to jump, in which case I will.[ii]

The keeping of diaries has been forbidden by SHAEF. Also, all overnight passes and leaves will be stopped as of April 5th. Seems a bit early. I would not be a bit surprised to see a change in target date for Overlord.[iii]

The situation over there remains essentially unchanged the past few weeks. Still 54 divisions. The Russian pressure in the Balkans is helping. If we could get the southern France front opened a week or two before our effort, that would help too.[iv]

---

i   They didn't. The division staff was notorious for doing very little and that not well.

ii Ridgway initially decided he would come in later by glider. He changed his mind the night before the jump and was inserted with the 505th, with Gavin jumping with the 507th.

iii At this point, May was the month with the day to be determined. This was changed to June to allow more LST production.

iv At this point, the southern France invasion day was to be simultaneous with the Normandy effort. It was delayed so LSTs could be sent to the UK.

It is certain to be a hot place. I have been busy selecting the DZs. That does bring it close. They look good except for the prospects of immediate hostile interference. It is going to be a rough fight.

Leicester, April 3, 1944, 0800

Saturday devoted almost entirely to a tour of all of the Sidecar takeoff airdromes. Took from 1000 until 1900. Everyone in satisfactory bivouacs. The new regiments feel a bit imposed upon, so it will prove a good experience for them.

Weather bad, so the exercise had to be called off. Sunday also.

Received a call from Val Sunday morning informing me that I had won a case of whiskey at a charity affair at Claridge's Saturday evening. Not being there, I went down yesterday to pick it up. It had been moved from the hotel, so Val will pick it up for me.

The weather at this time is most unfortunate. The entire parachute force of the division is at takeoff airdromes sweating out what now amounts to three days of rain so far.

Yesterday the division's tentative outline plan for Overlord was drafted. I am to be given the parachute task force, going in the night of D-D[ay] plus 1. Gen. Ridgway follows with the glider force at daylight. It shows great promise for interest. It will be very exciting and a wonderful opportunity. With a break we will go to town, although I wish that the new regts had a bit of experience. We will be hit shortly after landing and during landing, of that I am quite certain.

I am worried about Val. She is a wonderful person.

Leicester, April 4, 1944

Visited each regimental headquarters. They are all taking much better care of themselves now. It has been a good thing for them. The problem had to be postponed another 24 hours. Worked some on operational planning. It is shaping up well.

Gen. R visited Col. Mendez's Bn at Barkston Heath. Mendez evidently had something nice to say about my critique of several days ago. Since Gen. R was pleased, I was doubly pleased. It is not very often these days that he shows many evidences of pleasure with what I am trying to get done.[i]

This is an odd job, Asst CG. There are none of the accomplishments, nor the satisfaction, that comes with a well-handled troop command. One is somewhat of a whipping boy and axe man, as well as general supervisor. If the Asst CG does not get along well with the C/S and the staff, things would be in a hell of a mess.

---

i   Here, two strong, ambitious personalities had to work in tandem without harming the units. Both managed a very smooth relationship despite the occasional friction.

Anyway, I have never had the feeling of solid accomplishment that I occasionally experienced in the 505th. Only in combat will that come, I suppose, although even that is problematical.

I may, if I am fortunate, get the division.

Leicester, April 5, [1944]

An all-night problem, Sidecar, involving the flight and drop of three regiments (Prcht). 136 of the C-47s not accounted for at daylight. They scattered to all points of the compass. Landed all over UK. Those that jumped did not do too badly. The present pathfinder equipment helps. The 508 looks fine, the 507 not too well. Millett may yet have to go. That will be hard on me, but it may have to be done. Very tired. No sleep last night.

Leicester, April 7, [1944], 1700

Left yesterday afternoon at 1600 for London, arriving 82 Portland Place at 1830. Went to Ciro's for dinner at 2100, returned 2400. Left for Newbury at 0715. Gliders loaded and marshalled for takeoff, but weather kept them grounded. Despite this, the troops got a great deal of good out of the exercise. Combat will tell us a lot about our glider capabilities.

Talked to Jack Thompson for a bit at Ciro's. He was escorting some girl whom he kept referring to as "Lady," with some emphasis on the lady. Americans put such great stock on a title, and some of the dogs that pass off for royalty make for quite a mess.

Very disappointed to find Val such a scold as she was last night. I am so anxious that this be entirely OK and workable. It is disheartening and discouraging, and most disappointing. What to do? I don't know the answer. I want — [Ends with this incomplete sentence.]

Leicester, April 10, [1944], 1600

The evening of the 7th I was called to London by Gen. Ridgway at 1900. Arrived down there at 2200 for a conference on personnel matters. Gen. R of the opinion that Billingslea could be gotten up to take over the 507th, which I heartily endorsed. What to do with Raff still a question. I neither want him now or if I had the division.

I went down to Newbury Saturday after spending the night at the Dorchester in London. Glider training organized and I returned to London at 1800. Dinner and billets and breakfast at 82 Portland Place. Talked over Thursday night with Val. Perhaps that sort of attitude can be avoided in the future.

Returned to Newbury early Sunday morning the 9th. Gliders took off at 1600 and landed at 1900. I called on Gen. W. C. Lee in the hospital at Hermitage. He left in the afternoon for America. A most difficult farewell. He has done a great deal for A/B troops. His heart was set on taking his division into combat.

Called Gen. Ridgway by phone and he told me that Gen. Hodges was to be present today, 10th, and for me to be at the Glebe Mount House at 0700 this morning. Came directly back and arrived at Leicester at 2200, thus missing an opportunity to spend a few hours with Val.

Later I will regret it, but at the moment this war is getting quite serious. After about one more fight I can see where I will not be worth a damn between fights. Even now I am not worth much. The old soldiers are all the same. It is very difficult to keep up the pressure when you know what is in store.

This afternoon Gen. Ridgway gave me for comment a letter that Gen. Howell sent him recommending the retention of Millett as regimental commander of the 507th. Too bad that we are at odds.

I am no doubt making many enemies in this army by refusing to retain or condoning the retention of inefficient unit commanders. I cannot see any other course. Many lives are at stake. If a unit commander does not have it, I do not see how in the world I can keep him. I have been a bit ruthless, and have hurt many people, but I have had many people killed too. Biazza Ridge should not have been fought as it was. Hagan was responsible for the plan of attack there. There will be many snafu affairs in the 507 as long as Millett is in command of it. This is a vicious system. It will turn against the hatchet man if he is not careful. If you do nothing, many lives will be lost needlessly, and your unit will not function satisfactorily. You may or may not be relieved of your own command. If you kick a man out, you make many enemies, lose lots of friends, and certainly make no new ones. I wish the goddamn war was over and I were back to blueberry pie.

Leicester, April 11, [1944]

Time flies. An interesting talk with Gen. Hodges. He is to command the American First Army. Bradley is to move up to the FUSAG. Hodges commanded a battalion in the last war. His tactical ideas are quite good. Some of them I wish I had heard ten years ago. He appears to be quite old to be an active field commander. I believe that Ridgway gets impatient with his slowness in getting about.[i]

A conference with Ridgway last night re Millett's relief. It looks as though he may take him into this first fight. Poor Zip is in a hell of a sweat and I am sorry

---

i   The 82nd rarely worked for 1st Army. Hodges was a careful, predictable commander which
     Bradley prized. Hodges relied to a great deal on General Collins as the fire within the Army and
     gave him all the tough tasks, from the Normandy breakout to the counterattack at the Bulge.

as hell for him. An officer should stay away from a high troop command unless he is especially fitted for it and supremely confident. The SOS also needs thousands of good officers.

Leicester, April 12, [1944]

Spent the morning in the office catching up on papers. Went to a pay drop for the 456 FA in the afternoon, then to brigade bazooka firing west of Nottingham. Returned by 5:30. Sometime in the war room and then to the Glebe Mt. House.

I still am unable to adapt myself to this Division staff setup. Nothing is ever done at night, or rarely. Everyone quits and goes home about 5:00.

Leicester, April 13, 1944, 1200

Visited the tank training at Strawberry Hills. Most beneficial. Just what these lads need. Had lunch with Vandervort. He is a good soldier. I hope that I can someday repay him for his fine Sicilian job. His battalion will do well in its next fight.

On the return trip Weber hit another car. Most unfortunate. Not exactly his fault, but I believe that he could have avoided it. He has been throwing his weight around a bit behind the star. This car just didn't move over, and the right fronts tangled. It annoys the hell out of me. A bad thing to have happen. I am sure that Gen. Ridgway does not like it, and it will certainly cause a lot of tongue wagging. This being a general is most painful at times.[i]

The brigade had two Bn jumps last night. Both did a nice job of reorganization despite the poor performance of the Air Corps. This matter of the Air Corps just simply not delivering is much more serious than most of us will admit. If we have another Sicily in France I am going on record as strong as I am able to. We have got to have better pilots, if necessary, bomber-trained pilots.

Hit a low, I guess. Val called.

Bagby came in and wanted to change the operational plan so as to use the entire TC lift the night of D-Day, preferably by lifting the entire 82nd and part of the 101st. Gen. Ridgway asked the purpose of his visit and, when I told him, he was very sharp and critical about the thing. I felt that he was showing some resentment because of the car crackup. Perhaps not.

This Asst Div Comdr is a hell of a job. Actually, one can do nothing, except in this division there is a training responsibility that at times becomes very confused between Brigade, G-3, and myself.

---

i   Gavin was used to acting independently as he saw fit with minimal restrictions. His promotion
    put him in a much more strictured and sensitive environment which was contrary to his impulses.

Leicester, April 14, 1944

A conference with Maj. Forward of IX TCC at which the DZs tentative [sic] were selected. Looks rather good.

Returned to Glebe Mount earlier than usual and got an hour's sleep before dinner. Talked to Gen. Ridgway for a few minutes. If I were on my toes I would stop in and talk to him regularly and have a drink with him before dinner. I have a hell of a time making myself do this, but I know he likes it.

He called Andy March and myself in for a drink. Talked Overlord. We are to have lots of artillery and TD. Bradley is giving us everything. I am positive that this generosity is based upon our work for him in Sicily. He certainly came to my rescue there and we did a job for him. I know he went over our position later at Biazza Ridge, and I suppose saw the graves. These lads will fight and, more than that, clean up if given half a chance and the means.

We get a TD Bn an SP Arty Bn, an Armd Recon Trp, a Recon Plat, and 155 support. The softening up is well underway. The kraut still moves about at night quite freely, however. I have no illusions about that.[i]

Leicester, April 15, 1944

The Ides of April. Time is flying. Visited the 505th for the first time since Eckman took over. Shaping up very nicely. The area and regiment are showing improvement. Heard that Billingslea cannot fly. Must be wounded. He is to come in with me. Raff returned by the 1st Division. He is to be my assistant, since there is no other job for him. That sort of thing is rather unbelievable and most unfortunate. Mark Clark made him a colonel and now no one wants him.

Went by brigade. They were crying about the jump the other night. About 10% casualties. The TCC did a very poor job. New groups 439th and 440th. Talked to Joe Crouch about pathfinder work. Seems to be coming along OK. It is difficult to get everyone, both TC and A/B, to accept it, yet if we had in Sicily what we have today it would be an entirely different story.

Val came up from London.

Leicester, Sunday, April 16, 1944

A conference or two on operational planning. Went to town to lunch with Val. Worked over the regimental missions with G-3. Got them in tentative shape.

---

i   The forces mentioned were to join the 82nd after linkup from Utah Beach. In fact, almost all of them were assigned elsewhere as the battle developed.

Downtown at 1700. Took Val to dinner at 2030. [Next line blacked out in the manuscript, presumably by Gavin himself.] I have always figured that the woman that I married next[2] would be very active in athletics, music, theatre, and have many and diverse interests. It is odd that Val so completely meets every standard that I have had in mind, yet she is not especially interested in any of the above.

Because of the war and its social deprivations, I have come to feel that a woman's honest, complete and full love is more important than anything else. Why marry an athlete or a public character? Nothing should be permitted to take the place of one's home life. The home must come first. Recognizing the fact that biologically sex is a very transitory attraction, and that a permanent union must be based upon something more permanent than sexual attraction [following three lines plus one or two words blacked out in the manuscript, presumably by Gavin himself].

Leicester, Monday, April 17, 1944

Completed regimental missions and tentative division order. Issued order to regimental commanders. It certainly helps at this stage to have had some combat background. They have many simple questions that would be hard to answer otherwise. Ekman and Lindquist will be OK. I am sweating out Millett. It will be a hell of a day at best for all of us. The mission looks OK.

Leicester, Wednesday, April 19, 1944, 0800

Left for Horsham Monday afternoon, arriving in the problem area at 2100. There met Gen. Taylor, Pratt, McAuliff[e] et al. Glider landings scheduled for daylight Tuesday finally came in at 11:40. Marshalled 50 gliders on takeoff airfield in 50 minutes. Time from takeoff of first glider until entire column was on its course to its objective: 24 mins. Time from release of first glider until last glider landed: 5¼ mins. A good show. Most of the Horsas were damaged beyond recovery. Of the Wacos probably about ¼–½ of them can be snatched out. The entire show was impressive. If we could only do it at night so as to eliminate the necessity for such great air coverage.[i]

Returned at 1800, landing at East Leicester, an RAF field that was supposed to be closed. Landed anyway, despite the red flares. Will probably get a letter.

Called Val at 2030. No reply. Went to a 325 dance. It is most regrettable to attend these regimental affairs and see the type of girls that are invited. Few if any of the officers would either wish or dare to escort them to a regimental affair back in the States. Yet they do here, where they and their army are judged by the type of

---

i   The British Horsa was made with plywood and was usually a total loss after landing. The smaller WACO was steel framed and much more survivable. The 82nd used the Horsa extensively in Normandy as it carried twice the load of a WACO.

company they keep. The English have not helped in that they have not asked any of our people to meet the nicer sort of girls. On the other hand, one can hardly blame them.

Leicester, Wednesday, April 19, [1944], 2100

Went over to North Witham Field this morning and talked to all of the pathfinder personnel of the division. It was something that had to be done very soon. They have a tough assignment, and probably the most important one in the entire airborne effort. Their attitude appeared to be very good.

Rec'd a call from Col. Twitchell of Gen. Bull's Ops Section in SHAEF re a British order to America for 96,000 equipment canopies. We have asked for 51,000 for Overlord, and Bull thought that someone was wrong. We advised him that the British requirement was excessive, based upon 8 canopies per ton of supplies and approximately 300 tons of supplies per division per day being needed.[i]

Went to a cocktail party given by the local British upper crust at 1830. Quite nice.

Called Val at 0730 after a bad night. Enjoyed talking to her. Called Edith Steiger and made a date for a division hop tomorrow night. I have got to do something. I have never let myself get so one-tracked before. It gets painful at times. Called again this evening at 2030. No reply. Some state of affairs. I've got to decentralize, and right now. Nice letter from N/B. There is someone who is loyal and OK.

Leicester, Saturday, April 22, [1944], 1230

Thursday spent checking training. Thursday evening went to the Division Officers dance. Dragged Ethel Steiger, ARC, and a hell of a nice person. Took her to dinner at the Grand first. A good hop. Stopped by her home afterwards. An air alert.

The following morning up at 5:45 and out to a 507 FX. Friday afternoon a cocktail party given by the local police chief. Mostly titles present. Had a very nice time. (This was Thursday afternoon.) Friday evening went to a dance given for the division by the Lord Mayor and Lord Mayoress of Leicester at DeMontfort Hall. They gave for Britishers. Danced, by request, the first dance with the Duchess of Rutland. Nice enough. Trouble was she had three grown children and was high-ranking in her own opinion. The British certainly fell all over her. An American resents that attitude. Left the dance at 2130.

Val evidently doing well.

The training is coming along as well as can be expected at this stage. Up at 5:45 this morning and off to a CPX. Capt. Downs, who will handle my communications, appears to be OK, a solid citizen as the boys say.

---

i   These were for the supply Parapacks and door bundles carried by the drop aircraft.

Gen. Ridgway has been sick in bed for three days. It has been a grand opportunity for me and I have made the most of it. I love command. My entire outlook has changed in these few days. The responsibility is good to get. I would like to get around now and see the men more often. I should get daily recreation schedules, as well as drill schedules, and they should be checked as well as training.

From recent indications it appears as though Gen. Ridgway is not as popular with the men of the division as he should be. Popularity of course must of necessity come second to command ability and tactical skill, but it certainly helps to have it. It should not be courted, but no opportunities to gain it should be overlooked.[i]

Leicester, Sunday, April 23, 1944, 0700

Stayed close to the CP most of the day except for an inspection of the 504 area, a visit to the 80th, and a conference with Gen. R. Most everyone in the usual Saturday afternoon spirit by mid-afternoon.

Felt rather low, as usual at these times. Called Val twice. Then she called me. Went to bed at 2100 and read.

Gen. R up for dinner, so he may now take over. I wish he would or wouldn't. I can see lots of things that I would like to go to work on, but I can't since it is not included in my functions in this division.

The train schedule cancelled, or rather postponed until 1000, today. At 0400 received a call to the effect that the train would arrive at 0500. I have just returned from meeting it. The 504 boys look fine. Talked to the S-3. Depressing and sobering to hear of the combat losses and commanding officer replacements as a result of combat.[ii]

Leicester, Monday, April 24, [1944], 1700

Rube Tucker came in at 10:30. Looked fine and all ready to go on the 2nd Front. Very disappointed that he is not to get into the assault wave.

Left at 1400 for London, arriving at 82 Portland Place at 1630. Val grand to see again. Left at 2030 to return and arrived here at 0115. Took a jeep and went out to a 505 night problem, arriving at 0200. Returned to camp at 0400 and to bed after a full 24 hrs.

---

i   Ridgway was somewhat aloof with the troops whereas Gavin mixed very well. Gavin was regarded by them as "their commander," a point that vexed Ridgway.

ii This is the arrival of the 504th from Italy. They had taken considerable casualties and were essentially combat ineffective, making them ineligible for Normandy. Some members provided augmentation to the assault force.

Up at 0700 and off to another day. Conference with officers of the 504th on policies, etc. Conference with Gen. Eddy, CG 9th Div., in PM.

Edith Steiger's father died, and she called. All of this is getting too complicated.

Leicester, Tuesday, April 25, [1944], 1330

A very busy day with several conferences. Working with Gen. R still leaves me frequently with a feeling of not doing well enough or not doing the right thing. One rarely experiences a feeling of complete satisfaction. I remember his attitude towards Keerans and Taylor. His present attitude towards March is at times embarrassing. I wonder if I am much the same with my subordinates. I believe that he likes more personal attention than I give him. I perhaps should stay at the Glebe Mt. House.[i]

Leicester, Wednesday, April 26, [1944], 1330

A conference with all regimental commanders at 0900 that lasted until 1200. Their plans were aired for discussion by the CG and staff. They appeared to be in rather good shape.

Gen. R flew up to IX TCC and upon his return went to bed again sick. This morning the doctor diagnosed it as malaria. If this is correct it will be most unfortunate for him. He got wind of a possible change in our operational plans from Gen. Williams yesterday, probably requiring a jump of all parachute regiments of both U.S. divisions the night of D-1. I like that idea very much. Our area is going to be an inferno the night of D-Day.[ii]

Leicester, Thursday, April 27, [1944]

A div CPX, the first, went along rather well. The staff was almost enthusiastic about it. Called Gen. Bradley re a conference, then changed plans and I am to meet him in London Friday AM. The current matter of discussion is the plan to drop all Para units the night of D-1 rather than spread them over two nights.

Received a good letter from Val. She is starting proceedings to divorce her present husband. Since it possibly means a loss of alimony, it is a big step for her to undertake. She is banking on her own affairs straightening themselves out. I have explained to her how long this is likely to take. I will be shot at an awful lot in the next few months, and after this we have the Asiatic front to clean up. If I live through it all

---

i   Gavin and Ridgway were still working out the relationship and roles. Gavin, as in most things, always stretched his activities, which may have made Ridgway uncomfortable and resentful. Regardless, he understood Gavin's great value as a combat commander, much like Collins at a different level.

ii Ultimately, exactly what happened.

I will be lucky. But it is certain to take time, perhaps years. I love Valerie very much. I believe that we could be very happy. I am afraid sometimes of her adaptability to a service life, and I am not yet sure of how well she will get along with people.

I also wish that her education were more along American lines. She has a typical English-Continental background that illy [poorly] lends itself to American society, particularly of the kind that I enjoy. I have always felt that a wife should have many and diverse interests, be capable and energetic, and be somewhat of a community leader. Val will bring to our union few of these things, but she will, I believe, make a happy home and a family.

Perhaps I am at the stage where a home and a family are what I will want above all else. In my career my wife will certainly play a large part. If I live through the coming battles of this war, I will do everything to make myself heard from in the councils of our government and national defense. Val at least will have her own independent means to enjoy many of the material pleasures that I will very likely not be able to afford. She is attractive, poised, and of impeccable behavior. Maybe she is it. I love her very very much.

Leicester, Saturday, April 29, 1944, 0730

Malaria again hit Gen. Ridgway Thursday afternoon. Fever up to 102°. I stayed at the Glebe Mount House Thursday night, leaving at 0500 for London, where I had a scheduled conference with Gen. Bradley. Met Gen. Bradley at 0800 at Bryanston Square.

The story was that our mission for Overlord remains unchanged, but that A. M. Leigh-Mallory had submitted a paper to Gen. Eisenhower stating that he could not deliver the present planned large glider lift at dawn D-Day without heavy losses, and that therefore he was recommending a complete parachute lift the first night, six regiments, with each division getting 50 gliders apiece.

The 82nd, due to its remoteness, is to get 200 gliders at dusk D-Day and 200 more the following 24 hours. He justified this delivery of 200 on the supposition that they would practically neutralize the GAF by dusk D-Day.[i]

Gen. Bradley discussed the probable enemy actions for some time. He is very optimistic about the whole affair, feeling that the peninsula will fall with much more ease than I at present expect. He does not think that the German will commit any armored units up the peninsula, especially if we cut it off even partially the night of D-1 D-Day. His attitude is a good one when talking with subordinates, and besides I am inclined to agree with him.

---

i   The 82nd had its first glider reinforcement at 0400 on D-Day followed by the main body of the 325th later in the day. More than 30 percent of the 325th were casualties due to glider crashes in the restricted ground.

Attended a conference later in the day, 1500, at Bentley Priory in Stanmore with A. M. Leigh-Mallory, A. M. Tedder, Gen. Bradley, Gen. Browning, Gen. Williams, and A. V. M. Hollingsworth. A. M. Leigh-Mallory is afraid of getting too many gliders into the air until he has the GAF beaten down, which he thinks he can accomplish in 24 hours if they will come up and fight. At present they are staying down. They will have to come up at H-Hour or be considered definitely beaten and out of the war.

The British plan over east of Caen was discussed at some length and does not look too good. They are having trouble coordinating with the Navy. Our mission will require a very high degree of coordination with the Navy and with our own air support. The operation is to be rehearsed in Eagle.[i] The preparation of that exercise is the next immediate task of the staff.

Gen. Ridgway is expecting a classmate by the name of Matthewson [Note: No such person in USMA April 1917.] in to take over the div artillery. It will be very hard on March. I caught a glint in Doc Eaton's eye when he was watching me discuss Matthewson's capabilities with Gen. Ridgway that may have indicated that Ridgway's plans go beyond having him take over the arty. He may have him in mind as the ultimate division commander. I certainly have not boned it, which I may well have at least worked at.

Leicester, Sunday, April 30, 1944, 0815

Another of those Sundays when everyone starts when he damn pleases. It never fails to burn me up. If a subordinate gets off to a late start on a particular day when someone in Div Hqrs wants to contact him or visit the outfit, one would think that the Army was falling apart from lack of a sense of duty of its officers. Yet on occasions, and whenever the whim strikes them, Gen. R or the staff merely get in about an hour late.

Lunch with Val yesterday. Also, dinner and to a dance at Market Harborough later. She was very attractive and rather popular. Gave me an odd and entirely unreasonable feeling for a moment.

Back to Leicester at one and I was in at two AM. Had a cocktail party for the local British upper crust at the Glebe Mount House. Went off very well.

Received a cablegram from the War Dept. authorizing parachute qualification for all glider personnel of the div, something that we have been waiting for for a long time. We are on the beam.[ii]

---

i   Eagle was a mass rehearsal of the airborne effort and was orchestrated by Taylor, now CG of the 101st.

ii   This was a plan to allow the 325th to be a source of replacements for the PIR as well as to bring them into the airborne community. They were viewed by the airborne as an outside element, not really part of them. This would change after Normandy.

Leicester, Tuesday, May 2, 1944, 0720

A busy day Sunday. Worked over the Air Support Plan to fit the changed operation. Received the regtl orders. Made final resupply plan. We are to ask for an automatic resupply daily for four days amounting to 250 tons. Our mission will be difficult of accomplishment. Although the resupply will come in, recovering it will be a task, if for no other reason because of the tonnage.

Took Tucker and Billingslea over to 52nd Wing and the Pathfinder School yesterday. For the first time Crouch expressed rather definite doubts on the efficacy of the Eureka. He now has four 717 sets of BUPS Beacon. They are the only four in the world. It appears to be the answer right now and most probably will not be jammed. Efforts are being made to get additional sets before the operation.[i]

I talked to Gen. R about it as soon as I came back in an effort to elicit his interest in cabling or calling Gen. Marshall or Gen. Arnold. I do not know of any single piece of equipment that could have such great effect on the success or failure of the 2nd Front.

Called on Miss Steiger of the ARC last night. I don't believe that I have ever been so well behaved. Valerie occupies a permanent place in my scheme of things that I intend to honor and respect.

Wish that this was one month from now.

Leicester, May 2, 1944, 2000

Waited around the office most of the morning for Gen. Clark, Cols. Petty and Brown from the 52nd Wing. When they arrived, we laid on a definite air movement table for Eagle and Neptune. It certainly helps to have had combat experience with that wing. I am quite satisfied with the plan. We would have preferred to have had nine serials, but the six decided upon should do the job.

At 1230 attended a lunch given by the English-Speaking Union. Harvey Gibson, Lord Trent, Sir Arthur Hazelwig et al. A very nice affair of high purpose and probable accomplishment.

In the evening played deck tennis with Gen. R, Doc, Lt. Kraus. Not particularly enjoyed.

Received a letter from Peggy. She followed the line expected, calling attention to the unfortunate plight of Barbara in the event of a divorce. I still feel, however, that for any child a home with love is far better than a home of distress and hate, or better to have one parent always present who loves her and keeps her happy than

---

i   This refers to the BUPS system which was far superior to the Rebecca-Eureka system. Ultimately, it did not arrive in time.

to have two parents who are always at odds. She said that she would divorce me as soon as possible after the war. Now all that I have to do is survive.

This all must be affecting my work. I don't really concentrate on things the way that I use to. Most of the time I figure that this is because I am stale and rather fed up with the war, but again I suspect that it may in part be due to my preoccupation with my messed up marital affairs.

Leicester, Thursday, May 4, [1944]

Some time with training. Visited brigade twice during the past 24 hours. The 508 is shaping up very nicely. They are destined to do a top-notch job. The 507 is still questionable.

Gen. Williams came in yesterday. The 82nd is to lead in. The P/F drop at 2350 and the first troops at 0022. I will be with that serial.

It is fine for the morale of the 505th that they are again to lead the invasion. The entire affair looks much better now than it did some time ago. I hope that I live through it. If I do, and the division does at all well, I have an excellent chance to inherit it. As a parachute division it would be wonderful, and that is what it would be.

Leicester, Sunday, May 7, 1944, 0830

Went to London Friday morning for a conference on air support. Held at Stanmore, Smith FH presiding. Concerned itself mostly with air support for the flight. Night and day fighters, intruders. 20 intruders to work over searchlights will be available. At time of takeoff fighters will be over German bases to intercept German fighters if they dare come up. Bad crossings of the coast are to be smoked.

Left Stanmore at 1800 and due to car trouble did not arrive at Leicester until 2300. Had dinner and left at once for the division field exercise, arriving at 0200. It was to be a ground rehearsal of Neptune. Came in from it last night at 1700 and so a full two days were passed.

Saw Valerie on Friday. She has never looked better. Hope to see her today.

Leicester, Tuesday, May 9, 1944, 0930

Critiqued field exercise Sunday AM and left for London at 11:30. Conferred with Cols. Bagby and Jones at Eastcote from 1430 to 1530. TCC promised to include all of our air support requests in their plan. It is interesting to have such frank admissions made of the fact that the TCC can get AS directly from the Air Corps when we would be denied under the same circumstances. It is quite evident that the AB troops and the AC should be together in the same "branch."

Joined Valerie at 1700. Supper at a pub, The Coach and 'orses. Early to bed and away to Stanmore for a conference on AS with the AEAF. Started at 11:00 and ended at 1700. A very enlightening session on air support and the capabilities of the Air Corps in bombing support.

H-Hour has not been set so that it was difficult to make a firm plan. The entire picture looks like an expensive one. This invasion is going to cost many lives. Although it is imperative that I present an optimistic front at all times, nevertheless I am not very happy about our prospects. It is going to be a bitch of a fight with many losses. I believe that we will be dropped on our DZs OK, but I also believe that the kraut will be either on or near the DZs also.

Shortly after our landing, elements of the 21st Panzer should hit the area. That is the present picture and, unless the Russian front moves damn soon or the French crack the southern area, the prospects will get worse rather than better.

Before combat for the first time a man has boundless faith in the high command and the staff planning. He feels that if worse comes to worst they will pull him out of every difficulty that they put him into. Avellino was the first rude awakening. Sicily was no better. You must look out for yourself if you expect to live and fight. Especially in AB operations is this true. It is entirely within the realm of possibility for a staff to sacrifice an AB unit without realizing it or even giving a damn.

Well, I want to come back from this one. In Sicily I didn't give much of a damn except to want to do a good job. Now I know that these lads will do a good job anywhere and I am supremely confident of my own tactical ability. The difference is that I have a complete and full reason for coming back. Valerie and I should have a full and interesting life ahead of us.

Smith told me that Tokyo is to be bombed May 15th with B-29s. Just a token drop. The gas must be ferried across the MTs to the takeoff bases and is entirely impractical for regular use. As he put it, it will get a few more thousand votes for Roosevelt.

D-Day and H-Hour are still not set. Since Y-Day is now June 1st, I expect D-Day to be within a day or two of that. H-Hour will be about 0700.

Leicester, Wednesday, May 10, [1944]

A very full day. Conferences with the G-3 and Gen. R in the morning. Luncheon with Mr. Gibson and representatives of the Red Cross upon the arrival of 13 donut trucks. The Red Cross is doing a splendid job for us in this war.

Conference on Eagle at 1500. Conferred with Regt COs of Task Force A on Neptune later, winding up at 1700. They are in good shape and will give an excellent account of themselves. Played deck tennis until 1900. Dinner and then to the office and to bed at 2230. Called Val.

Leicester, Thursday, May 11, [1944]

Studying the 52nd Wing order for Eagle roused my suspicions that all was not as it should be. Went over to the Wing and to the P/F School and talked to Clark and

Col. Crouch. I have never seen such a mess. Our DZs are different. The TCC is going to drop our people on different DZs than the Division FO gives them missions on or thinks that they are to be dropped on. Most unfortunate, and little that can be done about it now. Our G-3 Weinicke is miscast if I ever saw an officer miscast. He has plenty of ability, very smart, a smooth talker, but lazy as hell.

Photographs taken Apr 28th came in yesterday. Hill 110 continues to be most intriguing. The spots are continuing to expand. We cannot tell what they are. We are still going to jump on them.[i]

S. Sauver has been bombed. Five bombs. Probably some kid on the way home jettisoned his load. Didn't hit anything.

The Germans are flooding the river down near Lessay, an excellent sign. They may be organizing a defensive line along the river near Lessay. That is the best sign we have seen yet. They are continuing to build up their divisions, now being up to 56. The Russians have done nothing for a few weeks. As soon as they attack again, and especially if the southern France attack comes in, it should help us. It is going to be some affair.

Leicester, Saturday, May 13, [1944], 0800

Left for takeoff airfields at 0730 Thursday. Checked all fields during the day. Takeoff at about 11:00, drop at 1:30–2:30, landed back at Saltby at 4:15. Back at Braunstone at 5:30. Left by air for First Army CP at 9:30. Lunch with Gen. Hodges, Ridgway, Kean and staff. Conference later on-air support. The AS plan getting rather well set. Despite the elaborate plan, however, we are learning more and more that the air support arm has very definite limitations. The amount of accurate bombing that can be done on any one target at one time is very limited due to dust etc. On a clear target the accuracy of the AC is not very good.

Leicester, Sunday, May 14, [1944], 0800

Arrived at CP 21st Army Group at 11:45, a bit late. Remained in conference until 1300. It was agreed that the 82nd would get its bombing requests on D-1 provided that the German was unaware of the locale of our effort on the continent. If he were not, we would not get our targets bombed until D-Day. Since he is now flooding the Ay Valley near Lessay, it appears as though he has defensive intentions for the Cherbourg Peninsula. This is the best indication that I have seen so far.[ii]

---

i   Hill 110 was the dominant feature at Saint-Saveur, the center of the 82nd objective area.

ii   He probably means Lisieux rather than Lessay.

Hill 110 continues to be built up with anti-airborne obstacles. The attitude of the AC in our recent Exercise Eagle was most disheartening. My own pilot refused to use his Rebecca, relying solely on DR.

This operation will, I hope, settle a few things. If it is as snafu as Sicily I hope someone gets tried. I am afraid that if it is as bad as Sicily, I may not get a chance to settle with the TCC. I was inordinately lucky down there. Yet this airborne effort cannot limp along with the TCC screwing things up at every opportunity, more thru indifference than lack of equipment or means. Its future is limitless, restricted only by the imagination of its proponents.

Leicester, Wednesday, May 16, 1944

This has been a very busy period. Couldn't resist the temptation to run into London and see Val Sunday afternoon. After all, there is no telling when I may never [sic] see her again.

Returned Sunday evening at one AM, out to a drop at three, and back to camp in bed at six. To work at eight and a very busy day. Flew down to Eastcote to a critique on Eagle, returning at 1800.

I am afraid that again I was too critical of the TCC. That is the damnedest touchy problem, how to get them to fly better and show more concern for our aspects of the operation without becoming too critical of their technique. They are quick to resent it if we do. It is so evident that we would both be much better off in one unit with one branch, boss, promotion list, supply source, planning hqrs, but it will be very difficult to ever get them together.

Monday evening Gen. Joe Collins, the VII Corps commander, arrived for an inspection of the division and so we took him around from early Tuesday until noon today. An interesting type. Runty, cocky, confident, almost to the point of being a bore. Not quite appreciative of our problems in assigning us tactical missions, but nevertheless very much interested in our welfare. At least he expressed himself as so being.

I am certain that Ridgway would make a much better corps commander than Collins. They are classmates, and it is difficult to understand. Ridgway appears to be sick. His malaria, and what now appears to be jaundice, are getting him down a bit.

Leicester, Friday, May 18, 1944, 0830

A most profitable day spent cleaning up details about the office. Caught up with all or most of my letter writing and studies of the Overlord situation. Went to a 325 dance in the evening. Dragged their Red Cross girl, Edith Steiger.

Plans that were made to go to London Friday for a Saturday conference at St. Paul's had to be dropped because of a cancellation. I feel particularly bad about it because of the disappointment in not seeing Valerie. Sometimes I think that I would be better off if I had never met her. I am so damn much in love with her. Sometimes I can't quite figure out why, and how long it will last concerns me too. At the moment I feel miserable as hell. What's the answer?

Leicester, Saturday, May 19, [1944], 2130

Just returned from Torquay, having been down there for the past 24 hours. It was an interesting war game. All of the Div Comdrs and staffs in the VII Corps were present. The 82, 101, 9, and 90th. Like Old Home Week. There were many old faces that I haven't seen for years. It was nice to see them all again. The conference was as interesting from a view of the characters present as from a study of the tactical solutions offered.

Ridgway was outstanding as a divisional commander. Collins, the corps commander, was outstanding. Eddy of the 9th didn't look too good, nor did McKelvey of the 90th, although he didn't have much to say.

As a general comment, they all looked too well fed and behaved rather pompously to be very effective field soldiers. A few shots and they will change some, either that or lose their commands.[i]

A letter from Val awaiting me upon my return, which was very nice to get. I am still entirely unsatisfied about her continuing to go about so and about to give up on it. She has been the recipient of such attention for years and she is so good looking and attractive that she almost has to have constant attention. I am afraid that it has come to be part, an essential part, of her existence.

I am convinced of her faithfulness to me but, despite that, I find her gadding about extremely difficult to feel satisfied about. Having a continuous miserable feeling, knowing that she is spending the evening with another man, becomes after a while intolerable. She will not understand this, despite any explanations I may make, so an attempt at a clear break may be best.

It is an odd experience for me. Except for the remote possibility of a happy future for us, I would say that it was unfortunate that I ever met her. I am still not convinced that she will not expect to gad about after we are married. That would be the finish.

Leicester, Sunday, May 21, 1944

A call from Val at 0100, which was damn nice to get. Changed my serial and DZ.

---

i   McKelvey of the 90th was quickly relieved by Bradley during follow-on operations. Eddy, an Africa veteran and good friend of Patton, did well and ended up as a corps commander under Patton.

Monday, May 22, [1944]

Not a very busy day Sunday. Picked Val and Eileen up at Liverpool Station and went to 82 Portland Place. Stayed there until 11:30 PM, when it was time to pick up Jack Thompson, who I brought back with me, getting back at 0245. Wonderful to see Val again. She does love me; of that I am convinced.

Saw Al Ireland. He had the dope that our movement to the takeoff fields would be deferred until June 1st. This helps considerably, although the high command does not look well upon it.

Leicester, Tuesday, May 23, [1944], 0800

Gen. Ridgway talked to the 325 and 505th. Excellent talk to the 507th. This is a good thing. He is to talk to the others in the next day or two. I plan on doing my talking at the takeoff airfields. He does not look well. I am afraid that he is not well and is covering it up.

A conference at 1700 at which time all Bn COs outlined their plans. Worked well. Our Infantry is closer together than it has ever been before.

Leicester, Wednesday, May 24, [1944]

Visited the 504th and 505th with Jack Thompson. Spent several hours with the 505th talking over their mission. Kellam still looks weak.

Gen. Ridgway talked to the regt at 1800, at which time the Legion of Merit was awarded to Lt. Masters. The talk was well delivered and equally as well received.

Later a demonstration of the Gammon grenade was staged at the Gypsy Lane quarry in Leicester. Most impressive. Lt. Reiss of the 505th also demonstrated the throwing of 60mm and 81mm mortar HE shells as hand grenades. Powder increments are removed, the pin removed, the base of the shell struck on the ground until the setback pellet drops back and the fork flies out, then the shell is armed and will detonate on impact.[i]

Worked about the office in the evening. Called Val, or rather she called me. I am becoming worried about her condition. I don't really know whether or not she is as sick as the doctor leads her to believe. She looks the picture of health but may be run down. At all events, if she is as sick as he says she is it is a matter of much

---

i   The Gammon grenade was a British invention intended for use against armor by infantry. It was a black sock filled with C2 explosive with a string-pull fuse. The user pulled the string and then lobbed—not threw—the sock at the target. It exploded on impact. They were quite effective and prized. Most troops carried at least one. They were somewhat unstable and occasionally detonated if inadvertently dropped. The 60mm "hand grenade" was occasionally used but the 81mm was too heavy to be practical.

concern. Due to the cancellation of many trains, she may be unable to come up this week. I had rather hoped she would.

Leicester, Thursday, May 25, 1944, 1600

The seaborne left this morning. Present plans contemplate the departure of the glider and parachute lift on the 29th. Yesterday I took the T pinpoints to the Pathfinder School at North Witham. Talked over the 101st mission with Col. Crouch. It looks rather tough. Spent quite a bit of time last evening with our PIs. There are now cows grazing on the Pra[i]rie de M. This is beginning to look bad. If that is passable for armor, we will be in a tough spot.[i]

Visited the 505, 507, 508 this morning. They are in as good a shape as we can get them under present circumstances. I wish now that we could have given them tougher training such as we got in Africa. They are confident and certain of their ability to do the job.

It is inspiring to contact new parachute troops about to go into combat. They are so sure of themselves. They will do a good job, and it is just as well. Either this 82nd Div job will be the most glorious and spectacular episode in our history, or it will be another Little Big Horn. There is no way to tell now, but we are going in and they will, I am certain, do a hell of a good job. It is regrettable that so many of them will have to get lost, but it is a tough business and they all figure that parachutists have nine lives. Apparently, we are to get all of the air bombardment missions that we have requested.

Leicester, Saturday, May 26, [1944], 1300

As is always the case when there is a big change, there is too much to do in connection with it to take time to write about it. Neptune has been changed and we are now to jump astride the Merderet River with the mission of seizing the crossings, protecting the flank of the corps, securing a bridgehead over the Merderet, and being prepared to advance to the west to the Douve.

Gen. Ridgway was called down to Bristol yesterday and given the new plan. It was necessitated by a change in the German dispositions. They are continuing to build up in France, despite the pressure that is being put on them in Italy. It looks as though they may lose Rome. Presumably they would sooner lose it than weaken their reserves in France, a sound decision. Since we are now dropping much closer to the amphibious troops, our chances of survival are greatly improved. The entire picture looks much better.

---

i   The reference is to cows grazing on the Prairie de Marceuses, a vast swampy grassland to the south of Sainte-Mère-Église and adjacent to Carentan.

I will jump with the 508th and 507th. Gen. Ridgway is going to jump with the 505th. It looks like a real rat race and a grand show. There will be lots of fighting for everyone from the moment their feet hit the ground.[i]

Leicester, Sunday, May 27, [1944], 1420

Meeting of the regt COs, at which time the new situation was outlined to them. Lots of work. These damn changes. Complete sets of plans, terrain memory classes, plastic models, all wasted.

Valerie arrived at 1800. Took her to dinner and then to the 505th Officers Club. Grand to have her here.

The 505th looks fine. At this stage of the planning the new drop looks like a real snafu, confusion and indiscriminate fighting galore. It will be several days until any semblance of organization or tactical integrity comes out of the mess.

Leicester, Tuesday, May 30, 1944

May 30th. I just realized it. We are living in a different world these days. Drove down to London Sunday evening. Returned in haste, arriving at midnight. Planning still in a rather confused state.

Yesterday, Monday, visited the P/F School and 314th Grp, which will fly me in. Col. Meyers is to command my serial. Probably will work OK. Gen.

Bradley arrived in the evening. All of the unit commanders were in for dinner. He is still as confident as ever that we will swamp the German. It is difficult to fully share his optimism, although one really wants to.[ii]

The situation is shaping up a bit better daily. If I live through this one, I may be fortunate to get command of the division. Three excess field officers from the States arrived yesterday. A terrible system. They sent their castoffs to combat units on the verge of going in. Inexcusable.

---

i   The change was dictated by the sudden infusion of German troops at Saint-Saveur and the widespread new Rommel asparagus on the open fields. By shifting the plan about 15 kilometers east with Sainte-Mère-Église as the target, the 82nd would be less than five air miles from Utah. To hasten planning and dampen emotions, General Ridgway simply took the Saint-Saveur acetate overlay and shifted it to Sainte-Mère-Église. This covered all the likely avenues of approach with the three PIRs and eliminated much of the new work.

ii   Unknown to Gavin was that Bradley had to fight Leigh-Mallory for the airborne operation. Leigh-Mallory believed it would be a disaster and told Eisenhower so. Ike talked to Bradley, Taylor, Collins, and Ridgway, all of whom strongly supported it, Bradley to the point of stating it as a requirement for success.

Cottesmore, Wednesday, May 31, [1944]

Moved over here yesterday afternoon. Visited all of the fields in the past 24 hrs and everything is in excellent shape. The SOS[i] is doing a splendid job of taking care of us before takeoff. Just about our every wish is granted. Cots, blankets, mess kits, cooks, and the chow is well above average. These troops will enter combat with a much higher morale than we have ever had before. Regrettably they will lack some of the condition and toughness of our African-trained troops.

D-Day remains Monday, June 5th. Everything is in readiness. Even with the new mission I want to come back from this one, much more than I have ever wanted to come back before. I am not as uneasy about going in as I have been before, although it is certain to be a hell of a rough fight. Those of us who have been there before are all a bit more certain of ourselves and of our ability to handle anything that develops. There are not so many unknowns this time. It is the unknowns that bother the new soldier.

Cottesmore, Friday, June 2, 1944

Started the rounds talking to the 505th Hq and 1st Bn at Spanhoe at 1030. Ended with the 2nd and 3rd Bns at Cottesmore at 1800. During the interim spoke to all bns at all fields. Most interesting. Not sure who enjoyed it most. I certainly had a lot of fun. At this stage of the game, they are tops to talk to. Finally evoked some spontaneous cheers after 20 years of waiting. Their morale could hardly be improved upon. With God's help they will do their job well and return.

Last night had a conference with all Bn COs and Regt COs. Final conference. Gave the Regt COs the date of D-Day, still June 5th. Afterwards attended a training exercise in reorganization and assembly.

Back to Cottesmore by 0115. Mr. Walton of *Time* and *Life* and Sgt. Bucknell of *Stars and Stripes* joined yesterday. Lt. Col. Bolland, recently assigned to the division, joined the Task Force staff yesterday in order to get shot at. He does not look very good. It is a shame the number of graduates who are definitely inferior officers. This should never be.

Cottesmore, Saturday, June 3, 1944, D-2

Over to Saltby at 1000 and talked to entire serial on the reorganization and assembly plan. Difficult to say whether or not it will work. The degree to which it will work is the degree of enemy resistance.

---

i   SOS, or Services of Supply, was the organization tasked with managing all logistics for the U.S. forces in England and was led by LTG J. C. H. Lee.

Short conference with Gen. R at noon. Over to Div Hqrs at Braunstone at 1500. Read the mail, called Val, studied the situation. Anti-airborne obstacles are appearing all over the operational area, some in the fields in which we are going to jump. I figure that they are a desperate last-minute measure that it is hoped will deter a commander from committing his A/B troops in those areas. Actually, I do not see how they can be very effective. They may cause some casualties, but hardly enough to be decisive.

Dinner at the house with Gen. Clark present. Gen. Ridgway decided afterwards to go in by parachute. An unusual plan and one that hardly stands up under analysis. As it appears to me, he is particularly interested in getting a parachute combat star, but this would hardly seem to be proper reason for abandoning the entire glider-borne staff and Hqrs to go by chute.

Gen. Clark was strangely anxious for him to go by chute in a plane piloted by himself. After the decision was made, he stated that he would probably not be able to pilot the ship because he must stay back here. Strange things happen.

But at all events it does appear as though we will have an airborne division headquarters. It may be scattered a bit, but it will all be there.

Called Val in the evening. Away from her guileful influence I can question the wisdom of marrying her.

Returned to Cottesmore at 2300 and then went to an assembly problem at Saltby at 2400. Worked well.

Sunday, June 4, 1944, 0800, D-1

Visited all fields during the day. Things rather well in hand. Everything has been provided for as well as we are able to anticipate our needs. Late photo coverage taken June 2nd shows considerable activity in and around Etienville. The entire area of our landing, as well as I can see it now, will be a hotbed of fighting and activity. A hell of a place to put new troops, but they must learn sometime.

I wish sometimes that I were going in with the 505th. Getting new units in hand under fire gets tiring after awhile. The 508, however, looks as good as any new outfit that I have ever seen. If they cannot do it, it cannot be done by green troops.[i]

Monday, June 5, 1944, 1400, D-1 [Second date identified as D-1]

Received a postponement at 0900 yesterday. We can make good use of the extra time. All men were briefed anyway, since it had already started. Visited all fields

---

i   Ultimately, he decided to jump with the 507th targeting Amfreville, considered the most likely German concentration. His was one of the very few 507th aircraft to hit the general area. His great concern regarding troop carrier competence was proven well founded.

this morning. Troops are in top condition and morale couldn't be higher. They are ready, anxious and confident.[3] It will be a very mean and nasty fight if the German is better off than we figure him to be.[i]

I am going to get the AT stuff across the Merderet first, then go to the assistance of the 507 and 508 on the bridgehead. Whether or not the bridge south of Etienville is blown may prove critical and decisive. It is regrettable that security precludes its destruction prior to 0600 D-Day. I expect this to be my hardest fight, and I hope my last with unseasoned troops such as the 08 and 07. They will do well, as is becoming American parachutists.[ii]

Notes

1 Mis-dated as 1944 in original manuscript

2 Apparently Gavin and his wife Irma had by this point agreed to divorce after the war ended.

3 John McNally captured the moment of Gavin's pre-invasion talk to his unit in a letter to his sister: "Then General Jim Gavin came to talk to us, so we assembled in the hangar. A man of greatness if there ever was. There are many kinds of generals. There is the general's general; the public's general; the newspaper's general. Then there is another—the soldier's general. That's General Gavin.

"In all of our airborne drops, the first man out of the plane is always the General himself! All of the thousands of men who crouch in the door of a plane, ready to leap into the roaring, flak-filled night, know that someone else was down there before them. Imagine the terrific morale factor of the simple, stark fact: the General jumps first! If there is a mistake in picking the drop zone, the General is the first to pay the penalty.

"Picture, if you can, a general who, arriving a little ahead of time and seeing the waiting soldiers being entertained by a GI doing card tricks, would stand unnoticed and wait until the little act was over before coming out to speak. Then he started talking in his quiet way, punctuated once in a while by a slow, tentative smile. He has the intense eyes and lined mouth of a man who has fought the Nazis a long time and well. I watched the faces of the men as he talked. It was as though an electric shock had gone through the whole group. When he talked, every man felt drawn into the company of the elect who, for the space of a breath, risked their lives a thousand feet above the ground.

"When he had finished, he needed only to lift a finger and say 'Follow me,' and there wasn't a single man who wouldn't have followed him straight to hell." McNally, *As Ever, John*, pp. 41–42.

---

i The original June 5 date was postponed 24 hours due to weather.

ii Etienville was about five miles west of Chef-du-Pont in the 508th's sector. The bridge connected the area with many of the German forces west of the drop.

CHAPTER 7

Normandy and After

Leicester, Friday, July 14, 1944[i]

Took off on schedule.[1] Flight en route to coast of France uneventful. Many ground aids in the form of light signals of different makeup being used. A few squirts of flak came up from the islands off the west coast.

Shortly after crossing the coast, we entered a dense fog bank. The wingtips could not be seen. Upon emerging, then a few minutes from the DZ, my ship was all alone. The entire formation, which was beautifully held and flown, had disappeared.[ii]

At the last moment several ships appeared in the sky at some distance. The red light had come on as per plan. The green light followed and, after a brief check of the locality, out we went.

A riverbed appeared in the distance. It must have been the upper reaches of the Merderet. I was afraid for a moment that we were south of the Douve, but I had remembered something of the Merderet turning west at a point north of our area.

Upon opening there was a great deal of fire coming from the ground. Some tracers were mixed with it and the crack of the bullets made it clear that we were the ones that they were shooting at. Off in the distance, in line with our flight, there was a concentration of firing of all types. Houses or something burning in high flames, and to the right there was a lot of flak, some of it of large caliber.

The fire from the ground seemed bad and I sweated out landing. However, I hit hard in a clear spot in an orchard or pasture with a few trees and I could see someone land near me. It turned out to be Lt. Olson. No one bothered me as I freed myself from my harness and started out. Lt. Price of the G-2 section was encountered. He was as quickly lost. Olson and I moved east after checking our direction with a compass.

---

i   Gavin here describes the insertion to cover the period he did not keep a journal.

ii   The fog created huge difficulties for inexperienced pilots, who scattered at all altitudes to avoid collisions. They never recovered and all but the 505th PIR with the 52nd TC were grossly misdropped in both divisions. All the fears Gavin expressed came to pass.

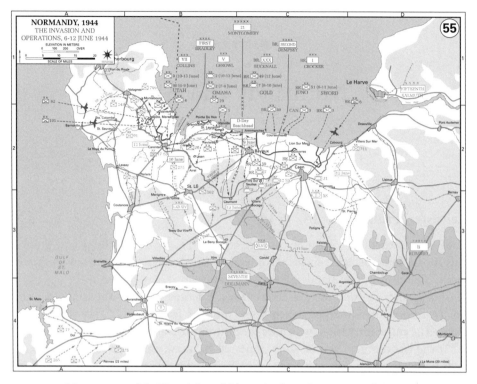

Map courtesy of the United States Military Academy Department of History.

We came in a few minutes to what appeared to be a wide marsh. I figured it must be the Douve or Merderet. From its size I thought that it must be the Douve, but its location indicated that it must be the Merderet.

We moved south and in about five minutes came across a large group of men assembling. It was my stick. Part of it had landed in the swamp. Two men were hit coming down and two injured. Lt. Scherer had a broken leg.

The river proved to be a serious obstacle. It was very deep, even along the edges. There were foxholes and gun emplacements that had been evidently dug by the Germans on the bank and farther inland.

More planes were coming overhead. Jumpers were coming out of them, especially to the north. Some of them went right out into the river. A blue assembly light appeared across the river on what appeared to be the far bank. I sent Lt. Olson to get what men he could and bring them to where I was. We continued to try to get our equipment or weapons out of the swamp.

A red light appeared across the swamp to the left of the blue light. I sent some of the Hqrs men to it to direct all men there to assemble on me. We continued to struggle with equipment. Practically none could be recovered in usable condition. Individuals and small groups of men started coming in. A sector was assigned to the 507 at once. Col. Maloney, and later Col. Ostberg, was put in charge of it, or vice versa.[i]

It was immediately obvious that the men did not realize the seriousness of the situation. They acted as though they were on maneuvers. Milled around in groups, no one taking control, all completely unappreciative that they were about to get killed if they did not act quickly.[ii]

Olson reported in that there was a railroad across the swamp and that we could wade to it, although it was very deep in places. I decided that we were on the west bank of the Merderet, several miles north of La Fiere. We had to be, although the Merderet never looked this deep in aerial photos. I decided to assemble as many men as possible and move before daylight to seize the west end of the La Fiere bridge.

It was evident that we were in a dangerous spot if at daylight we were forced back to the swamp by a superior force. It was imperative that we seize the bridge without delay. The only question unanswered was how many men to wait for. They kept coming in. We were about ready to start moving about 4:30 when two gliders appeared overhead, cut loose, and landed several hundred yards away. I couldn't leave then without getting out the 57mm AT guns. Besides, they would be very valuable to have in a fight at the bridge.[iii]

There was a strong possibility that they [the gliders] contained part of the division staff. Patrols were sent out. A report was received that one contained a 57 and one a jeep that they [++] in bad swampy ground that a big detail was needed to get the stuff out.

About this time the first shots were heard west of the gliders. There had been lots of firing all around before this time, but none of it obviously directed at our group. This was different. They appeared to be focusing their attention on us. Patrols were sent out, increased twice, until 30 men were at the gliders and the equipment had to be abandoned practically under water.

Details at the gliders were now under rather heavy machine pistol and rifle fire. The gun and jeep were destroyed. Several men had been hit. The new men were a complete loss. They cringed in their holes, unbelieving that the Germans were shooting at them. No aggressive action against the German patrol could be started.

The 507th group, of which I had at least 100, were completely ineffective. There was no control, no organization, no one able to get anything done.

---

i   These were mis-dropped battalion commanders in the 507th without their men. Both were highly competent and Gavin learned to rely upon them.

ii   He described in his book how no one was in charge or engaged. He had to "counsel" some to get them moving.

iii   At this point, Gavin was unaware of the successful 505th drop and their seizure of La Fiére. He was completely focused on what he knew or perceived as having the only force to accomplish the mission, assuming the 505th had been equally mis-dropped.

Col. Maloney was simply one man. He had no control over the regiment, although he himself was brave enough. Ostberg was getting most done, although he was having trouble. It appeared to me that all NCOs and junior officers ceased to function. They were waiting for someone to tell them what to do. Whether or not it would have been plain slaughter if the German attacked in force, I am not sure. Anyway, there were not more than ten Germans firing.

It was now too late to get to the bridge during darkness. We obviously would have to fight. The situation between our present position and the bridge was unknown except that there was enemy there. How many? Were we even at the bridge, or north of the bridge as we figured? As a combat force our own troops were at the moment, with few exceptions, ineffective.

The blue and red lights continued to burn on the far bank. Word was received that Col. Lindquist had moved down the RR with 100 men a few hours earlier. Patrols said that they could not get to the blue light because of the depth of the swamp. Olson said they could.

Practically no bazookas or crew-served weapons with their ammunition were recovered. No radios were recovered. I decided to move to the east bank, there pick up all available troops, and move and seize the La Fiere bridge from the east side. It was evident that there was considerable fighting going on in the direction of what I supposed was S. Mère-Eglise. Orders were issued and the move started.

The 507 couldn't get their orders down. No chain of command. Men were being left in their positions. The Germans were closing in, increasing their fires. We had to leave Lt. Scherer with the broken leg with the wounded.

The move across the swamp started. We were fired at and several men hit during the crossing. The railroad was reached, and the move south continued. To my unbelievable delight, at La Fiere the 1st Bn of the 505th was encountered in perfect order, under complete control of CP, set up and fighting to get the La Fiere bridge, exactly as per plan. Elements of the 507 and 508 were mixed up with them.

I left Maj. Kellam fighting to get the east end of the bridge and took all 507 and 508 men south along the railroad to force another crossing of the river south of La Fiere and get the west end of the bridge. He was having lots of trouble, losing quite a few men. Although the German force appeared very small, they were well placed, well dug in, and tenacious.[i]

It was impossible to cross the river. Too deep and swamp grass, and no boats. And Germans dug in on the far bank. The move was continued to Chef-du-Pont. A fight similar to that at La Fiere took place. Col. Osterberg and many men were hit.

---

i   The 505th was not able to secure the west bank until June 9. Gavin is referring to the Chef-du-Pont bridge south of La Fiére as the other crucial bridgehead. This was a 508th objective and was not secured due to major mis-drop issues.

The east end of the bridge was seized by dark. The Germans at La Fiere were counterattacking using armor. Maj. McGinity was killed. Many of the officers and men were hit. We managed to hold on. The 507 was given the Chef-du-Pont bridge and a reserve formed of the 508. The 505 was doing OK as well as could be determined.

I met Gen. Ridgway at the La Fiere RR overpass. No contact with amphibious troops yet. There were comparatively heavy German fires of all types all during the night. The 508 was placed between the 505th's left flank and La Fiere. The fighting continued all day.

At La Fiere the casualties were particularly heavy, all officers having been killed or wounded except a few lieutenants. A withdrawal started just before dusk in reaction

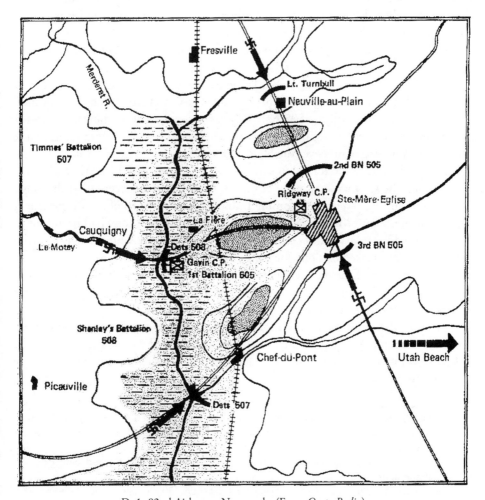

D+1, 82nd Airborne, Normandy. (From *On to Berlin*)

to a very heavy German attack. The German force was building up on the opposite bank. A serious and perhaps disastrous situation was imminent.[i]

They managed to hold on and in fact restore the position. Three German tanks were destroyed on the bridge and many Germans killed and captured on this side. 91st Div [sic]. By nightfall this day the situation improved, and contact was made with amphibious forces.[ii]

Rumors had been rampant that there had been no amphibious landing. There was an attempt made at air resupply during these two days. The Germans recovered a great deal of it. I liked the way they shot at the places where the canopies landed. We didn't need to get the stuff immediately, and it took their artillery off our necks.

A crossing was forced at La Fiere about the third day. Contact was made with Shanley and a bn of the 508 on the west bank of La Fiere about the second day. The division established two bridgeheads, La Fiere and Chef-du-Pont, and was passed through by the 90th Div. It had a frightful time.[iii]

The 82nd passed through the 90th on the Etienville-Renouf line and we moved to the west of the Douve, where the 9th [sic] passed through. The German was by this time being completely routed. A billeting party met us in S. Sauveur-le-Vicomte. It was an advance party for a German regiment that was moving up to that locality.

I spent some time with the 505th, which had moved north on the left of the 4th Div all of the way to Le Ham. One day, while observing and assisting in an attack with them, a message came over the SCR 300 that Slim Jim wanted artillery fire in a certain area. I hadn't asked for it, but since the 505th knew where I was, they asked for verification. The German had many of our 300 radios. We were certain of this now.

Many of our men were daily coming into our lines telling us of their experiences behind the Germans. Millett had been captured. Batcheller's body had been found. The division doubled back and crossed the Douve at Beuzeville and Etienville, finally occupying a defensive position along the line Bois de Limors–Pretot.

The 81 mortars of the regiment were able to be concentrated on one target. Very active patrols, although a number of men were lost. Lt. Olson was hit by mortar fragments in the Bois de Limors. That was a bad place.

I continued to visit each Bn CP daily and, whenever circumstances permitted, visited the company CPs. The high velocity artillery and mortars exacted a daily toll. The German was unable to use his artillery in mass as we use ours. Probably lack of ammunition.

---

i   During the course of the battle, Lieutenant John Dolan was the acting 1-505 battalion commander and Sergeant Bill Owens the acting company commander. Both would be recommended for the Distinguished Service Cross.

ii He is referring to the German 91st Airlanding Division, a unit specifically designed to fight paratroop units.

iii He is referring to Lieutenant Colonel Shanley and 200 of the 508th trapped west of the Merderet. They took severe casualties and were relieved on June 9 along with Lieutenant Colonel Timmes of 2-507 and 150 men trapped against the Germans and the Merderet to the north of La Fiére.

There were many Russians on our front. Ost Bns. They fought well. We occasionally blew up vehicles from our own mines. In one tragic case two vehicles and six men when mines removed with the safety fork replaced were hit on the shoulder.[2]

Leicester, July 19, 1944[i]

Took a two-day leave, commencing at noon Saturday, July 15th. Ar London about 1700. Did some shopping and then went to 82. Val arrived about 1800. Dinner at home and went to the Milroy, a new place. Champagne could be had for 8 pounds per qt., Cordon Rouge 1929. Consumed two quarts and had a night.

A close hit by a doodle bomb the next morning. They are very devastating. The blast breaks all windows for blocks around.[ii]

Went to a movie in the afternoon and then to the Mirabelle for dinner. Very nice. Off to a lazy start Monday morning. Lunch at Ciro's, very nice. Went to see a show, *While the Sun Shines*, in the evening and back to 82 for dinner, an omelet containing shrimp. Val can come up with the damnedest dishes. Talked to her and Eileen until after midnight, then to bed.

Val had to go to work Tuesday, so I returned. Immediately upon my return I was called in by Gen. Ridgway and told that he had been directed by SHAEF to form an A/B corps, and that further he had recommended that I be given the division. He later stated that Gen. Bradley and Gen. Eisenhower had approved my being given the division and that I could be sure that that was all set. However, my promotion to MG might take several weeks or longer because of the usual administrative difficulties.

Then followed the usual old-fashioned horse trading in key officers with Col. Eaton, who represented Gen. R. I will keep Weinicke, who will be my Chief of Staff. It now looks as though Ireland G-1, Winton G-2, Norton G-3, Morman G-4 will be the slate. The Asst CG is the toughest one that I have ever had to make. There is no one available who is fully qualified.[iii]

Leicester, July 20, 1944, 0740

No training being accomplished since 50% of the men are on furlo. Checked about getting a line on things. Talked to Gen. R and Doc re the staff. Wish now that this thing would shape up. Norton coming to duty today, Winton in a day or so. My period of resting is about up. I'm getting fat and lazy. Wish I knew what the next mission was going to be. Hope that it is occupational. It is beginning to look that way almost.

---

i   The division had just returned to the UK and was recovering.

ii These were the V1s, a sub sonic rocket.

iii Brigadier General George Howell was the acting Deputy Commander for Support in Normandy and landed with the sea tail. Gavin did not think much of him but eventually made him the deputy CG by default. He served throughout the war in that role.

Leicester, July 23, 1944, 0730

I have had a quiet and well-behaved weekend so far. Today is Sunday. Yesterday attended graduation exercises at Ashwell Camp with Gen. R. The graduating class made a fine appearance.

Left for Stanmore at 11:30, arriving for a conference at 1400. Conference was evidently called by Bagby or Henson. Regardless of which one called it, it was pointless and a waste of time. Since we had not received the agenda, we were not prepared to enter into protracted discussions of what they wanted. It had to do with changing the SOP on A/B operations.

My position as division commander appears secure. It has quite evidently been given the blessing of SHAEF. Last evening Gen. Ridgway wanted to know again if I wanted George Howell as a BG, and if not, if I had no use for him, my wishes in the matter would be transmitted to Gen. Eisenhower and he would take care of the case, apparently reducing him. I told him that this was a hell of a thing to put in my hands, the reduction of a superior who had been a BG for a long time, but that no matter what happened I did not want him as my assistant. Gen. R agreed with me and stated that he would report the circumstances to Gen. Barkley, Eisenhower's DCS, today.

The organization of the staff continues. I am a bit worried about Weinicke as Chief of Staff. He is very intelligent, but a bit lazy. A CS must apply himself relentlessly. Ireland will be OK as 1, Winton a bit impersonal but OK as 2, and Norton with a bit of experience brilliant as 3. Marin [Morman, as above?] as 4 will be about very satisfactory.

I will appreciate getting on my own. This is a difficult time when the old regime is still hanging on. I am sure that I can give the division lifeblood and warmth and give it a personality. It lacks that now. As soon as possible I want every man to know who I am and to talk to each of them.

If I only had a better Asst CG. That is the most difficult problem of all. Lewis will be cantankerous and unpopular. Parachutists will have absolutely no respect for him, particularly since they all know of his breakdown in combat. They will never understand why he is Asst CG, but who else?[i]

Leicester, July 24, 1944, 1500

Continued discussions with Gen. Ridgway on the subject of an assistant division commander. If I had any classmate or friend who would fill the job I could have him and get him made a BG right now—and I can't do a damn thing about it.

---

i   This refers to Colonel Lewis, commander of the 325th, who had a heart attack in Normandy.

I told him that I do not want George Howell, which may end in the reduction of George. After much palaver he suggested Gen. Cutler, whom I know but do not like particularly. He has a sour negative personality but is professionally capable. He is capable of commanding the division in case of my departure for any reason. So, it looks like Cutler. Jerry Higgins is to be Asst CG of the 101st.

I am going to try my damnedest to have a tiptop division. It will not be easy. In fact, it will be very difficult, much more difficult than anyone realizes. The loss of the staff will be hard-felt. We continue to waste a great deal of time, no effort being made at strenuous training because of our present post-combat policy of granting leaves to everyone. Idleness makes me madder than hell, and people are loafing all over this place now, so I am rather unhappy.

The international situation is breaking nicely, with a small revolution brewing in Germany and Guam in our hands.

Had a meeting this morning at which time the matter of possible airlanding operations was discussed with all unit commanders.

Leicester, July 27, 1944

Went to London yesterday to confer with ETOUSA JA and IG re my new staff. The IG most cooperative, lined up Lt. Col. Dunnington, who looks most promising. The JA rather difficult. Wanted to see something in writing before he would make any effort to be of assistance.

Upon my return this morning I talked to Doc Eaton about the situation, and it does not look so good. Eisenhower has held up all the papers, my promotion, Howell's relief, the formation of the corps. So it goes.

Saw Val for awhile. Eileen talks too much. She did not look so good, and I am afraid that at times she does not think too charitably of me. Probably feels that I am a stuffed shirt. It will all probably affect Val and me sooner or later. Val is a grand person. I wish that she had a different job, or no job.

The division is still dogging along. Training will be intensified next week.

Leicester, Saturday, July 29, [1944]

An officers dance Thursday evening at the Bell Hotel at which I did not do myself very proud. This matter of how to behave as a general officer at a unit dance appears difficult of solution. Going as a stag is not too good, since there is an unconscious resentment built against such rank cutting or wolfing. Dragging is hard on the drag, since no one else will dance with her. Being too sober of mein, one is a bore and stuffed shirt. Being a gay eager beaver is improper and conducive to loss of respect and consequently command. Should one not go to hops at all?

Spent the day in reconnaissance of training areas. Had a tooth filled at the 505 in the afternoon. Dinner with Gen. Ridgway at Lord Trent's in Nottingham in the evening. By far the nicest affair of its kind that I have had the pleasure of being present at since [sentence fragment ends here].

Sunday, July 30, [1944], 1000

Graduation at the Parachute School. 175 student replacements. Capt. Rosen among those who matriculated. Reconnoitered the site of the coming review for Gen. Eisenhower in the PM. Also laid out the problems for the coming training period with Jack Norton, G-3.

Went to Nottingham to a 508 Prop Blast in the evening. Dragged Hillary Holloway, blue brunette and yum yum. Back at 5:30. Good training for my new driver. Weber's battle nerves finally bested him, and he asked for relief.

Monday, July 31, 1944

The first day of training under the new schedule. 504 off to a slow start. If Tucker does not do well, it will be his scalp. I will not fool with him. A number of his men still on furlo.

Had an interesting but brief discussion with Gen. Ridgway on the merits or lack of merit of keeping a diary. Maybe something to what he says, but I am going to give it a better try. I believe it is imperative that one be kept in combat, for official purposes if no other.

The weekend was a typical weekend with the English taking a holiday. Unfortunately, our soldiers are learning the English customs too well.

Still nothing can be done about forming a division staff if Gen. Ridgway leaves. He is leaving it up in the air and refuses to take any responsibility for the corps. It continues to keep the new division staff in a ridiculous spot.

The Normandy affair is going great guns.

Tuesday, August 1, [1944]

First Bn Ex at Big Moor. All night affair. Stopped in Nottingham to call on Hillary. A div show *Let's Sing Together* in Leicester, very good. Called on Ireland, now a Maj.

Saturday, August 12, 1944

The longest period ever, and at the same time the most unsettled. Gen. Ridgway has been going to turn over the Div and then he doesn't. We have been threatened with almost immediate operational commitment and we don't. Training has been redirected and intensified; more attention being focused on air landing. The results clearly point out the advantages of parachute operations, both as a time and ship saver.

Gen. Eisenhower came up for a review of the division yesterday. I had a feeling that I was under scrutiny. I still do not know if my recommendation for promotion has been forwarded to the States. Oddly enough, I give little damn about it, feeling at this stage that I can command this division efficiently and well. I would like to take it in, but another affair like Normandy makes petty things like promotion fade into insignificance.

Have been seeing a lot of Hillary, an inordinately attractive girl. Valerie came up last night for a day or so, the first time we have seen each other in weeks. She looks wonderful.

The new staff is unquestionably the best in the business. I am quite proud of them. Would to God that they could take over and start running the division. The thing that I dislike most, feel most keenly, and am most uneasy about is the fact that neither myself nor my staff is getting any opportunity to command the division, and yet we may have to take it in any day on a few days' notice. Gen. R and staff still hang around. It is a hell of a state.

August 16, 1944

Well, this is it. Gen. Ridgway and the staff left a few minutes ago. I am in the damnedest position imaginable. I just wrote the Babe [his daughter Barbara] a letter which follows in part:

"Well, there will be a lot of tch tch-ing before we are through. I have a thousand ideas and I am going to carry them through, in combat and out, with zeal and determination, come what may. Either this division will rise to heights of combat attainment in our service unprecedented or rush to oblivion. In either case I will be with it all the way.

"To those of us who have had a lasting and firm faith in the efficacy of airborne troops as a means of waging war, there is of course no doubt about the future of this or any other parachute division, nor is there any doubt or concern really with what value posterity will place on what we do now. We are supremely confident of ourselves. I suppose that we would not be in the hazardous business we are in if we in the slightest degree lacked this confidence.

"Since the day I entered this airborne service there never has been a dull moment. Always a new challenge, always a new horizon. That is the way it should be. Despite the alleged hazards and apparent uncertainties of it as a way of service, we love it. With this abiding confidence in our professional creed, and a determination to excel in combat unmatched in any army anywhere, all airborne soldiers look to the future certain that they have a rendezvous with greatness."

Notes

1   Gavin is here just getting around to writing about the Normandy invasion during which they had parachuted into combat on the night of June 5/6, 1944. No doubt he had been fully occupied in the interim.

2   Later Gavin wrote reflectively on the landings and subsequent fighting. "From the moment of landing it was a hotly contested affair," he recalled, "with the experience of the 505th tilting the scales in our favor. The 82nd Airborne Division captured all its objectives and went on to sever the peninsula, thus sealing the fate of Cherbourg. In early July it made a last attack to the south, seizing La Haye-du-Puits and starting the opening that ultimately led to the debouchment of Patton's Third Army into Brittany. The 82nd returned to England after 33 days of fighting in Normandy, all objectives seized and no terrain lost. It had been our costliest battle in the war, 3,927 troopers wounded and 1,142 killed. The rifle companies as usual took the heaviest losses and some were down to about 50 men."

CHAPTER 8

Division Command and Nijmegen

Monday, August 21, 1944

Well, the summer flies and here we sit. Attended a conference in the office of Gen. Brereton the other day on the current continental situation. The necessity for several weeks of planning is working a hell of a hardship on the commitment of airborne troops.

In the present affair there appeared to be an excellent chance to use them on the crossings of the Seine. A. M. Tedder wants to use them to invade Calais. Brereton calls his force the First Air Army. Ridgway watches the Americans, and closer still watches Browning, who has designs on the entire force. It is some clambake.

My interests are solely concerned at the moment with the 82nd and that is a full-time job. Prospects for the commitment on the continent look rather remote at the moment. Possibly in an occupational role.

Wednesday, August 23, [1944]

A field test for a bn of the 504 yesterday.[1]

Leicester, Wednesday, Sept. 6, 1944

Sunday, August 27th attended a tea at the home of Gen. Brereton at Ascot. There given first intimation of an impending mission.

Tuesday attended a conference at the Hqrs of Lieut. Gen. Browning, now in command of the British A/B corps at Moore Park. Given a mission of participating in a proposed landing north of Tournai to seize and hold the crossings of the Escaut River to prevent German withdrawal. The drop was to take place Sunday morning at about 8:30. Participating were the Poles, British, and 101st U.S. A/B Div. Plans were pushed, orders prepared, ammo etc. issued, chutes issued, troops disposed at proper airdromes, all by dark Friday evening.

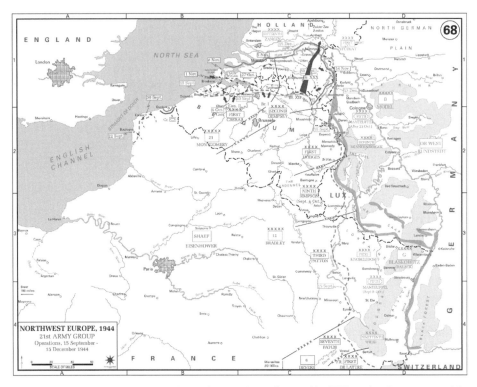

21st Army Group Operations, 15 September–15 December 1944. (Wikimedia Commons, public domain)

It was raining and continued to rain more. The U.S. armor continued to drive the Germans back, actually threatening to get to our DZs before Sunday. They did, Sunday morning. Besides, the weather was lousy. Knowing that the armor was going to beat us to it, Gen. Browning changed our missions to seize and take over Lille, Roubaix, Tournai, etc. so as to assist the armor in its passage. A hell of a mission for A/B troops.

But Gen. Browning was not to be denied and, for some unexplainable reason, the high command was hell bent on getting the 1st U.S. A A/B A in the fight, whether or not the commitment was decisive or even sound.

Well, Sunday morning I was called to Moore Park, Gen. Browning's Hqrs, and given a new mission. We were to jump of [sic: on?] the west bank of the Meuse, opposite Liege, to again block the retreating Germans. The historic Liege Gap. By now the troops were aware of the apparent lack of necessity of our participation in this type of role, or so it seemed. Again, weather intervened and was conveniently, and also typically, lousy. The British ground troops were overrunning our DZ and LZ areas in addition.

Consequently, by Sunday night the mission was called off. We reverted to the U.S. XVIII Corps and back home we came, a bit wetter but hardly the wiser.

It was an interesting and physically trying staff experience. The new staff did wonderfully well. I do not believe that there is a better combat staff in the army, certainly not in the A/B business.

Gen. Browning shed considerable of his professional aura and under pressure became the disheveled frustrated officer that so many of us are in combat. It was interesting to observe his functioning under these conditions. He unquestionably lacks the steadying influence and judgment that comes with a proper troop experience basis.[2]

His staff was superficial in its fullest sense. They were all there and, whenever possible, gave reasonable answers to questions asked, but totally lacked follow-up or even apparently an appreciation of what our requirements were. Why the British units fumble along, flub the dub as the boys say, becomes more and more apparent.

Their tops lack the know-how. Never do they get down into the dirt and learn the hard way, and really the only way to fully learn. Our supply, for example, was to be A/B for ten days, regardless of ground contacts completed.

I regret that he is to no doubt be one of the most influential advisors to the supreme allied councils in post-war days. He is personable and impressive, but completely and entirely impractical.

Gen. Ridgway is in for an interesting future in our War Dept. blocking Browning's schemes. With Churchill and Roosevelt so close together, little can, in the final analysis, be done to curb Browning. Now we are threatened with a drop on Dusseldorf or some similar German industrial area. Certainly, the time has come when we must drop from here within a week or so, or move to the continent or move to Asia. I am for the latter.[i]

This affair is practically wound up. I am going to have a difficult time adjusting myself to civil life in the U.S. away from troops.

Leicester, Thursday, Sept. 14, 1944

Last weekend Valerie came up for a day, returning Sunday. I drove her down to London, arriving at about 1400. At 1600 I received notice of a meeting at Gen. Brereton's Hqrs at 1800 so I took off, arriving a few minutes late for the meeting.

It was conducted generally by Browning and had to do with a new plan envisioning a drop for the 82nd to seize the bridges at Grave and Nijmegen and the high ground

---

i   General Browning would be a continuous thorn. Ultimately, it was pressure and persuasion that created *Market Garden* despite intelligence showing a reconstituted German armor force near Arnhem. His staff buried this interpretation and the rest is history.

between Nijmegen and Groesbeek.[i] That the plan would go through was all agreed to. Browning was to command it and had it all set up.[3]

The troop carrier lift was not set, however. That was arranged at Eastcote Monday morning. After the conference I went to Moore Park to get the latest dope on the area from the British. Left there for Northolt and then took off for Leicester.

Missed field landing at Derby and, after securing an RAF truck, arrived at the Glebe Mount House at 0030. Had a staff conference at once and put the G-2 section to work. After an all-night session they gave me their studies at 0530 and I took off for Eastcote at 0600. There DZs and LZs were picked, taken to Moore Park, and approved and, upon returning to Leicester, the tactical plan started. It was given to the regtl COs in about—actually 0800 Wednesday morning.

There were many plans. The TCC could not make a turnaround, so could not deliver the division in three days. The plan was D-Day 480 prcht and 50 gl, D+1 450 gl [sic: prcht?] and 400 gls. Resupply D+2.[ii]

D-Day has been changed from the 14th to the 15th to the 23rd and now to the 17th. Takeoff airdromes are not settled yet, nor is the lift, this latter because they have been unable to decide whether or not the full TCC lift will be available or whether the bombers will do part of the resupply or all of it.

The flak in the area is terrific, the krauts many. It looks very rough. If I get through this one, I will be very lucky. It will, I am afraid, do the airborne cause a lot of harm.[4]

Nijmegen, Netherlands, Oct. 8, 1944[iii]

And so, the Grave and Nijmegen bridges were captured as ordered.[5] Also the high ground was captured and held. A very marginal performance, and one that will not be duplicated in this war. The perfect airborne show.

Tucker crossed the Waal at 1500 on D plus 3 and by nightfall the bridge was ours. Vandervort with the II/505 took this end. In this final effort we were aided by the Guards Armoured Division. The Irish Guards one bn of armor assisted Tucker in clearing out to the boating point. One bn of Grenadier Guards helped Vandervort, and one bn of the Coldstream Guards were made available to the division as a reserve.[6]

At the time of the Waal crossing the German 6th Para Division attacked in a coordinated effort, hitting Beek and Mook and succeeding in penetrating the position for about 1,000 yards at each place.

---

i   This was Operation *Market Garden*.
ii   This meant less than half the division per day.
iii As above, this is a recapitulation of events written post operation.

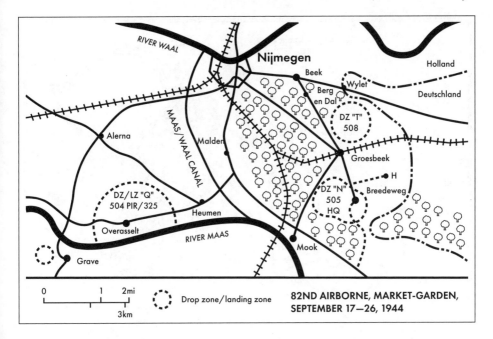

82ND AIRBORNE, MARKET-GARDEN, SEPTEMBER 17–26, 1944

The situation was very critical. Repeated attacks, up until about four days ago, have been made against the division position, all without success. The latest have been very costly to the German.[i]

My relations with the British have been most satisfactory. Although I dislike their professional methods, or lack of method, I nevertheless find them superb to work with. We have gotten along well together.

I am afraid that Gen. Ridgway has resented our success and in a small way is rather jealous of Gen. Browning's success. Unfortunately, I am in the tug of war, right in the middle. In the heat of the third day's fighting Gen. Ridgway visited my CP and, when not immediately approached, left in a huff, later writing a letter demanding an immediate explanation. Such a lack of trust and confidence between his and my command can only do us both and our units harm.

I have therefore asked that I be relieved of command of the division and assignment to his corps, the XVIII. This is a big step, but a necessary one at this point. We cannot continue to serve in a strained critical atmosphere.

It is most regrettable that he is so sensitive about the British. Several years ago, I would never have understood my feeling in a matter such as this. I am confident now that I can command a division, or any other unit, successfully in any combat adversity. I can successfully train any size unit for combat as well.

---

i   He downplays how extraordinarily well the 82nd did, a fact recognized by all the senior officers participating, the British in particular.

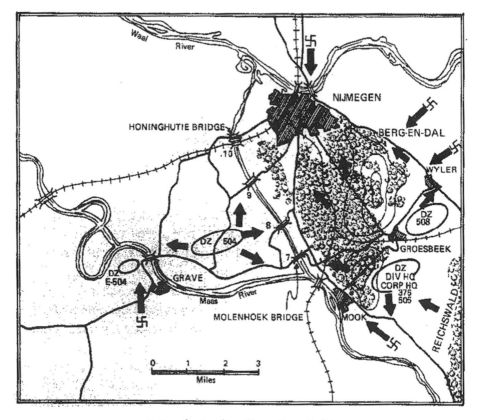

Action after Landing. (From *On to Berlin*)

I know airborne operations as well as anyone in our service. I have been very lucky. Four combat jumps are a lot.[7] I am ready to leave the service and try my hand a something new. I care not what. The only thing against this is a means of livelihood. I can fare reasonably well on what retirement I have earned. In the meantime, I'll try anything.

Whatever it is, I want to get completely away from the army and war. This letter of Gen. Ridgway epitomizes all that I have never liked about our army. After 20 years of service, the past three years as a parachutist, the year and a half in combat with this division, to have successfully undertaken an extremely difficult combat mission, then to be sent a letter by my corps commander asking for an immediate explanation in writing why I flagrantly violated the tenets of military courtesy during the heat of combat upon the occasion of a visit to my CP.

He has not seen fit to make any remark, good or bad, on our battle. And, worst of all, I was extremely considerate and courteous and always have been. Time to get out of his outfit. Perhaps the army too.

The division is still on the Nijmegen Heights. One combat team is with the British XII Corps north of the bridge. Gen. Horrocks of the XXX Corps has been most anxious to use us in a ground role. Gen. Dempsey of the Br 2nd Army spoke to me about it, but I demurred. Gen. Montgomery spoke to them about it, representing I believe Gen. Eisenhower's views, and they decided on a defensive role until after their big attack. At that time, we are to return to our base, which rumor has it will be near Rheims.

Horrocks has asked me to make a limited objective attack anyway, which I did not enthuse over. This morning I meet him and Gen. Browning, at which time I hope to be transferred to the Br XXX Corps. Gen. R will, I suppose, blame this transfer on me.[i]

Nijmegen, Oct. 12, 1944

Gen. Horrocks inspected the division yesterday. A hell of a nice person, as well as a good general. I like him very much. Very human and closely interested in the well-being and comfort of the soldiers, always the mark of a good soldier.[ii]

No word from Gen. Ridgway. Sent Chief of Staff to his CP yesterday. Should soon hear something. Gen. Parks, C/S First Allied Airborne Army, came by the CP and spent the night. I do not know whether he was inspecting me and the division or not. At all events he got an eyeful, I am sure.

The British have been high in their praise of the division and Gen. Horrocks on his inspection, accompanied by Parks, spoke very highly of the division. Gen. Horrocks and one of his Gs, Col. Jones, and I stopped by a haystack and had lunch during the course of the inspection.

Gen. Horrocks was very frank in his analysis of the future of England. He said that, in his opinion, England would be reduced to an outpost of the empire. Heavy industries would be prohibitive and in any future foray England would take a merciless pounding immediately. The heads of the government should therefore move to the American continent and establish a close relationship with the U.S. government. He distrusts Russia, even at this point, very much. A separate peace would be greatly to her advantage. We are agreed that Japan must be reduced to a world nonentity and kept that way. France and Germany pose the most difficult problems.

I am worried about my troubles with the XVIII Corps. This is a hell of a thing to have on one's mind at a time like this. It detracts from my efficiency about 25%. It's a ridiculous situation.

Nov 1st our date home.

---

i   The British were very anxious to use the 82nd rather than their own troops who were both tired and not of the quality the 82nd possessed.

ii He and Horrocks got on extremely well throughout the campaign.

Nijmegen, Oct. 16, 1944

Accompanied by the regimental commanders and Col. March, went to the XXX Corps CP at Wijchen and there met King George VI. A very nice person. Trying very hard to be nice to everyone. Except for his speech impediment, an easy person to talk to.

Gen. Montgomery and Gen. Dempsey accompanied him, and they were very nice. Gen. Montgomery an interesting study. He has, as the British say, "no side." Nevertheless, this lack of side is cultivated, I am sure. I can understand why the troops like him. He has mastered the system of being personally kind to the troops, using the chain of command, and being exacting with his officers.

He is evidently ruthless when a change must be made. His trail of ascension to command is littered with the broken careers of strong but, from his viewpoint, unsuitable officers.

Sent the C/S to visit the XVIII Corps in UK. He had a long talk with Gen. Ridgway and Col. Eaton. Gen. R said that he sent the letter in a moment of hasty judgment, that up to that moment he had not heard from me, and that the whole affair was to be regretted. He will see me about it later.

I believe that I got out lucky, although it is not over, nor will it be as long as R is in the service with me. I hope that I have learned a lesson of restraint. I must learn to not be hasty in anger. I've got to learn this.

Gen. Parks was in from the First A A/B Army. He said that my promotion had gone forward from SHAEF to Washington. The most pressing problem now, however, is that of effective command under present conditions. The troops are in good spirits, rations are excellent, and the enemy opposition measured in terms of casualties very light. But for this type of soldier, it is not good to sit in a foxhole for weeks on end.

Yesterday I suggested to Gen. Horrocks that, if the Canadians could not clean out the Antwerp estuary, we could do it for them. Right now, the entire war awaits the opening of Antwerp and the arrival of fillers, both personnel and supplies.[i]

Went to a movie of the Holland A/B operation yesterday. Very exciting. Could hardly stay in my seat. Met a very interesting newspaperwoman yesterday, Mrs. Hemingway.[ii]

The 13th A/B Division is on the way over. Will arrive UK in December. CG XVIII Corps says that, if Germany is to be given an A/B occupation, this

---

i   Antwerp was the key to the ability to drive into Germany. To this point, all supplies for all armies had to be transported from Omaha and Sword beaches, several hundred miles in the rear. While Antwerp itself was captured, the long Scheldt estuary was strongly defended by the German 15th Army. Heavy flooding prevented effective ground operations against it.

ii This is Maggie Gellhorn, a first-rate journalist and the wife of Ernest Hemingway. She was one of the very few accredited females in the war zone.

The huge crowds, the many flags, and the perfectly marching troops showed what a splendid day this was, but there was also a more solemn aspect, captured by John McNally: "There was not a single man in those ranks who did not hear the noiseless tread of the ghosts of glory that marched beside him, the other 82nd Airborne Division, the spirits of those whose broken bodies made this day possible. Their silent tread echoed in our hearts louder than the drums and cheers." (Gavin Papers, Army Heritage and Education Center)

Gavin proudly marched at the head of his division in the January 1946 New York City victory parade. (Gavin family collection)

Gavin at his March 1948 farewell to the 82nd Airborne Division, which he had commanded for nearly four years, talking animatedly with his beloved sergeants. (Gavin Papers, Army Heritage and Education Center)

Gavin and wife Jean with their three daughters (Pat and Aileen in front and Chloe left rear) and Jean's daughter Caroline (right rear) in this undated family portrait. (Gavin Papers, Army Heritage and Education Center)

Incoming President John F. Kennedy did Gavin the honor of appointing him Grand Marshal for his inaugural parade. The parade, supposed to take two hours, dragged on and on. When the last unit went past in near total darkness the only people left in the reviewing stand were the President, Gavin and his wife Jean, and one or two aides. Kennedy's remark to Gavin: "You know, Jim, this is the longest two-hour parade I have ever seen." (Gavin Papers, Army Heritage and Education Center)

Gavin and his wife Jean are tickled by the gift of an attaché case from his colleagues at Arthur D. Little. Gavin was given a leave of absence to accept appointment as Ambassador to France. Not quite two years later he would return to ADL and serve there with great distinction for some 15 more years. (Gavin Papers, Army Heritage and Education Center)

Ambassador Gavin leaving the Elysée Palace after presenting his credentials to President Charles de Gaulle in March 1961. (Gavin Papers, Army Heritage and Education Center)

Gavin and his wife Jean with John and Jackie Kennedy. (Gavin family collection)

Gavin, newly arrived as U.S. Ambassador to France, with Charles de Gaulle. Gavin looked forward to the challenge, especially dealing with de Gaulle, viewed by him as a man of great integrity who combined a powerful ego and a prescient mind. (Gavin Papers, Army Heritage and Education Center)

Gavin speaking in front of the town hall in Sainte-Mère-Église in the 1960s. To this day, an American flag still hangs, which was first raised over Sainte-Mère-Église in the early hours of June 6, the first American flag flown in a town on D-Day. In front is Marker 0 which marks the beginning of Liberty Road, reaching to Bastogne in Belgium. (Gavin family collection)

Portrait of Gavin for the French Embassy by 82nd Airborne veteran Linzee Prescott. (Gavin family collection)

Gavin in the Soviet Union, July 1971. He was there with Senator Frank Church (adjacent in the photo), David Rockefeller and other prominent American businessmen as the US delegation to a meeting of the US–USSR Trade and Economic Council. (Gavin family collection)

Gavin's gravestone at the West Point Cemetery prominently features the badge of a Master Parachutist with the added four smaller stars indicating the four combat jumps he made during World War II. (Gavin family collection)

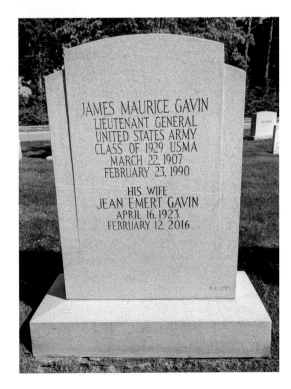

Gavin as Commanding General, 82nd Airborne Division, at Sissonne, France, in November 1944. (Gavin Papers, Army Heritage and Education Center)

division will drop on Berlin. It appears as though we are destined to stay in this theatre. The move of the 13th over here makes it appear as though that decision was made at Quebec.

The administration is dangling before the public the necessity of an international police force. Concurrently it is being built up of the A/B divisions in this theatre. Browning is getting lined up to head it. That is the way it looks to me now. It looks like a long time in Europe.

Nijmegen, Oct. 21, 1944

Made a trip to Rheims to look over the new camps at Suippes and Sissone.[i] Flew over and drove through last war's battlefields. Most disheartening.

Promotion came in yesterday.

Fighting going along rather quietly. Germans definitely on the defensive. We are still awaiting the fall of Antwerp. The Philippines were invaded several days ago. Too bad to have missed it.

Nijmegen, Oct. 27, 1944

Time flies in some ways. Gen. Horrocks in yesterday. Predicted the date of the British attack as Nov. 10th. That should get us out of here by the 15th. I am prepared to stay until December 1st. We are making plans for our Thanksgiving dinner in the foxholes.

Many visitors from the War Department and FAA/BA. We have a routine tour that we take them on now that takes them into Germany, near the front, to an OP where they can see the German foxholes. We can guarantee everything except the intensity of the firing. That the aides are trying to arrange. I am getting tired of the front. Six weeks without relief is a long time.[ii]

Nijmegen, Nov. 1, 1944

November, here it is. Fall, winter approaching and prospects of spending it in the trenches of the Lowlands. The front is definitely tougher. Last night the 325 lost six men killed and ten wounded with no prisoners captured. The other night two were killed. Tonight, and for the next several nights, we are not going out, hoping that the Germans come after us. This is a hell of a way for us to have to fight. The best offensive troops in the theatre and we sit in foxholes for two months.

---

i   These would be the camps for the 82nd prior to the Battle of the Bulge.

ii   The 82nd was in a purely defensive posture, which was bad for morale and combat efficiency. It negated the offensive nature of the unit mentality.

The Germans are reported using dogs. The 504 quickly found the solution and rounded up the most attractive bitches in Nijmegen. Results uncertain.

The British, so Billingslea says, are pinned down by digging 400 yards to the front.

The looting problem is in hand, I believe, although there are reports that continue to trickle in.

Wedemeyer replaced Stilwell in China, which means that Mountbatten rides high. Probably decided in Quebec. Wedemeyer knows nothing about infantry fighting nor how to command troops. Perhaps it will not be necessary. Maybe Vinegar Joe knew too much about it.

I am afraid that we will be available for the Rhine crossing show, which I want no part of. This war here is going into next year. Boy! will we be tired of it by next spring. In the next war we must plan on a scheme for providing short furlos from the front. This continuous long period away from the homeland is not too good.

Nijmegen, Holland, Nov. 10, [1944]

About Nov. 6th Gens. Bull and Bonesteel came up for a visit. Bonesteel, I believe, is a hatchet man, but not for me, I hope.

The 7th Gen. Ridgway came up with a report from SHAEF G-1 on the subject of looting. Some of the allegations made by a Dutchman of Gen. Krules' clique were most serious. The SHAEF IG, Gen. Haines, came up the 8th and has been here since. A potentially serious situation. We are apparently all clear. We should be.

Our relief by the Canadians is speeding along. Max Taylor hit yesterday. Shrapnel in the leg. Jablonsky in as a War Dept. observer. Said some significant things about Bud Miley. Despite this, I cannot see him as an A/B higher unit commander. Jabo talks too much.[i]

The Dutch political situation looks not too good. I am sympathetically inclined to look with favor upon the younger element headed by Prince Bernard. Gen. Krules of the older reactionaries should be run out of office and control. To be here in between both of them, with both sides endeavoring to prove the other side incapable of controlling the local civilian population, is most unsatisfactory.

Nijmegen, Holland, Nov. 13, [1944]

Turned over the sector to the 3rd Canadian Division at 0030 this morning, so now am entirely free. Everything very quiet. Extremely quiet. The German is most probably concentrating in front of the First and Third U.S. Armies. It is heartbreaking to completely abandon this salient that we have given so many lives to obtain.

---

i   Miley later retired as a major general.

Yesterday official notice was received that the Nederrijn was up to flood stage and that the Germans could put the "island" under water. The "island" is all of the land between the Waal and the Nederrijn extending out to the sea. The Germans can put Elst under three feet of water in a matter of hours.[i]

Upon relief all infantry and eng. units march to Oost, a distance of 23 miles. Quite a march for men who have been in foxholes for eight weeks. It has rained intermittently for the past several days so that the ground is generally rather muddy. Not a very pleasant prospect.

The Canadians looked fine taking over. They have much better uniform discipline than I have. I have so damn much to do that I almost wonder at times how in the hell can I possibly do it.

Lynch declined to come as Asst. Div. Comd'r. I do not want Sink, although he may be forced on me. Lindquist continues to do the wrong thing at the right time. Now reports reach me that he is favoring the 508 at Sissone, where I have him in charge of all arrangements.

Gen. Hains, the ETOUSA IG, is still with me checking on looting. Yesterday and the day before complete showdown inspections of the bags and musette bags of all men of the division were conducted. Units in the front lines are to be inspected today after their relief. I have never seen or heard of anything like it. It is most unfortunate.

The British moved out yesterday scot-free, taking with them cars and loot unlimited. Uncle Sam is known the world over for his generosity and these people are going to make the most of it. The men of the division have little if anything that they have not purchased or received as gifts.

This is becoming a regular way of life, too regular. I don't want to get away from how to live in peace or how to live as a civilian, but I am. No social contacts for eight weeks, and I am getting to where I accept that as a normal state of affairs.

Notes

1   Gavin later noted that, shortly after this date and before his next journal entry, "the time had come to organize our first American airborne corps. It was activated on August 27, 1944, as the XVIII Airborne Corps with General Matthew B. Ridgway in command." And, said Gavin, "at that time I was given command of the 82nd Airborne Division."

2   Later Gavin would write of a session soon after these events. On September 10, 1944, when he was in London visiting with some friends, he received a phone call directing him to go to the Headquarters of the First Allied Airborne Army, located in a country club about 50 miles west of London. "When I arrived," said Gavin, "the Army Commander, General Lewis Brereton, Major General Maxwell Taylor of the 101st Airborne Division, and General Roy Urquhart of the British First Airborne Division were all assembled. Lieutenant General 'Boy' Browning joined us.

i   The 101st occupied this as related in Stephen E. Ambrose's book *Band of Brothers* and the related HBO series.

He was commander of the British Airborne Corps. I noticed at once that, although two U.S. airborne divisions were represented, the 82nd and the 101st, corps headquarters was represented by an Englishman, General Browning. General Ridgway should have been the corps commander, since two of the divisions were from his corps. As the battle ultimately developed, it seemed to me that it would have made a tremendous difference to have an American general like Ridgway, with his combat experience, in command of the corps."

3   Gavin recalled that Browning had just come from the Continent, where he had conferred with Field Marshal Montgomery. "He brought with him orders for the three parachute divisions to land in Holland in four days, under his command. We pointed out at once that obtaining and distributing maps, aerial photographs, distributing food and ammunition, briefing the troops and getting them to departure airfields would take a least a week. Our orders were changed accordingly and the projected landing date was then September 17."

4   Gavin later recalled the mission. "I was ordered to land by parachute and glider in the area encompassed by Nijmegen on the Rhine River, Groesbeek, and Grave on the Meuse River. I was to seize the big bridges over those rivers and a bridge over the Rhine-Meuse Canal. I planned on taking three parachute regiments in the assault. For the first time we were to jump in daylight and there was some concern about the dangers of being shot down. All of our preceding jumps had been at night."

5   Again there is an understandable delay between the actual operation, usually dated as taking place September 17–25, 1944, and when Gavin can get to describing it in his diary.

6   Gavin had met King George VI and Field Marshal Montgomery and admired them both. The British Army, he observed, "seemed to be much more relaxed about the war than we, making themselves as comfortable as they could whenever they could, and at times seeming to enjoy the war. They were fine soldiers."

7   Later Gavin would learn that he had broken two vertebrae upon landing in this operation, an injury that plagued him for many years thereafter.

CHAPTER 9

The Winter War

Sissone, France, Nov. 15, [1944]

Arrived here the afternoon of the 13th. The 508th arrived yesterday, the 14th. 504 due today. The Div Arty and the 505th are to be stationed at Suippes, about 70 miles away.

The Sissone area was occupied by the Germans. Before that the French. It was a large post. The Germans had done an excellent job of training and the remains of their training arrangements show evidence of lots of work.

If we have the time, we should get a lot out of this stay. I am counting on three months. The weather will preclude any winter A/B opns. The only thing that will curtail our training will be the premature breakup of the present German government. This might necessitate an occupational mission into the heart of Germany itself. The problems of discipline are manifold.[i]

Sissone Nov. 18, [1944]

One year ago today, I arrived at Prestwick from Africa. Things are moving along. Need our base echelon things badly. Had a long talk with Chaplain Woods.[ii] He and the other chaplains are very much concerned with the attitude of the men towards continued operations. They do not want to go to the Pacific, feeling that they have already done more than their share.

The four [word inserted in pencil: star?] jump people are sweating out any more jumps, feeling that they have used up about all of their luck. I understand exactly

---

i   The troops were very exuberant and relieved after *Market Garden*. Liberal leaves were granted to Paris as well as nights in the local bars. As in the UK, there were constant fights between the airborne and the "legs." Concurrently, standards of individual dress and in living areas became quite relaxed. Gavin tried to correct this with a large intramural athletic program as well as inspections.

ii Chappie Woods was a Protestant chaplain who was renowned for his dedication to the troops and his upfront presence under fire.

how they feel. I feel the same way myself. They have always done a fine job, but now their ranks are thinning. Many of them are banged up from combat and hardly fit mentally or physically for further parachute operations, yet they have no other prospects.

It hardly seems right. There should be some way out other than being killed or wounded. There is no other now. Someday there is going to be a hell of a mess when complete units refuse to jump in combat again. There should be some relief for them or some promise of relief.[i]

Sissone Nov. 21, [1944]

Twenty-one planes from base over. Biggest trouble at the moment is with our lack of clothing and equipment that is being held up in base.[ii]

Gen. Ridgway called yesterday. His hqrs moving over. I still have to make an effort to get along with that hqrs. It would be much easier if Eaton were out of there.

An imported French show in last night. Terrible, but funny. It promises to be a long stretch here. I wouldn't be surprised if we were here in May. It is difficult to see how the United Nations can mount a large-scale effective attack before spring. Any immediate show will no doubt be done by the 17th. Later the 13th will be available. We can use a few months of rest and recreation, as well as reorganization and training.

This winter should bring to a head many problems in the European governments. There is a very strong and well-armed underground movement afoot. In Holland my sympathies were with it. They are the people who risked their lives, gave their fortunes, sacrificed their careers and homes for an ideal of self-government. They and they alone should have the say of how it should be created, not the reactionary entrenched interests.[iii]

There will be bloodshed. The young vigorous resistance movements are not to be denied. I do not believe that they in any [way] espouse the political ideology of Russia. In fact, most of them want no part of Russia. Russia and the communist

---

i   There was no real replacement system established that would allow long-term troops to rotate to the States. Troops remained with the unit so long as they were physically capable. They understood from experience that there is an arithmetic for the infantry that causes every man to eventually become a casualty. While Gavin recognized this, there was little he could do.

ii The division had suffered severe losses in weapons as well as personal gear. Winter clothing had not yet arrived.

iii The Dutch Underground was of immense help to the division allowing Gavin to "see" the battlefield better than anyone else. Their ability to call behind German lines using the phone system to develop intelligence allowed Gavin to make troop deployment decisions based on actionable rather than predictive intelligence.

party, however, want part of them. Want, in fact, complete control of them if it is possible to get it.

Therein lies the rub. They are, and will be accused of being, in sympathy because they are desirous of governing themselves. Nothing could be farther from the truth. They want no part of communism, no more than they want part of the corrupt rotted governmental bodies of 1939 and 1940. The governments that precipitated them into a war, and a war that they lost because of that government's lack of foresight and tolerance of corrupt individual practices.

It will be a rough winter for many people in Europe. We have a rough time ahead of us in the U.S.. The war is barely started if by war we include all of its implications, ramifications, and complications.

Sissone Nov. 28, [1944]

The reorganization and reequipping continues. Attended a Thanksgiving luncheon at the home of Gen. Thrasher in Rheims on the 23rd. Met some nice French people.

On Friday afternoon the 24th went to London. Travel time 2 hrs. Landed at Northolt and obtained billets at the Grosvenor House. A most enjoyable night with Valerie. Went to Ciro's, where they have an especially prepared and very good dinner.

Saturday went to Cottesmore. There had a short visit with Gen. Clark of the 52nd Wing. Went to Leicester for lunch with Lt. Col. Ostberg, the rear echelon comdr. Returned to London at 1500 and stayed overnight. Had a wonderful time. Just what I needed. No champagne this night.

Returned at noon Sunday and learned that Friday night in Rheims troops of the division raised so much hell that at the request of the Oise Base Section CG, Gen. Thrasher, all of our troops were restricted. Jumped right into the affair and had a meeting of all unit COs. A special guard is being formed of one officer and ten NCOs from each regiment, making a total of 5 and 50 hand-picked guards. The number of men on pass is to be reduced to 5% instead of 10%.

The trouble seems to center in three things. There is no way to get a girl of easy virtue, all houses are off limits and guarded, food cannot be bought in town anywhere. Champagne can be bought by the bottle anywhere any time. At present the situation is well in hand.

Sissone Dec. 14, 1944

Everything apparently in fine shape at last. Just concluded our war bond drive. Sold $1,280,000 worth of bonds. A high per capita record for this theatre. We don't know about the other places.

The payday troubles were at a minimum, probably as much due to the bond drive as anything. First three prizes get a trip to U.S. Gen. Lee, CG ETOUSA, called several days ago, ostensibly to see his son. The talk led to the excellent appearance and behavior of our lads in Paris. Gen. Lee said that he was talking to another general about their alert appearance and the other general said, "Alert. You're damn right they look alert. Hell, you are looking at the survivors."

The training is just getting under full steam. Everyone has been encouraged to take some time off, particularly after Bud Milner, C/S of the 101st, committed suicide. The troubles with young officers are on the increase. I have four cases to be tried by general [court martial] now.

Rec'd a nice note from Martha Hemingway. She wrote a grand article for *Collier's*. She is a very nice person, unusually nice for a war correspondent. I have asked her up for our Prop Blast of the 19th.

Dec. 31, 1944

On Sunday the 17th received a warning order from Hqrs XVIII Corps to be ready to move on 12 hrs notice to the front.[1] A German attack was apparently making unprecedented headway between the First and Third Armies.[2] First order received at 1900. At 2100 received notice to move as soon as possible.

Orders issued to the 82nd to move at 0900 the next day. The 101st to move at 1400 the next day. Oise Base to provide the transportation.[i]

I left at 2300 for the CP of the U.S. First Army, arriving at 0900 the 18th. Things in an uproar. The Germans about ten miles away and coming on. CP at Spa. Germans at Stavelot. Decided to put me at [Whebarmont] [or maybe Werbomont?]. Div started to arrive just before dark.

First Germans, and AG of the 1st SS Div knocked out by a 30 Div roadblock at Hablemont at about 1800. Div concentrated and ready to move by daylight. A quick move executed to the line Trois Ponts-Vielsalm-Samchateau-Regne-Fraiture. Contact made with the 7th Armd, 106th, and 28th Divs, which were almost cut off.

Held line against determined and strong German attacks for several days, during which time we mopped up the cut-off spearheads of the 1st SS at Cheneaux and covered the extrication of the 7th Armd thru Vielsalm.

Withdrew to the line Trois Ponts-Floret-Manhay. Right flank up in the air and never covered by the 3rd Armd Div nor the 7th Armd. Badly chewed up several German attacks against the new line.[3]

---

i   At this time, Gavin was the corps commander in addition to the 82nd CG. Ridgway could not get to Belgium from the UK due to fog. Gavin had to manage the dispositions of both divisions. As the 101st was on trucks ahead of the 82nd, he directed it to Bastogne where he met the VIII Corps CG, Troy Middleton, who was in the process of retreating west. He and Gavin agreed on the initial 101st position, with the 82nd holding the "Northern Shoulder" with the remainder of the XVIII Airborne Corps.

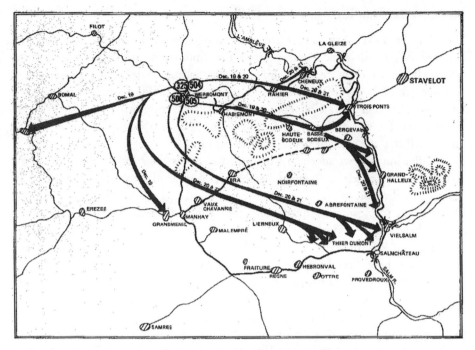

82nd Airborne Deploys in Belgium, late 1944. (From *On to Berlin*)

Right now, today, the Germans are thinning out on the division front and what the future holds is a big question. He is capable of making a very strong attack to the north out of his salient, but on this front, he is definitely falling back. What is the answer?

This has been an experience the like of which I hope I never have again. It will be invaluable to me in future years. Our army has a hell of a lot to learn, but at present these airborne troopers of this division are making monkeys out of the Germans opposing them. They are better trained and far superior combat soldiers. The German has better armor, Panzerfausts, mines.[i]

---

i   The 82nd completely blunted the German attack, stopping Kampfgruppe Peiper at Trois Ponts and along the defensive line that Peiper had to breach to reach the Meuse River. The division was augmented by two airborne battalions from the 13th Airborne Division. Regardless, the 82nd fought at slightly more than half strength with many weapons still in repair. Winter clothing would be brought in after a week of summer uniforms on the line. Gavin made a point of visiting every battalion and regimental CP each day as well as many isolated positions, a schedule that rarely saw him back at the division HQ before 2200.

Nonceveux, Belgium Jan 14, [1945]

The division moved into a rest area extending from Chevron to Pepinster two days ago. We finally attacked and retook the Thier du Mont, crossed the Salm at Grand Halleux, and entered Vielsalm and Salmchateau. In the attack we completely destroyed the 62nd Volksgrenadier Division, taking 2,500 prisoners, including 5 bn COs. One regt CO, Col. Franks of the 190th, committed suicide. His Adj. surrendered. He was guilty of advising his troops against taking prisoners, so it is just as well that we did not get our hands on him.[i]

The division was wonderful in the attack. That is their forte still. Several days ago, FM Montgomery, at a press conference, very kindly told the world that he ordered the division to withdraw after it had saved the 7th Armd, 106th and 28th Divs. Ordered it against the protests of the division commander. Published in the S&S. It helped a great deal.[ii]

In the attack I lost some very fine officers, notably Vandervort, who lost his left eye just outside of Arbrefontaine. Crossing the valley from Arbrefontaine was very rough until the 508th captured the west end of Thier du Mont, thus denying the krauts observation.

Capt. Olson, my aide, was again hit, this time in the right leg. We were together, following a connecting platoon of the 325 working between two battalions, when the krauts threw lots of arty at us. Tree bursts. I was very lucky. The boy between Olson and myself had his leg severed just above the knee. I put a tourniquet on him and to our surprise we saved his life. Olson gave him morphine. His leg flew across the road and for a minute Olson thought it was his. Woods was hit a few days earlier when we were up with the 517 [sic] trying to push one of their attacks.[iii]

This business of making green outfits go is positively dangerous, but it must be done. During the past few weeks Barney Oldfield has been very helpful with the publicity.

The XVIII Corps is now attacking with the 75th, 106th, 30th, and 7th Armd Divs. We are in corps reserve, and I believe that Army has a string on us, although corps will not admit it. Our position is unusual. Army, I believe, wants to keep us out of further fighting to save us for an airborne mission later. This may be a SHAEF directive. Ridgway, who commands the corps, his first corps in combat, is most anxious to commit us. It will undoubtedly make his attack a success. Otherwise,

---

i   The 82nd swung south and then east to clear German defenses—all this on foot and in deep snow.

ii   Both Ridgway and Gavin strongly protested Montgomery's orders to withdraw to "tidy the battlefield." As Gavin said, endorsed by Ridgway: "The 82nd has never lost or given ground throughout the war." Both recognized that it could cause a severe morale problem to give ground that had been won in blood. However, both understood the logic as being correct.

iii   Gavin is referring to Chaplain Woods.

the attack will very likely bog down. Our regular divisions appear at this particular time to be, with few exceptions, of poor quality.[i]

There is little doubt, in view of our losses of the past few weeks, that continued attacks will do the division irreparable harm as an airborne division. Ridgway is very ambitious, however, and it is unlikely that he will ever command a ground corps again. At least it doesn't happen every day. I do not believe that he would hesitate to exploit the 82nd to the utmost, regardless of the long-range harm it may do.

Came close to getting shot at Grand Halleux when I had to dive into one of our own foxholes to avoid a Schmeisser that was squirting in what a quick estimate led me to believe was my direction. Conditions have been very rugged. Temperature around 18° F., snow, wind.

It is amazing how these lads live sometimes. In all of my good paratroop units they attack in ordinary combat uniforms. Hoping to bring up the overcoats and blankets later. Rations are cold entirely unless they can heat them in a hole if and when they get to one. Most regular outfits wear overcoats.

Soldiers must be taught to be tough and, in teaching them, officers must set the example. There is a fundamental difference between combat and maneuvers. Combat is the payoff. There is <u>no</u> discomfort too great if it will bring victory in even the smallest fight.[ii]

Most outfits bring up hot chow when they can, which is frequently often. We eat cold chow entirely in the forward areas. Trench foot is a source of casualties in some cases greater than gunshot wounds. One bn, my 551, did not wear its overshoes in an attack and sustained about 230 trench foot cases in three days. Gunshot wounds and shrapnel were about 190. That bn is comparatively ineffective now.[iii]

We are now training with Panzerfausts, which are damn good. They will punch the front plate of a Tiger tank. We are also training our men to drive tanks and tank destroyers, since our armored supporting people frequently abandon their vehicles when threatened in an attack.

Commanding this division is quite a task and a feat. I hope that I measure up to it well. These troops are the best in the world and are deserving of the best leadership. Given it, they will do anything.

---

i   This is correct. Ridgway wanted the 82nd to deliver some punch to a less than energetic performance by his other units.

ii   This is a base point of his leadership ethos—lead by example, be tough, train tough.

iii   The 551st was a green airborne unit. Winter shoepaks had not yet been issued to them. The combination of severe cold with moisture and friction destroyed the skin and created both frostbite and blood disorders. Trench foot was a problem throughout the Army and not resolved until galoshes and winter boots were issued.

Nonceveux, Belgium Jan. 18, [1945]

Still in a rest area. A most unusual state of affairs. If our infantry would fight, this war would be over by now. On our present front there are two very weak German regts holding the XVIII Corps of four divisions. We all know it and admit it, and yet nothing is being done about it. American infantry just simply will not fight. No one wants to get killed. Not that anyone else does, but at least others will take a chance now and then. Our artillery is wonderful and our Air Corps not bad. But the regular infantry, terrible. Everyone wants to live to a ripe old age. The sight of a few Germans drives them to their holes. Instead of being imbued with an overwhelming desire to get close to the German and get him by the throat, they want to avoid him if the artillery has not already knocked him flat. This is the fault of our training. Our paratroop infantry is superb, close quarters killers.[i]

Nonceveux, Belgium Jan. 24, 1945

Still in the rest areas, but with promise of moving into the attack. I am pleased with my feelings in the matter. The fact that we are again going to attack I found rather pleasant. The troops are ready also. Sitting around gets rather tiresome, especially in a place such as this. If the war must be finished, why then let's get at it.

The other night I had dinner with Gen. Hodges and his staff. Gen. Keen, his C/S, had asked me. Nice for a change, although as usual it is always disturbing to go back to a higher headquarters and encounter their lack of familiarity with the things that go on in the front. They were all most outspoken about the *Stars and Stripes*, claiming that Gen. Patton gets all the headlines.

I have a feeling that it is not the best staff in the world. They are much more capable than personable. Keen told me that, in his opinion, the div would be in the lines about another three weeks and that in that time we would attack with the First Army to the east towards the Rhine. He must have been given this impression of our stay by SHAEF. He said that he would like to keep us, but that he doubted if he could. He would also like to keep Gen. Ridgway with the XVIII Corps staff, and of this he felt that it may be possible, reasoning that there is little chance of an A/B corps operation.

Ridgway, on the other hand, is hell bent on keeping us in his corps and he will never let us go without a direct order from SHAEF. It is all most unfortunate from an A/B viewpoint. I believe that SHAEF would promptly act on his recommendation to send us back for A/B preparation if he would so recommend. This he will never

---

i   A reference to the airborne elan that set it apart from basic foot infantry.

do until he is ordered to command an A/B operation. Quite a mess with all of the complexities of ambition and subterfuge involved.[i]

We are at present under orders to attack on the 27th, perhaps the 29th. During the past week I have talked to quite a few of the troops, talking to each battalion for about an hour and a half and at the end giving them an opportunity to ask all of the questions they desired. It seems to do a great deal of good. It is foreign to many of our teachings and a bit unusual. Some people would feel that my office was being improperly used, but I do not believe so. Many odd and sometimes questionably proper questions are asked. The usual is when are we going home.

Gen. Prickett, CG of the 75th Div, was relieved yesterday. Gen. Porter, formerly of the 1st, now has his division. The elimination rate among division commanders is very high. I can understand it. One gets quite a screwy attitude after a bit that was [sic: must?] be carefully controlled. Akin somewhat to indifference, but more just simply "browned off," or maybe "I need a leave." The life of an MG is not much fun. Rather solitary. If one is too tough, just an SOB, it soon reflects itself in the division. There is bitching and griping about everything, with little cooperation. If one is too easy, things stay in order just so long and not a bit longer.

Needless to say, one must know everything that goes on and learn the business from the ground up. There is where I believe that most of them make a mistake. They do not spend enough time in their front positions. Soon they lose touch, lose confidence, make bad decisions, and generally do not get the performance out of their troops that one would normally expect. But to command a division for a long period of time in constant combat is difficult and trying. The mental problem is greater than the physical.

Hugo Olsen is back on the job. I'll have both for the attack.

The Russians are doing wonderfully, thank God. We may yet end this in 1945.

Holzheim, Belgium Feb. 3, 1945

About six days ago we jumped off from the Wallerode-Medell line just NE of St. Vith with the mission of punching the Siegfried Line near Udenbreth and Neuhof. Yesterday we seized that portion of the line within our sector, and it was a very rough deal. Five days of attacking thru country entirely devoid of roads and even in many cases trails. Deep snow hampered all movement throughout and the krauts resisted quite bitterly.

Fortunately, after the first day we had him on his ass, and it was simply a case of going fast enough to keep him there. This we did. The attack was generally advanced with the main effort along the high ground, fanning out only to gain contact with

---

i   Gavin was consistent in his analysis of Ridgway's perceived ambition at the cost to the 82nd.

adjacent units and mop up. It is a preeminently fine technique and, although it means much sweat, it also means little blood lost.

The Siegfried Line was of considerable professional interest. It is a fine defense and could, with stouthearted, well-equipped, well-led defenders, accomplish its purpose. But the best defense is still to attack. The division is still in an interesting tug-of-war, with Gen. Ridgway holding on to the division for dear life and Gen. Brereton not knowing what to do about it and, as well as I can determine, doing nothing.

I would like to see the war in Europe brought to a successful conclusion and, if our retention on the Western Front will affect that, then we are being well employed, if not properly employed. The present situation is full of promise. The Germans appear to be beaten and beaten badly. With better troops I see no reason why we could not run all over them.

The public will never know nor never appreciate this. Our American army individually means well and tries hard, but it is not the army that one reads about in the press. It is untrained and comparatively inefficient. Certainly, our infantry lacks courage and elan.

I do not see how this can be acquired in less than several more months of war and careful digestion of the lessons learned in each operation. Some people say *The Battle Is the Payoff*. In fact, a book has been written about it, and a best seller at that. This is a fallacy. The digestion of the lessons learned, and their application is the payoff.

Ed Ostberg was hit and killed yesterday. Like most paratroop officers, he was hit exposing himself when he should have been using cover. We have all learned how to move and fight a division with efficiency and dispatch. It seems very clear to me that our higher headquarters take entirely too much time to put plans and orders into effect.

I wish that I could spend some time on an army, or an army group staff. We must learn to move more quickly, or we will be beaten. Gosh, I would like to fight troops with more speed and killing power than we now have. Only the airborne units have it.

Some say it's being overburdened with heavy equipment. Others say it's just their mental attitude. It is hard to say. Certainly, older officers get ideas that stay with them that they can neither rid themselves of, nor do they desire to rid themselves of them. The solution would appear to get younger officers in some of the higher commands or on the higher staffs.

To take 24 to 48 hrs to get a division rolling in the attack is ridiculous. How can it ever win a fight? Nowadays one must move fast, both to stay alive and to kill. If considerable confusion and chaos results, that is to be accepted as a normal component of such an operation. If all is orderly and well-conducted, speed is being sacrificed. It seems to me that this war could fold up any day now. Then for the Pacific.

Notes

1   Once again, the vicissitudes of combat delay Gavin's account of a major battle, as he is just now recording his comments on the Battle of the Bulge, which began December 16, 1944.

2   Circumstances at this time put Gavin in an unusual position. On the evening of December 17th, he received a call from Colonel Ralph Eaton, chief of staff of XVIII Airborne Corps, informing him that he was now acting commander of the corps. General Ridgway was in England and General Maxwell Taylor was in the United States, so it was up to Gavin to get the corps ready for rapid movement to the front, as a German breakthrough appeared imminent. After a quick trip to Spa, Belgium, and headquarters of the U.S. First Army there to get orders, Gavin moved south to Bastogne. There he met Brigadier General Anthony McAuliffe, then acting CG of the 101st Airborne Division, and ordered him to occupy and defend Bastogne. Gavin then moved north to the vicinity of Trois Ponts and Werbomont, where he placed the 82nd Airborne Division in blocking positions. "Thus began for us," said Gavin, "the Battle of the Bulge on the north shoulder. Here at one time the 82nd withstood the attacks of three Panzer divisions, while First Army succeeded in bringing the German counteroffensive to a halt after one week's fighting. From then on, combat for the division was continuous and took it into the high Eifel of the Ardennes in mid-winter and through the Siegfried Line. In late February the division was withdrawn for refitting and replacements."

3   Gavin's later comment: "On December 25th, we realized that we had just succeeded in withdrawing through a hostile withdrawing force, which was a rather novel maneuver." This, taken from an article on the Battle of the Bulge in Buck Dawson, *Saga of the All American*, is identified as "extracted from Gen. Gavin's personal report to a War Department historian."

CHAPTER 10

Germany

Rott, Germany Feb. 10, 1945

To our dismay and disbelief, the penetration into the Siegfried Line at Udenbreth was not exploited. In fact, the entire 1st and 82nd Div sectors were taken over by the 99th Div as a holding mission.

The background is that FM Montgomery obtained the go signal from Gen. Eisenhower to launch an attack with the British and Canadian Armies and the U.S. 9th. The U.S. 1st is protecting its southern flank. Thus, the buildup is to be abandoned and much of our sweating and losses were in vain. Difficult to explain this sort of thing to the troops.[i]

It is surprising how influential Montgomery is. It is understandable when one looks back over the futile efforts of the U.S. Armies during the past winter. Definitely decisive action was lacking. The German succeeded amazingly well in spoiling all of our attack preparations. We have, just simply have, got to learn to take risks to gain combat successes. Nothing ventured, nothing gained never was more true. Mental courage and confidence are essential.[ii]

Up here the 505 and 508 have been working with the V Corps to assist in capturing the dams along the Roer River. Nasty job, and one that could have been done by anyone. Next, we are to attack across the flank of Montgomery's effort.

Even if Montgomery's effort succeeds, it will not accomplish a great deal. The snow has melted, uncovering many of the dead and decayed of the past several months on this front. The 28th Division evidently took a bad beating in this area. A discouraging sight to see. Much of their tanks, jeeps, weasels, arms etc. abandoned. Their wounded and dead left on the ground now rotting. If only our statesmen could

---

i   This is the outgrowth of Montgomery's insistence for a single supported thrust by his army with the Americans providing flank support. It enraged the U.S. generals. The U.S. 9th Army was assigned to Montgomery for this operation.

ii   This is a continuation of the necessity for units and leaders to take calculated risks, move quickly, and exploit conditions.

spend a minute hugging the ground under mortar fire next to a three-months-old stiff. We just simply have got to stop wars.[i]

Hurtgen, Germany Feb. 15, 1945

A comfortable CP in a cellar of this what once was no doubt lovely German town. Under direct observation of the Germans across the Roer River, but not receiving much fire. I get the impression that the German is about through. We have been planning a river crossing for some time now. It has been delayed because of the deep water. Just a few minutes ago we received word that we were to return to our base at Rheims without delay. That will be good news to all of these lads. This type of ground fighting, where everybody sits around in the mud and no one wants to fight, is most unpleasant. I am ready to return.

It seems to me that it takes two different temperaments in this army, one for regular ground divisions and a different one for an airborne division. The airborne trooper gets furious, impatient and finally disgusted with the vacillation and delay in getting going in a ground fight with ground units. They take forever to plan and stage a show, and then they get nowhere after they start. The analogy of hitching a racehorse to a plow is no fallacy.

The airborne trooper wears himself [out] fighting the system. He is a bit too high strung to be wallowing in the mud indefinitely.

Our first cases of lice showed up yesterday. Came from occupying former German billets. The German army is ripe for airborne attack. They could be taken apart now.

Camp Sissone, France, Feb. 26, [1945]

Returned at last to our base. The area has been taken up by two general hospitals, but with their quota of about 190 nurses they are rather welcome. The troops have been moved under canvas, rather comfortable, however.

Attended a 504th Prop Blast several nights ago. Lots of fun, much like old times. Wellems talked about their attack to capture Herresbach. They were, as the saying goes, down to their uppers. The men were finally so exhausted that they dropped in the snow, which was in places waist deep, unconscious. Their company commanders and platoon leaders would drag them to their feet and slap their faces until they came to, then make them continue walking.

---

i   Gavin walked up the Kall River Gorge to Kammerschiedt and Schmidt and was shocked by the number of abandoned bodies and equipment left by the 28th Division, now commanded by Major General Cota, the hero of Omaha Beach. There was a SHAEF investigation of the events that decided Cota was just very tired and unable to get an accurate picture of conditions, violating Gavin's dictum that commanders must visit and know their front.

German snipers, which was all that there was finally, were practically ignored unless some men got hit. Finally, they staggered to the ridge north of the town and attacked down it. They surprised the Germans, who had no idea that any human could have gotten there and killed 62 along the road and into the town. The 504 did not lose a single man. The perfect battle.

Met a Lt. Peggy Knecht of the 242 at the Prop Blast and dragged her to a movie last night. Rather interesting.

The crossing of the Roer finally underway.

Camp Sissone, France, Mar. 12, 1945

A very busy three weeks. Reorganized and re-equipped about 75% to date. Given mission for the jump near Worms to get the Third Army across the Rhine about two weeks ago. Today it was definitely called off. Given mission for a jump on Berlin about a week ago. Operation Eclipse.

Attended a dinner in Rheims with Gens. Eisenhower, Ridgway, Chapman, Miley and Capt. Butcher, USN. Butcher, evidently voicing the views of his chief, surprisingly frank in saying that Eclipse probably would never come off because the Russians would be there first. With that background, I have not been pushing our planning. Today, however, Eaton (C/S of XVIII Corps) said that the whole thing was firm politically and that it would go. Hard to believe, but it may be. How in the world can it be arranged for the Russians to wait at one street while we load up and jump a week later? Even now they are close to Berlin.

Had a wonderful three days in London. Val looking well and as attractive as ever. I really worry, though, about her attitude and how unhappy we could be unless she changes. Prospects do not look too good for us.

The division doing beautifully and having less disciplinary trouble than ever in its history. I believe that I have them all with me.

Jump tested the C-46 yesterday.[i] Lindquist, who jumped with me, told me this afternoon that he sustained a partially fractured upper arm.

I'd sure like to live through combat jump five. I believe that five are as many as one man should be given. Beyond that is too much. We all realize it now. There is a drain on the courage of a man that cannot be replaced. Leave, nor passes, do not make the fourth or fifth jumps any easier.

Went to Picauville to award gold watches to two Francaise who befriended us in Normandy Saturday. Quite an affair. Got in a good plug for the Division Fourigere.[ii]

---

i   The C-46 was a slightly larger airframe than the C-47 and could hold more men and equipment. However, it did not have self-sealing tanks making it vulnerable to ground fire.

ii This is the French *fouragèrre* recommended by Mayor Renaud of Sainte-Mère-Église to DeGaulle. It was approved and is worn to this day by all members of the 82nd.

Camp Sissone, March 18, [1945]

A full week of jumping and glidering. Jump tested the C-46 Sunday, jumped with the Div Hqrs flight Tuesday, jumped with the 508 Wednesday. During the AM drop on Wednesday a C-47 lost a propeller, dropped into the pattern, and took six jumpers along in its crash to the ground. Thought it was a good idea to jump with the troops in the PM and so did, uneventfully. Lost 12 men, including four Air Corps.

Marlene Dietrich here Tuesday. A bit demanding and expectant and in a way surprisingly unattractive.

Had an interesting conversation with Mrs. Ernest Hemingway last night re this bright and happy world that we are all looking forward to so eagerly. She was particularly interested in my political views and stated that the press had been told by one Maj. Kirksey that the airborne troops would be rugged well-led troops that would keep America safe for fascism in the post-war world. She said that she had come down from Paris particularly to find out how I felt about this thing. Interesting. What will the post-war years bring? She seems to be trying to align someone up for something. My sympathies are essentially with the people, certainly not the interests well-entrenched and honored only by time.

Camp Sissone, March 22, [1945]

Well, Miss Gellhorn turned out to be quite a person. I have never met her likes and would just as soon not in anyone else. She took the damn place apart. It was wonderful. There will be no more visits with her here.

Tuesday, the 20th, went to Hqrs Ninth Army at Munschen Gladbach for a ceremony at which FM Montgomery made several British awards, my DSO included. A nice affair. Lots of rank—Hodges, Gerow, Simpson, and a half dozen MGs.

The staff gossip is that the Germans have practically no organized resistance on the far side of the Rhine. The crossing is to be made by Montgomery on the 24th. His technique is interesting. His patience and thorough buildup is extremely conservative, but undoubtedly what it takes in this kind of fighting.

Patton is roaring along on the southern front and may cross the Rhine today, and to hell with an airborne bridgehead. That is good fighting.

Talking before dinner last night the staff seemed quite taken by the well-known anecdote concerning the 504th's efforts to get prisoners on the Nijmegen front. The patrol leader would slip up on a foxhole, reach in, and attempt to pull the kraut out. Cringing in the bottom, he couldn't quite be gotten hold of. The patrol leader would drop a grenade in and go to the next hole, looking for a bigger kraut who could be reached. That is their report. The story is, however, that they would pull the krauts out of their holes and, if they were not big enough, they would drop them back in, drop in a grenade with them, and go on to the next hole until they found one of satisfactory and suitable size.

Camp Sissone March 25, [1945]

Yesterday took off at 0815 and went to Munschen Gladbach. Took off from there at 0940 and was over Venlo at 0955. There we sighted the U.S.. 17th and British 6th on their way into Opn Varsity. Quite a sight. As far as the eye could see, wave upon wave of planes. Fighters darting about. And ahead billowing clouds of dust and smoke from the battle area. They appeared to hit their DZs a bit early. The flak initially was heavy in both sectors. The Americans were on the right and the British left. As the dropping progressed the U.S. flak stopped, but the British continued quite heavily, finally throwing up bursts after the last landing was made.

Counted over a dozen ships shot down. The C-47s got in trouble with their poor gas tanks. In some cases, the crews bailed out. In most they went down in a ball of fire. Crossed over into the German sector to get a close-up view of the DZ area and was fired at by small arms fire. Was down to about 1,000 ft at the time. We had been observing at 2,500. The U.S. TCC formations were beautiful. The British not as tight, bomber stream in fact, and they flew finally at 3,000 ft. The DZ patterns did not look too bad. At least some of them were excellent. But all in all, it was a very rough show and, in fact, it appeared a bit dangerous.

Weiden, Germany, near Cologne, April 2, 1945

Attended a conference at FAAA CP at Maison Lafitte Thursday afternoon, March 29th. Two plans advanced for the use of Abn Trps before the war ends on the continent. One, dropping ahead of the armd spearheads for the purpose of supplying petrol and infantry; two, dropping separate bns on PW camps to protect the prisoners from fanatical civilians.

After the conference visited Gen. Parks and he told me that Gen. Bradley had just conferred with Gen. Eisenhower and had secured permission to use the 82nd and 101st on the west bank of the Rhine in order to release about eight divisions. SHAEF approved. The orders were issued Friday and here we are.

The Div has been assigned to the XVIII Corps of the Fifteenth Army. Called on Gen. Gerow on my way up Sunday the 1st. We are relieving the 86th, a very green but very fine-looking division. This was their first position and not too good a one. The krauts apparently have pulled out. The division frontage is 35 miles, generally centered on Cologne, or what is left of it.

It definitely appears as though the German is through. We were ready to leave Sissone. Six weeks out of the line is plenty, although I appreciated the opportunity to absorb and train the reinforcements.

Made a delightful acquaintance in Peggy Knecht of the 242nd General. A nice girl and we get along very well together. However, it was time for me to leave.

Weiden, Germany, April 3, [1945]

The boys still arriving. Those by motor coming into Stolberg near Aachen. The motor serials closed last night. The 86th still holding eagerly, but very greenly. Captured two prisoners in the six days they have been on the front so far. Had a patrol over night before last that picked up and talked to a German who convinced them that they should not take him prisoner because the patrol would be shot up going back. They had seen a MG which tracked them, but which they did not disturb. He said it would be very hard on his family if he surrendered. (He was already captured.) He was carrying a bucket of pea soup. Said that was all that they had had for food the past three weeks. They let him go instead of killing him. An American boy is not a killer and, short of combat, it is hard to make him one. He has got to see killing and be shot at.[i]

Weiden, Germany, April 9, [1945]

Took over and holding 35 miles of the Rhine River line, as well as governing about 650 square miles of Germany. This includes three displaced persons camps which are quite a headache.[ii] The Germans across the river, although in what is clearly a hopeless plight, are nevertheless very tough.

On April 5th a German colonel, Corps Surgeon of the 81st Corps, accompanied by a Second Lt. who spoke excellent English, came across under a white flag. He had with him a letter signed by Gen. of Inf. Kochling and a map showing two areas in which they had concentrated their wounded civilians and soldiers. His mission was to request us not to fire into those areas. This we certainly would not have done if they were properly marked anyway. He got as far as a company CP in a cellar in a house in Merkenich.

My first reaction was to take him prisoner, as I always have in these cases, but after some thought I figured with his rank and XVIII Corps' newness they might overrule me after he reached the corps PW cage. That would then be a hell of a

---

i   This reflection is very much like Patton's analysis of what it takes to create a quality soldier.

ii At this stage, the Allies were faced with thousands of refugees and released POWs streaming away from bombed-out cities and the advancing Russians. The military had to create camps where they could be reasonably fed and sheltered. These were the displaced persons (DP) camps Gavin mentions. Concurrent with military operations, the advancing forces also had to establish law and order as well as get the basic infrastructure restarted. Each division had a civil affairs element designed to do this, so the tactical elements did not have to divert resources.

mess since he would have seen all of my area. It also was possible that higher Hqrs would be interested in them as emissaries to the surrounded krauts.

I therefore called Gen. Harmon, the corps CG, who in turn called the army CG, who said let them return. This was done the following morning.

The night of the 6th A Co 504 was sent across and took over the town of Hitdorf. The German reaction was strong and violent, evidently thinking that it was a bridging site. We had a hell of a fight and finally had to withdraw the company with about 30–35% loss the night of the 7th. Had quite a fight with CG Corps, who seemed to fear leaving them over there. It was best to withdraw them finally.

We have had numerous patrols cross the river, although it is quite a gamble. The krauts wait until the boat is just about ready to touch down on the far shore and then they blast it out of the water. No future in that.

Bob Capa and Martha Gellhorn arrived for several days' stay on the 8th. Nice to have them and they are very interesting. Martha is a very nice person.

The displaced persons, slaves really, are quite a problem. Especially the Russians, who love nothing more than to beat up or rape a German. Next to burning his home to the ground or robbing and looting, they like this best. I have 7,500 of them, as well as several thousand Poles and more miscellaneous.[i]

Gen. Gaither visited.[ii] He would like, when the division returns to the States, to have me take over the Prcht School and he take the division. Rumors rampant. Are we to return to the States shortly? We are apparently being held back for some reason. It may be.

Weiden, April 13, [1945]

Heard this morning that President Roosevelt had died yesterday. A shock, and an irreplaceable loss at this particular time. Regardless of how much any of us disagreed with him, the facts were that he was a great man and a real war leader. I do not see how we can replace him. His Vice President, Mr. Truman, appears totally inadequate. We Americans are due for dark and trying days and years ahead, and the world peace efforts have been done an irreparable harm. Willkie was a great man.[iii]

What for the future? At least it will be interesting. Humanity is on the march and we for a change are not in the van. As long as our markets last and our natural

---

i   The Poles, in a controversial decision, would be turned over to the Russians regardless of individual desires. Most went straight to a gulag.

ii Ridgley Gaither, then a brigadier general and head of the Army Parachute School, would participate in the Rhine River crossing, Operation *Varsity*, with the 17th Airborne Division. Later he would command the 11th Airborne Division and XVIII Airborne Corps.

iii Wendell Willkie ran for president against Roosevelt on his third term run. He was a liberal Republican and greatly assisted Roosevelt after the campaign in working congress for Lend-Lease and assistance to Britain before the U.S. entered the war.

resources are full and plenty, we can afford the luxuries of a purely capitalistic nation, but our days are numbered, and we will have to join the march.

Our front is becoming more and more quiet. Soon there will be no enemy whatsoever.

Had General Harmon in yesterday for lunch. He allowed as to how our fighting on this continent was over. On the other hand, I visited Hqrs XVIII Corps and learned that General Ridgway had elicited and obtained the backing of Gens. Hodges and Bradley to get the two Abn Divs to the eastern front for the final clean-up.

Gen. J. C. H. Lee, who was in a day or so ago, said that he did not think that the fighting up there was now worthy of the 82nd. There may be something to that. The fact of the matter is that there is practically no fighting. The daily advances are hardly more than marches, the biggest problems being those of supply and transport.

Last night we had patrols across the river into Hitdorf. We used for the first-time infrared flashlights and beacons to signal to the patrols. It was preeminently successful. Next, we want to develop the PND, or "mouse detector" as it is affectionately called.

Miss Gellhorn still around. I like her very much. She is brilliant and charming. Had her land at A-58 with Bob Capa when they arrived. That way we found out why the airport was not being used.

The krauts in the sack are still being tough. When they are wiped out, we should know more of our future. We all suspect that it is destination New York. I want to get to the Pacific. As this thing approaches a wind-up, I realize that I will have a frightful time adapting myself to the years of peace and ways of peace. Fighting and excitement have become my daily sustenance. I miss them after awhile. I will die as a quiet civilian. I will get used to it all too soon, as so many have in the past, but the adjustment will be a painful process. I will not go back to my regular rank without leaving the service. There is so much to be done, both in the development of abn techniques and means and for our people in the fields of economics and politics.

Germany, April 15, [1945]

Received movement imminent orders yesterday. No idea where. It is about time. We are far too comfortable here.

Have stayed up until about 0100 and 0200AM the past week talking to Martha. She is by far the smartest woman that I have ever known. She is most sincere and genuine too, one of the few genuine people, completely devoid of pretense, that I have ever met. I like her ideas very much. Mentally we could be very happy, but sexually I believe that we are far apart.

She writes only as she feels, and the public can go to hell if they don't like it, which I admire very much, but it isn't necessarily going to make her a lot of money. She has been a wonderful influence and experience for me. I need to know people like her. She frankly criticizes me and the army and whatever strikes, or fails to strike, her fancy, which is good for me and I do not get enough of.

Germany, April 17, [1945]

The movement imminent was apparently a staff officer's ill-considered haste, but that we are moving soon is quite apparent. We are to be in SHAEF reserve and to move to the area Wesel-Frankfurt-Kassel in what I believe will be an occupational role. Gen. Harmon told me yesterday that he had it from a very high level that we are on a high priority for shipment to the Pacific.[i] I have also had it from another source that we are on a very high priority for shipment to the States.

So far everything fits into the picture. We are being held back for ready preparation and shipment to the States, and then to be refitted and shipped to the Pacific. But, as always in war, anything may happen. The front is moving along nicely, and contact should be made with the Russians within the week.

Germany, April 18, [1945]

The First and Ninth Armies remain on the Elbe, where they are now closing. The Third advances to the east to join the Russians. We continue in our present occupational role and in SHAEF reserve. We all feel a terrible letdown. The war on the continent is over. The mopping up of the redoubt area should be not too difficult a problem, really just what the new divisions will need, and they are anxious for it.[ii]

My 417th FA Group, just off the boats, has been given a definite occupational assignment. Their guns are to be put in cosmoline for long storage and they are to start guard duties of the occupied areas. It kills them. Fortunately, they fired about a dozen or so shots when we had some front on the Rhine.

Germany, April 21, [1945]

The place and time of meeting the Russians now looms large as the most intriguing thing of the moment. Our staff pool, amounting to 22 pounds, is at stake. Dresden looks good. My choice is Uebigau. The most important thing is that a meeting is to take place at last after these four years.

Inherited 9,500 more Russians yesterday. They are all doing well. They are a fine people. The division's future is as much in doubt as ever. I believe that we will be

---

i   Operation *Olympic*, the invasion of Japan, required a number of the European units. Army staff was identifying those units that should participate.

ii   The redoubt was southern Bavaria where it was believed large groups of Wehrmacht guerrillas, "the Wolves," would attempt to hold out. This included Hitler's house at Berchtesgaden.

given a good idea as soon as the Russian corridor is opened and SHAEF can feel certain of a clear unobstructed road to victory.

Weiden, Germany, April 25, [1945]

Received information yesterday that the division would go with the XVIII Corps to the 2nd British Army for participation in the severance and clearing up of Denmark. We should move in about three or four days and be closed up near the Elbe by the 30th. It cannot amount to much except considerable physical discomfort and very little fighting. I do not like to go with the XVIII Corps. They take away everything that is not nailed down and give us nothing.[i]

Made a trip to Versailles and talked to Col. Kessinger, ADCS G-1 SHAEF, yesterday regarding redeployment. I am sweating it out. Then went to FAAA at La Maison LeFitte and talked to G-1 re our Nijmegen citation. Back at Sissone called G-4 Oise Base and found out that we are again being moved out of our home.

The redeployment program sounds all screwed up. The 13th, which has not heard a hostile shot and, which has to be mere coincidence, just missed participation in a local abn show, has been given top redeployment priority for return to the States. Wow! They have only been away six months and haven't been in combat. What will happen to us Christ only knows. My heart is set on the Pacific. I would die if I had to sit in the States with a war in the Pacific and not get in on it.

Weiden, Germany, April 25, [1945]

Visited Gen. Ridgway for a few hours yesterday. Finally received our plan for the operations in the vicinity of Hamburg. I asked him about our citation for Nijmegen. He has asked Gen. Eisenhower about it and has been given some assurance of favorable consideration. No guarantee, however. He told me in the course of our discussion that Gen. Eisenhower had not approved of the 101st citation at Bastogne, that the War Dept. had jumped on the bandwagon and ordered it without consulting him. A splendid public relations job.

He told me that there is little chance of our going to the Pacific after this winds up. This was a shock. We have had our hearts set on it. I asked him to do all that he could to arrange it, and he said that he would. I believe that he may be in error. Rumor has it that we are going.

---

i   SHAEF received guidance to ensure Denmark was occupied by U.S. or British forces, not the Russians. XVIII Airborne Corps received the mission and completed it very quickly, moments ahead of advancing Russian columns.

He also told me that there are to be two Abn Divisions and two separate regiments in the post-war army. Where I will fit into this god knows. I am not anxious to return to the States to sit and decay.

We move to the 2nd British Army area today.

Hohenzethen, Germany, April 27, 1945

Arrived here last night. The division CP in the assembly area of the division six miles from the Elbe River and 40 miles from Hamburg.

The 26th I returned to Sissone for a short visit, principally to talk to CG Oise Base re our having to move from Sissone in connection with the redeployment program.

We apparently were in priority one for return to the States to parade in NY on VE-Day with one Armd and one Inf div. When the 13th was not sent in they took our priority and they are to return first, evidently for transit to the Pacific or breakup.

Here we have a new division that has never heard a hostile shot that is being sent back to the homeland to parade as a representative combat division because of a staff convenience, while a veteran division sits and fights. This will never be understood by a staff officer. It is unbearable to a combat soldier.

Anyway, the prospects are that we will have to move from Sissone to make room for divisions going back to the States, a most unpleasant prospect.

Had a short visit with Peg Knecht, a hell of a nice person. Loyal, sweet.

This sector looks OK from here. Thousands of DPs wandering about, and a number of PWs. Had a guard murdered in the motor pool of the 456 last night.

Haven't seen the actual front yet, but I understand that it may be wet. To our right, on the Ninth Army front, quite a number of Germans are coming into their lines to avoid the Russians. I have been advised by higher hqrs to be prepared to receive the Russians in traditionally good style with gifts, etc. It nauseates me. Why gifts? We give gifts to only our proven friends and to no other living being. We'll fight them if they want to fight. We would sooner do that than give them gifts.

Bleckede, Germany, April 29, 1945

A small tidy pretty German town on the Elbe. The CP is about a half mile from the river. The town has been held by the 5th British Division. We are taking it over in about an hour. We plan on crossing with the 505th tonight. The division will not close for several days, but the crossing must be made as a political necessity.

The British are intent on seizing the Kiel Canal before the Russians get there and take over. In addition, they want to take over control of Denmark. The Russians can't be very far away. No one knows how far. Consequently, the British crossed the Elbe on our left at 0200 this morning, three days before the planned crossing. We are to protect their right and meet the Russians.

The krauts on the river are in a disputative frame of mind. We apparently lost some men in a patrol last night. Reached the depths the day before on reconnaissance in Hitzacker when I came across a pig eating a dead kraut. The noise that he made was more bothersome than the act. I could hear it at lunch.

I have seen enough of war for a lifetime. The current practice of the kraut of making fertilizer of their enemies gives factual proof to the exponents of the theory of reincarnation. They can at least prove that one of their apostles turned up as a turnip.

Ludwigslust, Germany, May 3, [1945]

There will never be a day like this again, nor a week for that matter. The division crossed the Elbe with one regt, the 505th, the night of the 29th-30th. Moving with its usual elan and speed, the bridgehead was established by daylight, the crossing having been started at 0100. I followed at 0430 and by 0500 found myself in the heaviest artillery concentrations that I have experienced for some time.

We encountered something new in a sea mine, a mine activated by a magnetic-activated switch preset for a certain number of fluctuations.

The 505 was followed by the 504, which attacked to the south and cleared Darceau in an hour, thus uncovering another bridge site. The 325th came up from Cologne, crossed the Elbe, and attacked with the 7th Armored Division, CCB of which had been attached to the division. The German resistance up to this time had been spotty but mean. Lots of sea mines, which were most fatal and undetectable.

The 2nd an attack was ordered to seize Ludwigslust to Domitz. First the Germans fought and killed a number of our men. By noon they were surrendering in groups, and it was difficult to pass through towns without picking up large groups of willing prisoners. By early afternoon complete units were passing through our lines, ignoring everyone and everything, ready for surrender.

By mid-afternoon I arrived in Ludwigslust and there found a steady stream of Germans, civilians and soldiers alike, passing thru our lines for surrender. Families were riding halftracks. Soldiers were accompanied by their women. Complete units were coming in.

At about five o'clock I had established my CP in the palace of the Grand Duke of Mecklenburg in Ludwigslust when the CG of the 21st German Army had three staff officers visit my CP to arrange the surrender of his wounded and allied PWs. I told them that I would accept the surrender of his complete army only, and on unconditional terms only. He said, after some talking, that he would transmit these terms to his CG.

The son of the grand duke was present and wanted to stay overnight in the palace. This I refused to let him do, informing him that he would be processed as a PW if he remained. He told me that the house was the property of the English crown, etc. I reminded him of the English bombed homes. And so it went.

At about 2000 Lieut. Gen. von Tippelskirch arrived with his staff to arrange the final surrender. After much talking and lengthy discussion, in which he asked me my plans and wanted obviously for the U.S. troops to move out and accept the surrender of his army where it stood, I accepted unconditionally the surrender of his complete army.

There was little choice for him. I told him that the Russians were our allies and that I proposed to move against him and destroy his army in conjunction with them if he did not surrender. He surrendered, returning only to work out the details of the withdrawal of his troops.

All day yesterday and today his army has been coming into our lines. It has been a sight like nothing else in history. Their troops look well. They are well-disciplined. They are, however, outnumbered and completely out-quantitied with equipment. Our prisoner take must total near 70–90,000. I have never expected to see the equal of it.[i]

Late this afternoon contact was made with the Russians and a meeting took place with the CG of the 8th Mech Corps, Gen. [Denit?]. We agreed on a final location of our front lines and on a kilometer of no man's land between us. Tonight, they visited the division CP and I had Gen. Ridgway and the staff present for some palaver, champagne and brandy.

I visited their CP also and it was an experience. I understand why the Germans do not want to surrender to them. They kicked in store windows, looted, rolled a big keg of wine onto the city square where anyone who came by with a bucket could have a fill. Drunks swanned about the streets, flagging down vehicles.

Their military courtesy was unusually good. Very enthusiastic, and very rough on the Germans. They tear everything apart and loot everything. It is an experience to watch them work. Their common hatred for everything German seems to bind them together. With much drinking of champagne and brandy, they were sent on their way tonight. I would as soon fight them as anyone. The quantity of U.S. equipment in their possession was remarkable.[ii]

Ludwigslust, Germany, May 6, [1945]

The days have been filled to overflowing. The 4th I visited the concentration camp outside of town and there met a sight the equal of which I have never even imagined

---

i   At this time, German units were surrendering en masse to avoid having to surrender to the Russians.

ii   The Russians were supplied to a large degree by U.S. manufacturing through the Lend-Lease program.

nor expect to see ever again. About 200 dead were scattered about, most if not all of them having died from beatings and starvation. It was horribly gruesome.[1]

It is inconceivable to imagine such things happening in a civilized world. I ordered all unit COs to visit the place, and as many troops as possible. Those guilty of fraternization are to be punished by visiting the place and assisting in removing the bodies.[i]

This morning we had a funeral, burying the 200 unburied in the local city square. The most prominent citizens in town were required to dig the graves and remove and lower the bodies into their graves. The services were very good, and I am sure brought home to the local Germans the error of their ways. Perhaps it did. I'm not sure.

Yesterday had a meeting with the CG of the Russian 5th Guards Cossack Division, at which time he presented me with a silver plaque in commemoration of the occasion. It is a beautiful memento.

This afternoon Lt. Gen. Dempsey met Lt. Gen. Greishen, CG of the Russian 49th Army, at the Div CP. It was a very nice affair. I still think that Gen. Dempsey is one of the finest that I have known in the war.

At noon word was received from Gen. Eisenhower that all hostilities were to cease, that the German armed forces had surrendered unconditionally. This is it. After two years. One doesn't know whether to cry or cheer or just simply get drunk. It is difficult to give full expression to one's feelings while in uniform in command. Now for the Japanese.

Ludwigslust, Germany, May 8, [1945]

A visit yesterday from the 385th Infantry Division at 1100. Visited the Hqrs of the 5th Guards Cossack Division at 3:00. Greeted by a band and assembled staff, that followed by some toasting with some excellent hair-raising vodka. Then dinner, which was quite an affair.

We were shown their 120mm AT gun and I rode in their T-34 tank. After dinner we all sang, and they did some dances outdoors. Then the movie and home shortly after midnight. All in all, quite a day.

The JA was the only one who got combat fatigue. They are fascinating people and without exception are well-liked by our people. I was presented with a Cossack sabre and a Russian tommy gun.

Things are shaping up well. The apparent prospects are that we will stay here for several weeks and then God knows what. Extra officers are beginning to arrive. My talk to them, I am afraid, was anything but inspiring. Everyone is trying to jump on the bandwagon, the 82nd, the proven outfit where reputations are made, and fame is everywhere.[2]

---

i   This was common practice by all senior troop commanders if a camp fell within their territory.

Ludwigslust, May 17, 1945

Returned the visit of the 385th and that was some affair. Next returned one with Gen. Dempsey to the Russian 49th Div and that was almost as rough. My aide passed out, so I had to relieve him. Rumors of our ultimate demise continue to fly about with far too great a number and improbability. It seems certain that we will not see the States before the fall, if not Xmas.

Yesterday I had a long talk with Gen. Ridgway about the possibility of the 101 returning first. That would be a tragedy. We expect to leave here for our south Germany sector in about two weeks. It should be interesting, but few things are now.

Ludwigslust, May 20, 1945

An affair with the 5th Guards Cossack and the 385th. Very enjoyable. We like the Russians very much. They had a film for us, *The Red Star*, plainly propaganda, and an orchestra that was excellent.

Have been informed by XVIII Corps that our priority for shipment back to the States is being reconsidered. We were placed after the 13th and 101. That would be extremely unfortunate, and I am not sure if I would survive it. Our next area and assignment are in doubt. It does appear certain that we have from four to nine months to do on the continent.

Ludwigslust, May 29, [1945]

Being relieved by the British 5th Division starting the 31st. We are returning to the Sissone area, where we will catch up with our tails and prepare for redeployment. I personally doubt that we will be redeployed now, but everyone says that there is a strong possibility of it.

Gen. Ridgway is in Washington and should get some decisions. I received word that I am to return on June 10th to participate in a war bond drive in San Antonio, Texas, followed by two weeks' leave. It is hard to believe after all this time. My feelings are mixed. I do not want to leave the division at this time. Dominating all else at this moment is worry about P.[i] Overdue. The possible consequences are, well, death and disgrace. It is hard to accept calmly. Going back to Sissone will not help matters. I have used poor judgment. I'm extremely unhappy.

---

i   Promotion.

Ludwigslust, Germany May 31, [1945]

This, the last night in Germany. Tomorrow will tell a great deal. I am still worried but hoping for the best. Called on Gen. Moore, C/S of the Ninth Army, today. Had a long talk with Billingslea. He was surprised at Rommel's mental state in Africa. I told him that I was not. No one but one who has been through it can appreciate the mental strain and anxiety of a combat commander faced with independent decisions.

We agreed that there are two things that are outstanding in war for an officer, fear and anxiety. Of the two, fear is the least bothersome and the easiest to overcome. In peacetime we must have realistic training in airborne units, accepting a loss of about 1% per year from small arms, artillery, etc. I am not exactly looking forward to my return to the States.

Notes

1 Gavin later wrote movingly of the impact of this experience. "As much as we had been exposed to the horrors of war, from Sicily to Germany, we still derived great personal satisfaction from what we were doing together and we all respected and admired each other. It seemed to be that kind of a war and the German, while a tough opponent, was simply another opponent until we arrived in the town of Ludwigslust in Mecklenburg. At that moment the war changed. We came upon our first concentration camp—the sights, and sounds, and odors of which defied anything we had ever imagined. [John McNally's] description of that camp—and particularly its impact upon us—has impressed me tremendously. Although I have tried to drive the memories of that camp from my mind, they frequently come back at unexpected moments. We were changed by that experience as much as we were changed by the war itself." Gavin, Foreword to McNally, *As Ever, John.*

2 This was VE Day. Colonel John McNally took the occasion to write movingly (in his book *As Ever, John*, p. 63) about the British. "Today is England's day. Gallant, courageous England. God knows they are hardheaded and proud and sometimes damned smug, but all in all we Americans have come to admire their deep appreciation of their 'duty' and their abiding love for their English soil which transcends all else. So today will rank with Armistice Day and Waterloo, Crecy and Tilbury. Once more, as so many times before through the centuries, the Westminster bells are ringing to celebrate a victory. Once more England, and the world, are free."

Berlin

Berlin, Germany, August 2, 1945

June the 5th the division closed back in Sissone. There a few difficulties with the Assembly Area Command, which was about to use the area for redeployment. June the 10th I left with Capt. Thompson, ADC, for San Antonio, Texas, where we arrived June 13th.

Quite a celebration. Met Fraye Gilbert of WOAI. From there went to Washington to rejoin Peg and the Babe [Gavin's wife Irma, also known as Peggy or Peg, and their daughter Barbara] after two years. They were fine. To NY for several days, then to Mt. Carmel. In NY met Martha Gellhorn, a remarkable person, went to a show. In Mt. Carmel had a Hollywood homecoming and sold war bonds. Returned to Washington. Later went to Fire Island, NY, where I spent several days with Martha at Point of Woods. A delightful place, the first real vacation.

Returned to the division, which had now moved to Epinal, France, on July 3rd. Flew via Newfoundland, Azores, in a C-54 both ways. The division in fine shape, splendid relations with the local populace.

Our entry into Berlin tied up so that the 2nd Armd is to go in first. We are to go in about August 1st. While in Washington talked to Gen. Ridgway about Pacific prospects. Appears to be little chance. I am to go to Berlin, and that's that. The division was slated for demobilization.

Called on Gen. Marshall and Pres. Truman. Both delightful to talk to. Attended a tea at the home of Sec. of State Stimson.

Epinal very nice, Mon. Parisot and family very fine people. He is the Prefect of the Vosges. His Chief of Cabinet, Mon. Lelay, OK also. The Berlin sector is interesting, to say the least, at this point. The plan worked up last winter at SHAEF provides for a Berlin District that in theory operates under Group Control Council of Gen. Clay.

Clay, despite his nation-wide role, is taking over close control of the U.S. sector of the city and everything in it.[i] Parks, who runs BD, is gradually being pushed into a useless role.

There are at present 80 general officers in the city. Parks' staff refer to them as the political carpetbaggers (they are Clay's specialists). There are 40,000 troops in the city, far too many. I hope to get the number reduced. Relations with the British are apparently fine, with the Russians touch-and-go. I arrived with an advance CP yesterday. Today will be the first full day of business.

Berlin, August 3, [1945]

Called on Gen. Parks and Gen. Collier. Continued reconnaissance of training areas. Does not look too bad. I can see where one could get settled into a routine, and not too unpleasant of a routine, here. The weather continues to be bad.

Berlin, August 4, [1945]

Continued reconnaissance of training areas, generally out towards Potsdam. All evidence shows that the Germans turned in a good fight even after the city was captured. Made a short broadcast for AFN-Berlin. It opens tomorrow.

Accompanied Gen. Parks to the locale of the Group Control Council meeting to start on the 10th. Needs a hell of a lot of work. Parks informed me that he is taking a three weeks' leave in September and that I would represent the U.S. in the Berlin District meetings, quite an opportunity to learn a few things. I would like to make a name for myself at these international conferences. This International Security Council is the biggest thing that has hit this world in our time. To qualify for sitting with it is worthwhile.

Berlin, August 5, [1945]

Reconnoitered the NE boundary. Looks none too well. The Ruskie units in that sector nowhere near up to the standard of the 5th Guards and 385th Cavalry.

Accompanied Gen. Parks in a call on Gen. Clay. Interesting to see and talk to him again. Call ordinary. Apparently, the Group Control people have been quite incensed by the possessive attitude of the 2nd Armd towards all recreational and athletic facilities. Took a walk with Tommie through the Gruenvald.

---

i   General Lucius Clay was the commander of all forces in Berlin, less the Russian sector. It was his guidance that managed the Berlin Airlift when the Russians attempted to chase the Allies out.

Berlin, August 8, [1945]

The division arriving. Many difficulties with the Russian handling of the trains. Yesterday flew to Helmstedt to look for four missing trains. Figured on resupplying them by air if necessary. German propaganda excellent still. They tell our troopers that the war was not their fault. They could do nothing about it. The new men seem to believe them, and I am afraid are beginning to feel that the older soldiers of the division are unreasonable in their hatred of everything German. They tell the troops that the Russians are not to be trusted and thus get the troops bitching and blaming all their difficulties on the Russians.

The Germans will be disappointed and, I believe, surprised if we do not come to blows with the Russians before the winter is over. I take the sector tonight.

Berlin, August 10, [1945]

Took over the sector at 0803 August 9th. So far all is well, although there is a great potential source of trouble in this place. Yesterday attended the first Kommandantura meeting. Most impressive. It is truly our first experiment in real international government. There is the small amoeba of peaceful government, fuel, food, transportation, news, radio, all controlled in a central headquarters for the common good. It is a wonderful thing.[1]

News of the first atomic bombing of Hiroshima still crowds everything else off the front pages. It is frightening and unbelievable in its implications.

Last night Bob Capa brought Jack Benny and Ingrid Bergman by the house for supper about 2300. Had a nice time. She is lovely.

Berlin, August 12, [1945]

Japan has accepted the Potsdam terms and we have started negotiations with a view to their surrender. It's all over over there. So ends our chances for the Pacific. Right now, however, we could not be better situated. This is interesting and instructive.

Attended the opening of the Berlin Press Club Saturday night. Quite nice. Three German girls there. Very difficult to accept that, much more difficult than I suspected it would be. Having a hard time getting close to the Russians. Someone gave them a chill. The 2nd Armored shot four of them.

Berlin, August 14, [1945] [or August 15, a strikeover]

No surrender from Japan yet, but it is certainly in the offing. Dated Katharine Clark of CBS Sunday evening. We started making a broadcast at 1500 that wound up at 1380530 [0530 on August 13th?]. She says what the Russians are saying: "See, when the Red Army threatens the Japs surrender. You have been fighting them for three years and have done no good." Propaganda. But it is passed around by the best people.

Saw *GI Joe* last night, a wonderful movie. Dinner at Gen. Parks'. The French are having difficulties getting started. We are feeding them. They are to start feeding themselves in Sept., but very likely will not be able to make it.

Berlin, August 17, [1945]

The war is over, and peace is here at last. It made little difference to the soldiers, i.e. there was no celebrating.

What the future holds in the way of a quick return is the closest thing to their hearts now. The C/S hung up a sign: "Mr. Weinicke Life Insurance." Billingslea called me "Capt. Gavin." And so it goes. I don't care a hell of a lot.

The division is doing a fine job. I am having my usual troubles, more than usual I guess. My present position and rank are such that I can't seem to keep out of it. I hardly know how to cope with it. Must learn to discipline myself.

Berlin, August 31, [1945]

This winds up August, one of the busiest months that I have ever known. Tomorrow I take over the command of Berlin District, so next month should be worse.

Yesterday we had an airborne review for Gen. Eisenhower. He seemed quite pleased with it.[2]

The Kommandantura meetings have been an education. The U.S. sector is rapidly becoming overcrowded with DPs and refugees from the other sectors of the city.

The Russians, or deserters from the Russian army, of which there are many, seem to like to raid, rape and loot in the U.S. sector. The food requirements in the U.S. sector are not being adequately met. This winter there will be no coal for the civilians.[i] All in all it promises to be a winter of starvation and riots. Many heads will fall, I believe.

Within the 82nd I have started checking all supply agencies carefully to avoid the growth of leaks.[ii] It is a serious and difficult problem. If I survive this winter, I will be a hell of a lot better informed by spring. The Russians are not very easy to get along with compared to the combat units in Mecklenburg, but in time may melt.

---

i   The coal shortage became a major issue. The German mines were largely shut down due to lack of labor. Coal was procured in France and the UK, but it was a program slow to get started.

ii   By this he means pilferage into the black market—a very lucrative business.

Berlin, Sept. 1, [1945]

An airborne review for Gens. Baranoff, Gorbatov, and Antinov. It was taken over, however, by Marshal Zhukov and staff, the others scared away. It was very well done. Unfortunately, there was one fatality. A trooper became tied up in an equipment bundle that finally landed on his chest.

Later in the day I called on Baranoff. He had a Russian translation from a recent S&S. He objected to the article which implied that the Russians were aiding the black market.

In the afternoon Congressman Luther Johnson of Texas and party visited the CP. In the evening two troopers refused to obey the order of Col. Hughes, GCC, to release a German whom they had apprehended. To bed early. Attended a soldier show in the div arty area.[3]

Notes

1   Reflecting on these days, Gavin described the first tasks as cleaning up the city, removing and burying the dead bodies, and feeding and caring for the living. There were, he said, estimated to be more than 3,000 bodies in the subway system alone.

2   At some point the old-timers of the division, 99 officers and men, made a parachute jump into Berlin. John McNally described how, boarding C-47s at Templehof Airport, they were "fulfilling a pledge that one day, in war or peace, we would jump on Berlin." "All in all," recalled McNally, "it was very agreeable, especially as the first man out, as always, was General Jim Gavin himself." As Ever, John, p. 73.

3   Gavin's journal ended here, at the beginning of September. Sometime in October a major controversy erupted when it was announced that the 82nd Airborne Division would be disbanded in Europe. Another unit, the 101st Airborne Division, would be the one kept on the Army's rolls in the post-war force structure. They were also told that the 101st was to be brought back to the United States to march up New York's Fifth Avenue in a victory parade.

Gavin was incensed. Clearly, he argued, the airborne division with the longest service and most time in combat should be the one honored and retained. Gavin suspected that the 101st's commander, General Maxwell Taylor (who had recently been named to be the next Superintendent of the Military Academy at West Point and was by then back in the United States), had lobbied successfully for his division to be given these honors.

"It was difficult to describe how devastating the blow was," said Gavin. He turned to General Matthew Ridgway, then commanding XVIII Airborne Corps, for help. Of course, Ridgway had commanded the 82nd in Africa, Sicily, Italy and Normandy. He sided with Gavin on the matter, writing a memorandum to the Chief of Staff of the Army comparing the records of the two divisions (both then under his command). He recalled that the 101st had been cadred from the 82nd, and thus that the 82nd was the matrix from which American airborne forces in the war were developed and indoctrinated. Both divisions had splendid records, observed Ridgway, but the facts showed a much longer and at least equally brilliant battle record in the case of the 82nd. Then the closing zinger: Personalities of former and present commanders should not be factors in arriving at a decision, which should be based solely on records, in and out of combat.

Meanwhile Gavin also made his case to some friends in the press corps, particularly John "Beaver" Thompson of the Chicago Tribune, who had jumped with the division in Sicily, and Bill Walton of Time, who jumped with them in Normandy. Both were now in Berlin.

A month passed and then, while he was on a training visit to a troop carrier unit, Gavin received a cable forwarded from division headquarters. The War Department had changed its mind. The 82nd was to live and march up Fifth Avenue when it returned to the U.S. in early January.

Meanwhile, on November 3, 1945, Gavin was given command of the First Allied Airborne Army, then occupying Berlin. In December he finally received orders to return to the United States with the division.

Editor's Epilogue

Gavin's final entry in the World War II journal was dated Berlin, September 1, 1945. The 82nd Airborne Division was stationed in that city in the immediate post-war period, tasked with working alongside British and Russian troops to provide security for the Allied Government. "It was a duty of which we were proud, and the veterans responded with all the professional competence that came from over three years of war," Gavin later wrote. "We were certain that there would be an airborne division in the post-war Army and that it would be the 82nd."[1]

"Then," continued Gavin, "came the blow." In early October they received a cable from Washington informing them that the division would be disbanded in Europe. A different division, one with less combat experience than the 82nd, had been chosen to be retained in the post-war Army. "It was a shocking blow, and we were in despair."

At just that time, recalls Gavin, he received an anonymous letter signed simply "A Lieutenant," and he quotes its concluding words: "And we know that somewhere there will always be an 82nd Airborne Division. Because it lives in the hearts of men. And somewhere young men will dare the challenge to 'Stand up and hook up' and know that moment of pride and strength which is its reward."

That was very heartening to Gavin, and of course the Army's post-war plans soon changed to make room for continuing the 82nd Airborne Division on active duty and, thrillingly, bring it back to march up New York City's 5th Avenue in a magnificent victory parade. John McNally later recorded his impressions. "On a cold January day, the 82nd Airborne Division marched down the grandest street in America to the proud beat of the division band and the roar of a million people. In the lead was the tall, impressive General Jim Gavin with a rifle slung over his shoulder."

And: "There was not a single man in those ranks who did not hear the noiseless tread of the ghosts of glory that marched beside him, the other 82nd Airborne Division, the spirits of those whose broken bodies made this day possible. Their silent tread echoed in our hearts louder than the drums and cheers."

And: "General Gavin, at the Normandy briefing, had put the thought into unforgettable words which had burned their way into his heart. 'Some of us will lose our way,' the General had said. Now each man on parade walked a little straighter, and a little prouder, because he wasn't marching by himself at all. He was marching with those buddies who had 'lost their way' and who had found it again in his steps."[2]

***

Soon after the conclusion of World War II Gavin published his first book, appropriately entitled *Airborne Warfare*. While acknowledging that such warfare in the modern sense had been originated by the Russians and developed by the Germans, the introduction to Gavin's book also cited as "historical fact" that "the American Army took this new instrument of warfare and, with the British, refined and improved it and unleashed upon our enemies airborne forces of such power and perfection as even they had not dreamed of."[3] Given Gavin's key role in that endeavor, his views were highly influential, especially as he sketched much of the development based on first-hand knowledge and participation.

Gavin's friend and fellow airborne pioneer Major General William C. Lee wrote the admiring introduction for this book. "To understand modern war, one must have seen it at first hand, shared in it, shouldered a part of its terrible responsibilities, and known the cost in toil and blood and destruction," Lee stated. "I know of no man better fitted to write" a book on airborne warfare than Gavin, "either by experience or the ability to think clean and clear. His qualifications are complete."[4]

Gavin's reputation as an officer who led by example and was devoted to his soldiers was well-earned. On four combat jumps—into Sicily, at Salerno, then Normandy and the Netherlands—he was the first man out the door. Two Distinguished Service Crosses, two Silver Stars, and the Purple Heart rewarded his service.[5]

Gavin also took pride in the fact that throughout his wartime service he did not take a day's leave, nor spend a day in the hospital, despite being wounded in Sicily and breaking his back in the parachute jump into Holland.

Gavin later contributed a *Foreword* to Margaret Bierbaum's collection of letters her brother John McNally, a paratrooper, had written to her during World War II. She dedicated the book to all paratroopers who, she wrote, like her brother "went into battle not as others may have done, quietly and grimly, but rather in the thunder of planes in the night, to leap into tumultuous darkness."[6] That is a marvelous evocation of what Gavin and others like him experienced.

***

Much useful work was still ahead for Gavin after the war ended. He remained in command when the 82nd Airborne Division returned to the United States and was stationed on familiar ground, back at Fort Bragg. There he had in command of one of the division's elements, the 504th Parachute Infantry Regiment, Colonel

William C. Westmoreland, later to become commander of U.S. forces in Vietnam and then Army Chief of Staff. Westmoreland found the command climate in the division very much to his liking. "I found Gavin an excellent division commander to work for," he later recalled. "He gave general guidance as to what he wanted and left his commanders alone to exercise their own initiative."[7]

***

By the end of January 1946 what remained of the 82nd Airborne Division was augmented by remnants of the 13th Airborne Division, which had just been inactivated, and by the 555th Parachute Infantry Battalion.

During this time things changed in Gavin's personal life as well. He and his wife had not been compatible before the war, he said, and had even talked about divorce shortly after their marriage. Now it was, as many couples were finding, difficult after more than three years of war-time separation to pick up the loose ends. They accordingly mutually agreed to obtain a divorce, which was accomplished a year or so after he returned from the war.

In the following autumn Gavin met an attractive young woman named Jean Emert Duncan. From Knoxville, Tennessee, she was at Fort Bragg to visit her sister, who was married to an officer in the division. Two days later she and Gavin had their first date.

Jean had been married to an Air Force officer, but they too divorced after the war. Jean had a two-year-old daughter, Caroline, from that marriage.

Soon Gavin took Jean to West Point for a football weekend. The highlight of the visit, and indeed its purpose, was for him to propose marriage to Jean. On Flirtation Walk he asked, and she accepted.

By March of 1948, with over six years in the 82nd Airborne, about half of that in combat, Gavin was given a new assignment as chief of staff of Fifth Army, headquartered in Chicago.

At a farewell division review in Gavin's honor, they surveyed the troops then assigned to determine how many had been with it from the beginning and had made the four combat jumps. There were 24. Gavin said they took their picture, "and they certainly were not a very friendly lot, but they exuded confidence and sureness."

Gavin found the Fifth Army assignment complex and time-consuming, but he enjoyed it. Along the way he had a temporary assignment as Chairman of an Army Advisory Panel on Airborne Operations. After several months, when he felt he had the new job in hand, he went to Knoxville, where he and Jean were married on July 31, 1948. It was a quiet marriage, the second for both of them, and right away they moved to Fort Sheridan near Chicago. Years later Gavin reflected that it had been a very happy marriage and that, in addition to having a daughter apiece from each of their former marriages, in the next few years they were to have three children together, making a fine family of five daughters.

***

The Fifth Army assignment lasted only a year or so, then Gavin was called to Washington. There he was posted to a newly formed entity to be known as WSEG, the Weapons System Evaluation Group, an element of the Office of the Secretary of Defense, where he became Chief of the Military Studies and Liaison Division. That proved to be an influential and challenging billet, one where his interest in innovation and modernization could have full play. During two years in that element, he came into contact with some of the nation's leading scientists, men such as Dr. Edward Teller and Dr. Robert Oppenheimer, and had the opportunity to observe such historic events as the nuclear tests at Eniwetok in the Pacific.

In the spring of 1949, Gavin reflected, an argument was raging in Washington and throughout the country about the meaning of the atomic bomb. Would it bring about the end of land warfare? Was it the ultimate in airpower, as Giulio Douhet and Billy Mitchell foresaw it? He did not think so, admitted Gavin, also acknowledging that he had a lot to learn.

In Gavin's view, although the bomb (and what to do with and about it) had created wide divisions among civilian leaders, the divisions among military leaders were even greater, and this at a time when greater unity among the Services was energetically sought.

Soon Gavin was given a challenging mission, directed by the Secretary of Defense to take a team of three scientists to South Korea, there to spend six weeks visiting the combat troops and finding out what science could do to assist the ground forces. In company with the chosen three scientists, including the Nobel Prize-winning inventor of the transistor, the team arrived just at the time of the Inchon Landing. They went ashore on D+1 and accompanied 1st Marine Division assault battalions all the way to Kimpo Airfield. Gavin was getting around.

As Gavin laid out the issues of the day, there were some serious impediments to innovation. Clearly the land Army of the future would need much greater dispersion, hence greatly improved communications, longer range weapons, and more internal mobility.

Meanwhile the Air Force, given responsibility for procuring tactical aircraft for the Army, concluded that helicopters were unsound from an engineering point of view and that therefore the Army did not need them. Such parochial disputes, said Gavin, held the Army back in its early years of research, but its condition nevertheless steadily improved.

Gavin recalled that the first comprehensive test of armed forces equipment, clothing, weapons, tanks, and dwellings on an atomic battlefield was conducted at

Eniwetok in 1951. He was there. A 50-kiloton bomb was to be detonated, then the results observed and evaluated. The group that included Gavin was allowed to visit the entire blast area the afternoon before the bomb was detonated. For the blast itself they were stationed about ten miles from the bomb, backs turned to it, where they felt both the shock and the heat it generated. A day later they returned to the test area to observe the results. Gavin found this an impressive experience that left him with a very strong feeling of urgency that the Army get on with tests of its own combat formations in configurations that might be more survivable on an atomic battlefield.

***

In June 1951 ("fortunately," he said) Gavin was reassigned to SHAPE (Supreme Headquarters, Allied Powers, Europe) and soon afterward was appointed Chief of Staff of Allied Forces, Southern Europe, stationed at Naples, Italy.

En route to station in Naples Gavin stopped in Paris to call on General Eisenhower. He told him about the atomic tests he had witnessed and encouraged him to bring a leading scientist onto his staff. Gavin was gratified when Eisenhower did just that.

The NATO headquarters Gavin joined was just being organized. It was commanded by Admiral Robert Carney and, when Gavin arrived, he was the only staff officer Carney had. With help from the NATO headquarters in Paris and the Navy they cobbled together the nucleus of a staff and some of the requisite support elements.

Within a few weeks Gavin was joined in Naples by his wife Jean and her daughter Caroline, then five years old, and their daughter Patricia, who was two. Jean was then seven and a half months pregnant. They had yet to find an apartment, their furniture had not in any event arrived, and they needed to make arrangements with a suitable hospital for when the new baby arrived. It was for Jean a challenging initiation into the life of an Army wife.

This interesting assignment came to an end when, at the beginning of December 1952, Gavin received new orders taking him to Stuttgart, Germany, where he was to command the U.S. VII Corps.

The new assignment was good news for Gavin, who much preferred troop duty and command over staff work. They made the move just before Christmas, now with three young girls in the family entourage. Caroline was 8, Patricia was 3, and Aileen 1. (Jean was then herself only 29, while Gavin was 45.)

The children were amazed when at their destination the family was met by a band. And the two younger girls had never before seen snow, which was softly falling as they arrived. "Che bella sabbia," what beautiful sand, Patricia kept saying in wonderment.

After appraising the situation, he had inherited Gavin was somewhat concerned about the condition and combat readiness of the corps. When World War II ended virtually all the United States combat forces had left Europe. Only a relatively small constabulary was left, its primary role being to maintain law and order in West Germany. But now NATO had been created, and a buildup of forces was underway.

VII Corps occupied southern Germany, from the Alps north to above Nuremburg, responsible for an area that also included the historic cities of Stuttgart, Munich and Heidelberg. The American garrison included more than 65,000 troops, including two National Guard units, the 28th Infantry Division and the 43rd Infantry Division. Two armored cavalry regiments patrolled the border with Czechoslovakia. The training year included a winter maneuver, battalion-level tests, and periodic alerts. Given his background, especially the years spent in Weapons Systems Evaluation Group, Gavin was anxious to test the corps under combat conditions similar to those they might expect in the event of the use of tactical nuclear weapons.

Things got off to a less than ideal start when the Gavins had a dinner for the senior officers of the corps and their wives. Just as the main course was being served higher headquarters called an alert. This development provided further orientation for Jean Gavin on the life and times of an Army wife.

***

At about this time Gavin wrote an interesting and influential article, one he titled "Cavalry, and I Don't Mean Horses." His thesis was that vertical takeoff and landing (VTOL) aircraft could on the modern battlefield enable troops so equipped to perform the classic roles of the horse cavalry, making first contact with the enemy, delaying him and denying him movement against the friendly main body, and sending back intelligence regarding the enemy's composition and apparent intentions. This piece was published in the April 1954 issue of *Harper's* magazine. Noted Gavin ruefully, "It was not too well received in the Army."

***

In the spring of 1954 Gavin returned to the United States, and to the Pentagon, to be Chief of Plans and Operations, and simultaneously Chief of Research and Development, on the Army Staff. General Matthew Ridgway was then the Army Chief of Staff, and Gavin found him a good man to work for, "a man of incisive intelligence and great moral courage."[8]

Gavin felt he could not have been given a better assignment. This posting would provide him an opportunity to get the Army ready for the great changes he anticipated on the future battlefield. There was, however, the fact that it was for him and Jean and their amalgamated family the fourth move in the four years since they had married. Also, Jean was six months pregnant.

When Field Marshal Montgomery, then serving as Deputy SACEUR (Supreme Allied Commander, Europe), learned of Gavin's impending reassignment, he invited him for an overnight visit at his chateau outside Paris. Gavin had of course known Montgomery to some extent during World War II and considered that they were good friends. Montgomery also invited the distinguished scientist Dr. Vannevar Bush and a British major general, Sir Richard Gale.

After dinner they took seats in a circle in front of the fireplace. The topic introduced by Montgomery was whether troops operating on a nuclear battlefield should deploy in time or in space in order to defend themselves from the use of tactical nuclear weapons. Montgomery argued strongly for dispersal by time. Gale supported him (no big surprise there). Gavin, supported by Bush, took the opposing viewpoint, arguing strongly for dispersion in space rather than time.

What subsequently disturbed Gavin about that evening was that the Brits had never seen nuclear weapons fired, nor had they any idea of what the effects were except what they had read, and Gavin knew that was quite different than personal observation. They seemed to him to be trying to rationalize slight modifications of old tactics to meet this new phenomenon without understanding the phenomenon itself. Clearly Gavin's earlier experience at Eniwetok continued to have enormous influence on his outlook.

That, and what he viewed as the realities of continued relevance. In the intellectual climate of the post-World War II Pentagon, he believed, one had to show that he could live with nuclear weapons, either that or simply go out of business. The final lessons in readjustment for the future, whatever it might bring, had to be formed in the Pentagon, in new atomic formations, sky cavalry, missiles, space and improved communications.

In those days too there was extensive discussion about a war in Indochina. Gavin was therefore anxious to visit Vietnam, and in the autumn of 1954, he was able to do so, making visits to Alaska, Japan, and Korea en route. In Saigon he dined with Ngo Dinh Diem and other notables and visited refugee camps. He was struck by the role played by the various sects. After his few days there, said Gavin, he departed convinced more than ever that this was no place in which to get the U.S. Army involved. That attitude would only harden over the next few years, leading as much as anything to serious controversies both inside the Army and with external elements of the government and indeed the body politic.

***

In March of 1955 Gavin was promoted to lieutenant general and named the Army's Deputy Chief of Staff for Plans and Operations, and also for Research and

Development, a dual post he would hold until the two functions were split and Gavin, offered his choice of which to continue to head, opted for the Research and Development portfolio. This would prove a most challenging post during the coming years of enormous controversy and budgetary and bureaucratic struggle.

A major Army concern in those years was development of guided missiles with longer and longer ranges and progressively improved lethality. The major work was being done by an Army team led by the famous Wernher von Braun, and they were making excellent progress. Inter-service rivalries were not the least of the factors impacting on support for this program, or opposition to it.

Then rumors began that General Ridgway, whose initial two-year appointment as Army Chief of Staff was soon to expire, might not get the customary reappointment for another two years. Maxwell Taylor, back from the Far East, was in town and had been interviewed by Admiral Arthur Radford, Chairman of the Joint Chiefs of Staff; Secretary of Defense Charles E. Wilson; and even President Eisenhower. As Gavin would later point out, Taylor had assured his interlocutors that he could and would support the policy of "massive retaliation."

Gavin was a committed "Ridgway man." He had watched him as Chief of Staff taxed to the utmost in his efforts to maintain a combat-ready Army. In Gavin's view, the country owed Ridgway a debt that it would never be able to repay.

Gavin also thought it was not the Army's shrinking budget that was the problem, but the people Ridgway had to deal with. It seemed clear to Gavin that the Secretary of Defense and the Chairman of the Joint Chiefs of Staff thought Ridgway would be too difficult to live with for two more years.

It didn't take long for that drama to play out. General Ridgway retired on July 1, 1955, succeeded as Army Chief of Staff by Maxwell Taylor. Gavin expected reassignment at any moment, since customarily a new Chief of Staff brings in his own key staff officers. Surprisingly, that didn't happen.

Meanwhile the Army was being challenged in its dominance of long-range missile development by both the Air Force and the Navy. In an effort to retain its assets and the highly successful development program headed by von Braun, the Army created a new entity to be known as the Army Ballistic Missile Agency, giving it top priority among all Army research and development programs.

Gavin continued during these days to be deeply concerned about the policy of massive retaliation. Continuing to speak out against what he viewed as its sterility and unresponsiveness was considered by some to be anti-SAC (Strategic Air Command) and even unpatriotic. Support for Gavin's position was, however, widespread in the scientific community, and his friends there encouraged him to continue to speak up.

At a crucial point in this ongoing debate Gavin went to New York to participate in a June 1956 meeting of the Council on Foreign Relations. Among others taking part were Henry Kissinger and Roswell Gilpatric and flag officers from each of the other services. Kissinger functioned as the group's secretary, taking extensive notes on the discussion that later evolved into an influential book, *Nuclear Weapons and Foreign Policy*, welcomed by Gavin as the first book to challenge the effectiveness of the existing policy.

In December 1955 Gavin met with General Taylor to discuss his future assignment. Taylor had by then been Army Chief of Staff for about six months, and Gavin was finishing two years on the staff. Gavin wanted to talk about moving somewhere out of Washington. He told General Taylor that he assumed he would be bringing in his own man to take his place and, if that happened, he would like to go to CONARC (the Continental Army Command). That was a place, thought Gavin, where he could apply many lessons, he had learned to help get the Army ready for the future. Taylor said that sounded like a good idea, but declined to make a decision at that time.

***

In the spring of 1956, there took place a confrontation that Gavin found foreboding. Senator Stuart Symington announced that he was going to hold hearings on airpower. Gavin asked the Army Chief of Staff whether he would be allowed to appear as a witness on behalf of the Army. That was approved and in late May Gavin appeared before the Subcommittee on the Air Force of the Committee on Armed Services.

The first thing that happened was that Gavin was sworn in. He didn't like that, feeling there was an implication that he would not tell the truth unless he were under oath. Later Symington explained it. He knew the various witnesses were under considerable pressure in the Pentagon, and he wanted to put them in a position to respond, if they were criticized for their testimony, that they had no choice since they had sworn to tell the truth.

The hearings were in executive session and classified top secret. In due course Senator James Duff of Pennsylvania engaged Gavin in a discussion of the number of civilian casualties to be expected if the U.S. Strategic Air Command carried out a nuclear attack on Russia. Some horrifying figures had been cited in a recent *Fortune* magazine article, and the senator referenced those. Gavin said he would answer but suggested the Air Force or a proper study group should be asked the question.

Gavin said that current planning estimates were that there would be several hundred million deaths as a result of such an attack. And, he added, they might be mostly in the USSR if the winds blew in one direction but could be mostly in western Europe if they blew another. Gavin's numbers were several times higher than those in the referenced article.[9]

In reflecting on this testimony Gavin recalled a Corps of Engineers study that put anticipated casualties from such an attack at 425 million. He was deeply troubled by the results of that study and convinced of the necessity to find an alternate way to carry out a war.

A few weeks after these hearings the official censor, a retired vice admiral, cleared and released the fallout testimony. A June 29, 1956, article in *The New York Times* was headlined "Army Fails to Bar Bomb Testimony: Secret Hearing Told Millions Would Die in Many Lands if Soviet Were Attacked."

Gavin was in Naples when he received a cable from the Army Chief of Staff telling him that his testimony had been made public. The information regarding fallout casualties had appeared in the press, and he wanted an explanation of Gavin's role in the hearings.

Gavin was disturbed by the implications of the cable. There seemed to him to be more behind it than his testimony, that the Chief of Staff was seeking to protect himself from criticism in the matter. Returning to Washington posthaste, Gavin was informed that a bevy of high officials was extremely angry with him, including the Secretary of Defense, the Secretary of the Army, and the Chairman of the Joint Chiefs of Staff (JCS).

Pretty soon Gavin became aware of a JCS paper in which it was alleged that in the Symington hearings he had, in confirming a reference to *Fortune* magazine, made a misstatement of fact. Gavin got the article, then compared it with the transcript of his testimony. That confirmed that Gavin had not made such an error and that it was the JCS paper that was wrong. Gavin laid out the papers in his office and asked the Assistant Secretary of Defense for Atomic Energy matters, Herbert Loper, to examine them. He did and wrote in a subsequent memorandum that Gavin had been correct.

That should have put the matter to rest, but Gavin continued to be disturbed by the fact that all this had occurred without anyone speaking to him about it. He concluded it was intended to embarrass him. And Gavin continued to hear from the Secretary of the Army and the Army Chief of Staff about his fallout testimony. As late as December 1956, for example, Secretary of the Army Wilber Brucker had Gavin to his office to tell him that Secretary of Defense Wilson was convinced Gavin had knowingly erred in testifying before the Symington subcommittee.

Gavin acknowledged that, had he erred, he should have been relieved. But he had not erred. And, very disappointing to him, it was obvious that the Army Chief of Staff, Maxwell Taylor, had withdrawn from the action and stood aside.

Gavin attributed the failure to support and defend him—he had, after all, been in the right, and it had not been his decision to release the testimony that caused all the subsequent ruckus—to ambition to achieve higher position in the hierarchy that can only be done by having one's subordinates take positions based on truth, then dissociate oneself from them if they get into trouble.

A similar concern soon arose with respect to an element in the Army Chief of Staff's office known as the Coordination Group. That had been formed in Gavin's office a year or so earlier and then, when he became responsible only for Research and Development, placed under the Secretary of the General Staff, who in turn reported directly to the Army Chief of Staff.

The Coordination Group was tasked with developing positions expressing Army policies and views toward its role in defense. The materials it produced were intended for use by the Chief of Staff and the staff as witnesses before Congress. Brigadier General Lyal Metheny headed up the group. Four or five hotshot colonels worked for him.

Those in the Coordination Group were quite concerned about the Army's well-being, feeling that it was getting dangerously close to not being able to fulfill its missions. Gavin shared that view. One member of the group discussed these concerns with a reporter and soon they too were featured in *The New York Times*.

Gavin was not then involved in any way with the Coordination Group, but he noted David Halberstam's later comment on what happened then: "The story hit the Pentagon like an explosion. [Secretary of Defense] Wilson was in a rage and the Army brass quickly folded."[10] The resultant tidal wave coming from the storm center in the Secretary of Defense's office, said Gavin, reached all of them. And, Gavin added, the Chief of Staff backed off in a hurry, denying all knowledge of the Coordination Group and its members (despite the fact that they were serving in his own immediate office).

Gavin was appalled by this disloyalty and dishonesty, quoting Taylor's book *The Uncertain Trumpet*, in which he wrote that "an immediate investigation was started to try to determine the source. The investigation brought nothing to light to permit the identification or punishment of offenders, if such there were." Gavin knew better. But the Coordination Group was broken up, with the colonel who had been the source for the press account receiving a letter of reprimand from Taylor and he and the others being immediately transferred away from the Pentagon. They were, said Gavin, shocked and dismayed, because General Taylor knew who they were and what they were doing, and he had approved of their course of action.

***

Early in 1957 Gavin again raised the matter of his potential reassignment, discussing it with Lieutenant General Donald Booth, the Army's Deputy Chief of Staff for Personnel. Months passed and Gavin heard nothing, so he approached Booth again in the autumn. Booth said he had discussed the issue to a limited degree with General Taylor and it was his understanding that Gavin would be assigned to CONARC (a four-star billet) when the incumbent commander, General Willard Wyman, retired at the end of March 1958. That was to Gavin an attractive next posting, as it would enable him to continue organizing the Army along the lines, he considered necessary for it to be combat ready.

Then, in mid-December, Gavin was called to testify before what was called the Special Committee on Space and Astronautics, chaired by Senator Lyndon Johnson and convened to look into why the Soviets had launched a satellite before us. Gavin pinpointed failures in the Joint Chiefs of Staff system as it was then organized, identifying the "two hat" role of the various Service chiefs as the heart of the problem. They were at one and the same time heads of their Services and members of the Joint Chiefs. The resultant divided loyalties, said Gavin, led to dysfunctional behavior, especially when the perceived interests of their individual Services were at stake.

Bad news for Gavin was that General Taylor had testified before the same committee earlier that very day, stating that in his opinion the Joint Chiefs of Staff system was working fine and he would recommend no changes to it.

On the afternoon of December 23, 1957, General Taylor sent for Gavin and informed him that he would be staying in his current billet for an additional year to defend the budget. Gavin responded at once that he was not going to do that, but instead would retire at once. Taylor asked Gavin to discuss that intention with General Lemnitzer (then Army Vice Chief of Staff) and Secretary of the Army Brucker. Taylor then left on an extended trip to the Middle East.

Gavin returned to his own office, where he immediately prepared and signed a request for retirement (to be effective March 31, 1958). He had it in the office of Major General William Westmoreland, Taylor's Secretary of the General Staff, within the hour. The following morning, he talked with General Lemnitzer. Secretary of the Army Brucker was out of town, so a conversation with him would have to wait.

Meanwhile, recalled Gavin, the press went after him like a piranha after fresh meat. The politicians speculated that his retirement request was submitted out of disappointment that he was not being promoted. Gavin vigorously denied that promotion had anything to do with his retirement request. In a press conference following further Congressional testimony he stated flatly that "promotion has nothing whatsoever to do with my forthcoming retirement."

Then, returning to the Pentagon, Gavin was called to Brucker's office. After once again being assured by Gavin that he was intent on retiring, Brucker signed off on the retirement request and the deed was done. "I was on my own, at last," Gavin exulted. "I was thankful."

Gavin declined the retirement review customarily given to senior officers in the Washington area, opting instead to retire at Fort Bragg in a ceremony put on by his beloved 82nd Airborne Division. Many old friends and colleagues came for it, including such notables as Senator Barry Goldwater and General Matthew Ridgway. Secretary Brucker sent the Army's Under Secretary, Charles Finncane.

***

In his later years Gavin wrote four additional useful books, beginning with *War and Peace in the Space Age*. In its preface Gavin said this: "We Americans must devote more attention to our problem of national survival. And we must learn to think of the earth as a tactical entity and of space as the next great strategic challenge—space and the mind of man. This book is a modest effort to do this very thing."

In the book Gavin noted that "most informed people agree that the Soviets are ahead of us technologically, and some believe that they are ahead of us militarily. I believe that they are... As a consequence, they now have the initiative and they continue to outmaneuver us, diplomatically and strategically."[11]

***

General Maxwell Taylor was, of course, Army Chief of Staff at the time Gavin retired. The two had a long history of shared service, dating back at least to the early days of World War II when both played important roles in the fledgling 82nd Airborne Division.

Taylor was the elder and more senior of the two, having graduated from West Point and been commissioned with the Class of 1922, while Gavin was a member of the Class of 1929. Both were included in the famous list of outstanding officers compiled by Dwight Eisenhower soon after the end of World War II.

A recent work assessing Taylor's Cold War service began on the very first page with a description of how he was viewed by many contemporaries in negative terms. Gavin, it maintained, concluded Taylor "was a political operator who used his subordinates—men like Gavin—to score points or remove obstacles." But the same author found Gavin "notoriously cantankerous." Others cited were even more critical, finding Taylor "dishonest and untrustworthy."[12]

As Army Chief of Staff General Maxwell Taylor became fiercely opposed to the Eisenhower policy of massive retaliation, working away on a book denouncing it that he would publish immediately after his retirement in 1959. Meanwhile he relied on subordinates to carry the load in opposing the President's defense policies. "While Taylor made the argument for the army missile program," wrote a Taylor biographer, "in public and private he often seemed aloof and let his subordinates, above all James Gavin, carry the brunt of the fight against [Secretary of Defense Charles] Wilson, [Chairman of the Joint Chiefs of Staff Arthur] Radford, and the air force."[13]

Later Gavin described his view of Taylor and the trauma of working for him during these turbulent times. "It was an amazing thing that a man of his apparent integrity, polish and education would be so driven by ambition as to try to lead the Secretary of Defense and the Joint Chiefs of Staff to believe that he agreed with them in every action when in fact he didn't, while at the same time he failed to support the Army staff on issue after issue. It was a strange and puzzling phenomenon to deal with and, of course, in time it became intolerable. One could not lie to support him and his position."[14]

In a relevant observation Gavin's daughter Chloe described the Taylor–Gavin relationship as she saw it. "I'm pretty sure my father detested him," she said, "and I think the feeling was mutual."

***

Gavin landed very much on his feet in the civilian world, soon taking a senior position with Arthur D. Little, Inc., an industrial research, engineering, and management consulting firm headquartered in Cambridge, Massachusetts. After about a year he was named Executive Vice President of ADL and a member of its Board of Directors. In March 1960 he would be elected the firm's President and CEO.

After the executive succession committee had selected Gavin to be the firm's executive vice president, he received an unusual invitation. Accordingly, he travelled to Cambridge, where he spent the morning, followed by lunch, with senior members of the ADL staff. It soon dawned on him that his hosts, a collection of highly skilled scientists and engineers, were not necessarily pleased with the prospect of their firm being taken over by a general and were going to take this opportunity to put him through the wringer. Gavin warmed to the challenge, responding to a wide range of questions, not all relevant only to business.

When, several hours into it, one participant asked Gavin what he thought of Suetonius, he had his chance. It happened that he had read Suetonius only a year or so earlier. (Gavin knew, but maybe not all his interlocutors did, that the Roman historian Suetonius was best known for his lurid descriptions of the sexual mores of the Roman emperors.) Gavin's response: "Print it in paperback with a naked woman on the cover and it would be a best seller." His questioner laughed and that essentially ended the inquisition.

Gavin considered the type of planning and management he had been doing in the Army as something new, "both in its scope and diversity and in its pioneering use of the latest scientific advice and equipment, such as systems analysis, operational research, [and] data control." Gavin privately referred to all this as "technoplanning" and, in his new role as Vice President of Arthur D. Little, sought to implement it, the "chief business" being "the preparation and execution of complex plans."[15] His first major initiative was to explore ways of getting ADL into the European market in a major way.

A range of other affiliations ensured that Gavin would have wide influence, especially in educational and policy circles. He was elected to the Board of Tufts University, and soon after that to the Board of Trustees of the Fletcher School of Law and Diplomacy, soon becoming its Chairman, and to the American Academy of Arts and Sciences. Many of his new colleagues at ADL were also close to the greater Boston academic community, often working back and forth as part-time faculty members and part-time consultants.

***

When, early in 1959, Gavin was invited by Senator John F. Kennedy to join him and others for lunch and a policy discussion at the Harvard Club, another whole range of interesting relationships and issues was opened to him. The all-star gathering included Walt Rostow, Henry Kissinger, Kenneth Galbraith, Arthur Schlesinger, Archibald Cox, and Lincoln Gordon. Gavin was keeping very good company indeed. And he found Kennedy's grasp of the issues very impressive, concluding he was the man he hoped would be president.

As the election campaign progressed, and it was clear that the choice of the next president was going to be a tight contest, Gavin gave a lot of thought to what could be done to boost Senator Kennedy's campaign. He credits himself with coming up with the idea for the Peace Corps and introducing that in an address to a group of businessmen and educators in Miami only 11 days before the election. He was gratified when they responded with spontaneous applause. He contacted Kennedy by phone to tell him about the idea and how it had been received, following up by sending a briefing paper at Kennedy's request. Gavin was elated when, only days later, Kennedy spoke in San Francisco and urged creation of a Peace Corps. Said Gavin, "Thus it began."

Soon after Kennedy's election Gavin received word that the President-elect had designated him Grand Marshal of the Inaugural Parade. Gavin recognized this for the great honor it was. But it was also serious business, especially when a snowfall that amounted to eight inches began in Washington mid-day of the day before the scheduled January 20th Inaugural.

First there was the matter of getting the Grand Marshal to the parade site. Gavin, Jean and their family left Boston by air about 1:30 the afternoon of January 19. By the time they reached the Washington area Andrews Air Force Base was closed. They tried Philadelphia, Baltimore, and Richmond before finally landing at Patuxent, Maryland, where they deplaned in a driving snowstorm with the temperature just below freezing. Partway to Washington their two cars bogged down. The Maryland State Police rescued them, and they finally arrived at Fort Myer, just outside Washington, at 1:00 a.m. in a howling blizzard.

Herculean snow clearing efforts throughout the night resulted in a relatively clear parade route. When the 82nd Airborne contingent approached the reviewing stand President Kennedy called for Gavin to join him. The parade, supposed to take two hours, dragged on and on. When the last unit went past in near total darkness the only people left in the reviewing stand were the President, Gavin and his wife Jean, and one or two aides. Kennedy's remark to Gavin: "You know, Jim, this is the longest two-hour parade I have ever seen."[16]

***

The night of President Kennedy's inauguration, following the Inaugural Ball, a small group of his supporters, including Gavin, assembled at a private home in Georgetown for a nightcap. There he learned from William Walton that the new President was considering Gavin for an appointment in his administration, the post as Ambassador to France. A few days later, as requested, Gavin called on the President in the White House.

Kennedy explained that what he wanted most in the Paris embassy was someone who could get along with French President Charles de Gaulle. He viewed Gavin as that person. After a few days of backing and forthing it was decided. Gavin would go to Paris. Back in Boston he undertook emergency tutoring in the French language.

Gavin soon discovered, to his shock, a rather intense feeling of dislike and disdain toward President de Gaulle prevalent in the U.S. Department of State, an outlook he found profoundly disturbing. A briefing officer at State even told Gavin not to be concerned if he did not get along with de Gaulle, since nobody else had either. In fact, Gavin found, the State Department people not only seemed to believe that he could not get along with de Gaulle, but some of them even hoped that he wouldn't.

A planned visit to France by President Kennedy, to take place in May, further complicated matters. There would be little time to prepare for that, much less build any relationships in the new post. But Gavin looked forward to the challenge, especially dealing with de Gaulle, viewed by him as a man of great integrity who combined a powerful ego and a prescient mind.

Gavin and his family travelled to Europe aboard the liner *United States* from New York to Le Havre. Included in their entourage was dog Laddie, assigned to a kennel on the ship. After a notably rough Atlantic crossing Gavin observed that the last time he had gone to France from abroad he had landed by parachute and was greeted by gunfire.

Gavin's view of de Gaulle was soon updated as they had frequent contact with one another. Gavin perceived that national self-interest was always de Gaulle's motivation, even while Gavin questioned whether, in the current shrinking world, that was always the best policy.[17]

When certain matters as reported speculatively in the French press needed rebutting Gavin appealed to Washington. Among the responses received was one from President Kennedy himself: "In spite of the fact that this is a most difficult post," he wrote, "I am very anxious for you to continue to serve as my Ambassador because of your high reputation with the French. You are by far the best Ambassador we have had in that post since Franklin."[18]

For his part Gavin said he and de Gaulle had become good friends, noting also that he, Gavin, was "very much interested in how he saw the United States and the place of France."[19]

Gavin had hoped at the outset that his mission to Paris would last two years or less. He had made a commitment to ADL that he would resume duties there when the stint as ambassador ended. In fact, it was only about 18 months into it that he arranged with President Kennedy to resign and return home, that action effective in late September 1962.

The last event the Gavins attended before leaving Paris was the world premiere of Darryl Zanuck's film *The Longest Day*. A tremendous crowd, including members of the French cabinet, attended, as did Cornelius Ryan, author of the book on which the film was based, and his wife. After the film a sumptuous supper was served, followed by fireworks and a cannonade, then Edith Piaf sang songs of the war period from the first stage of the Eiffel Tower. Gavin recalled it as an evening the likes of which he had never seen. When they returned from Paris Jean began styling herself Jeanne and retained that version of her name thereafter.[20]

When the Gavins returned from Paris JFK gave a dinner for them at the White House. Gavin also called on President Kennedy in the White House soon after arriving home, then saw him once more late that same month when they talked about problems in the State Department.

Then Gavin, back at Arthur D. Little, was attending a Board of Directors luncheon meeting on Friday, November 22nd, 1963, when a waitress bent over and whispered to him that President Kennedy had just been shot. Soon she returned and added that the President had been taken to a hospital and a priest had been called. Gavin told the directors what he knew and ended their meeting.

Gavin and his wife Jeanne attended President Kennedy's funeral at St. Matthew's Roman Catholic Cathedral. There the eulogy was delivered by Archbishop Philip Hannah of the New Orleans diocese. Hannah had been a paratrooper in Gavin's 505th Parachute Infantry Regiment during World War II. Gavin found this sequence of events almost more than he could bear.

***

Back at Arthur D. Little Gavin resumed his duties as its President and subsequently as Chairman of the Board. The overseas growth program he had instituted earlier was flourishing, as was development of U.S. markets for European products and services. The firm had also become involved in the Apollo program, developing hardware for use on the moon's surface. Other new enterprises involved Africa, and especially Nigeria. Providing training for Nigerians led to establishment of a school in Cambridge, on the grounds of the ADL complex, where the first class graduated in 1963.[21]

Gavin continued as ADL's Chairman until retiring in 1977, then continued to serve in later years as a consultant to the firm. Among the interesting comparisons between when Gavin joined ADL and his retirement from the corporation were the number of employees (increasing from about 1,200 to over 2,000) and revenue ($16 million the year he joined and over $106 million his final year).

***

During these years opposition to America's involvement in a war in Southeast Asia, and especially to increases in that involvement, became for Gavin a central concern. A letter written by him to John Fischer, editor of *Harper's* magazine, laid out his concerns in detail and was the first articulation of what became known as his "enclave theory" for reduction of U.S. commitment. Gavin argued that the alternative to early extrication of U.S. forces would be escalation to a catastrophic confrontation on a massive scale with Communist China. The letter was published in the February 1966 issue of *Harper's*, leading to Gavin's further public involvement in the ongoing debate about the war.

Senator Fulbright summoned Gavin to testify before the Senate Committee on Foreign Relations. In anticipation of that appearance, opponents of Gavin's views arranged that General Maxwell Taylor be interviewed on a widely viewed television program, "The Today Show." That appearance took place on Friday, February 4, 1966. Taylor obligingly stated that Gavin's position was totally lacking in merit, summarizing his "enclave theory" as having U.S. troops withdraw to the coast and dig in where it was safest. That characterization infuriated Gavin.

On the following Tuesday, February 8, 1966, Gavin appeared before Senator Fulbright's committee. Only the day before President Lyndon Johnson, in Honolulu for discussions with senior South Vietnamese officials, had castigated those who counselled retreat from the war as belonging to a group that was "blind to experience and deaf to hope." Gavin felt certain the U.S. was not going to win a war with Ho Chi Minh, since that would in his view lead to also going to war with the powers behind him, Red China and the USSR. These, he maintained, were facts.

Gavin advanced these views during his almost day-long testimony before the Senate committee, then repeated them to Secretary of Defense McNamara in a subsequent meeting. Afterward Gavin complained that the only thing that interested McNamara was how to win.

Gavin's views, shown to be even more extreme, were elaborated in a later interview conducted for a study entitled *The U.S. Government and the Vietnam War* prepared under auspices of the Senate Foreign Relations Committee. Gavin was provided the text of the section of the study quoting his interview: "Gavin, who explained that the administration used Taylor to counteract his testimony, said that in proposing enclaves he was not suggesting that the U.S. forces should stay in those positions, but 'just use them to get out, that's all. We are getting out. We're not staying there any longer. It was stupid to stay there.'"[22]

***

Gavin continued to periodically produce several excellent and diverse books. These now included *France and the Civil War in America, Crisis Now,* and a memoir entitled *On to Berlin.*

The 1968 *Crisis Now* was the most controversial book. In it (written in collaboration with journalist Arthur Hadley) Gavin took renewed issue with the fact and nature of America's involvement in the Vietnam War, suggesting instead his by now signature "enclave theory" that never gained much traction operationally but did get a lot of media attention.

"Vietnam is the least understood conflict in our nation's history," wrote Gavin. "… unfortunately, there will be no 'victory' in Vietnam. Only more victims."[23] Gavin cited to good effect a Presidential statement issued after Secretary of Defense Robert McNamara and General Maxwell Taylor had returned from visiting Vietnam in the autumn of 1963: "Secretary McNamara and General Taylor reported their judgment that the major part of the U.S. military task can be completed by the end of 1965."[24] Now it was 1968, and a steady flow of American ground forces, responsive to General William Westmoreland's repeated pleas for more and still more, had resulted in over a half million U.S. troops on the ground in Vietnam. Gavin was incensed. But he undercut his own critique by characterizing Vietnam as "a guerrilla war,"[25] far from the battlefield realities then pertaining in which conventional combat between regular forces was the dominant mode.

A favorable portrayal of Ho Chi Minh further eroded Gavin's credibility as a Vietnam War critic. "The information we have indicates he is a patriot, an intense nationalist, albeit a Communist—a man who tends toward the combination of nationalism and Communism associated with Marshal Tito."[26] In an unfortunate mischaracterization, Gavin also claimed (in the "About the Author" profile in *Crisis Now*) that he had resigned from the Army in 1958, whereas in fact he had retired, not resigned, a far different matter. In that same brief profile Gavin revisited the circumstances of his departure from the Army, attributing it to his "outspoken concern over the policy of massive nuclear retaliation at the expense of a more flexible strategy."[27]

On a broader scale, Gavin deplored what he viewed as unwise over-dependence on nuclear weapons as opposed to conventional forces.

"I felt that the country had never faced a more dangerous and at the same moment a more challenging time," Gavin wrote in the book's preface, citing his feelings about "the sterility and inadequacy of 'massive retaliation at a time and a place of our choosing.'"[28]

At some point Gavin received an invitation from General Westmoreland, then still in command of U.S. forces in Vietnam, to visit the war zone. Gavin and Westmoreland of course knew one another well, including from the immediate post-World War II period when Gavin was still commanding the 82nd Airborne Division and Westmoreland was for a time his division chief of staff. Westmoreland's invitation included the suggestion that Jeanne accompany Gavin and that a shopping trip to Hong Kong be part of their trip. Instead, Gavin went alone and skipped the Hong Kong stop.

In Vietnam Gavin called on Ambassador Ellsworth Bunker, saw Westmoreland of course, and also met with his deputy General Creighton Abrams. At each stop Gavin declined briefings, asking only that his questions be answered. Apparently, the answers he got were not the ones he wanted, as his later statement was that after about a week he left Vietnam, sad and depressed about the tactical dilemma in which our troops found themselves.

Gavin was by now quite impressed with the amount of public support he was getting for his views on the war. That led to his exploring whether he might launch a campaign for the presidency. Discussions with Senator Prescott Bush centered on the need for a base of power, money, and an organization, none of which he had. There were, though, people organizing small "Gavin for President" groups in a few places. Somewhat bizarrely, or so it seems at this remove, Gavin also called on the chairman of the Republican National Committee. No help there, nor was there any from the Democratic National Committee. Gavin found himself in what he described as a familiar position, out in front and rather lonely.

Among those others consulted by Gavin was Nelson Rockefeller. When Gavin asked for his support, Rockefeller countered that Gavin should join his campaign. When Senator Eugene McCarthy and then Senator Robert Kennedy entered the race as anti-war candidates, Gavin's candidacy evaporated. He went back to his schedule of speeches, managing Arthur D. Little, and finishing his book. When Robert Kennedy was assassinated, Gavin joined the Rockefeller campaign staff.

Those then charged with pursuing the war in Vietnam were not favorably impressed by Gavin's "strategy." In March 1969 Major General Phillip Davidson, then the Military Assistance Command, Vietnam, J-2, spoke of "some such silly scheme as this one that Jim Gavin had of enclaves."[29]

But as time went on, with the Nixon administration mandating successive incremental unilateral withdrawals of U.S. forces from Vietnam, it appeared that something very like what Gavin had advocated was indeed being implemented. General Creighton Abrams, commander of U.S. forces during the latter stages of the war, spoke of this with anguish to his subordinate commanders at an August 1971 conference. "They've dug it out and dusted it off and said, 'Now, by god, in the end the U.S. has finally adopted what Gavin recommended in the first place—that's an enclave [words unclear].' Goddamn!"[30]

***

Many public service appointments adorned these later years. Gavin served as a trustee of the West Point Association of Graduates and on the Army Science Board and the American Battle Monuments Commission.

A robust correspondence with Sterling Lord, Gavin's literary agent and eventually very close friend, contains many examples of Gavin's reflections on his earlier service and the personalities involved. Among the most interesting is Maxwell Taylor, going back to World War II days. Describing for Lord the contents of a planned memoir, Gavin said of his two years in the Pentagon with Taylor, "This should be quite traumatic, dealing with Southeast Asia, the bomb, missiles and space, which terminated with my retirement rather than staying on." And, added Gavin, "I think now that the Pentagon experience can be written without emotion and without hurting people's feelings, although Taylor will not come out well at all."[31]

Gavin also in these later years reflected, often quite critically, on the senior level leadership under which he had served during World War II. He was especially negative in his assessment of General Eisenhower and his repeated failure to be on hand when needed, identifying four such critical occasions as "the escape of the Germans and Italians from Sicily; the escape of the two German armies at Falaise; the escape of the German army from Calais by barge; and finally, doing nothing about Berlin or Prague."[32] Thus, of Eisenhower, "His generalship was really one of absentee general or, in the critical moments, non-existent."[33]

While in his World War II journal Gavin often wrote favorably of Field Marshal Montgomery, his later views were less positive, especially when the existence of the Ultra intelligence, available only to the top-level commanders, became known. "The more I think about the situation the more I realize that the implications vis-à-vis the higher commanders, who were the exclusive possessor of this knowledge, are very far reaching," he wrote. "Montgomery should have destroyed Rommel and not have allowed him to escape to Tunisia to fight again."[34] And further: "Knowing now of all the intelligence that Montgomery enjoyed all the way from El Alamein, he was inexcusably cautious and hesitant, and the Germans could have delayed him just about as long as they pleased."[35]

Gavin leveled a similar criticism at Eisenhower. "There is also a serious question about Eisenhower's generalship in light of the accurate intelligence information that he had," wrote Gavin. "Seizing Berlin would not have entailed great risks and might have completely changed the post-war geo-political situation."[36]

Reporting on research for a planned memoir, Gavin said he had read cable traffic from the World War II period and talked to Generals Bradley and Bull. The more he got into it the more he "realized the very overriding role that was played by the great volume of ill will that pervaded the higher commands."[37]

Another frequent target of Gavin's criticism was the Joint Chiefs of Staff system, which he held responsible for the loss of Berlin and Czechoslovakia. "It was the first occasion in which the Joint Chiefs worked without consulting the State Department or the White House in matters of highest importance," he stated, "and I think that the pattern established then persisted, in a way, through the Vietnam War."[38]

In 1978 Gavin published his fifth and final book, a work entitled *On to Berlin* and sub-titled *Battles of an Airborne Commander 1943–1946*, essentially the same period and events he had recorded serially in his World War II journal. He dedicated the work, somewhat misleadingly, "To Jeanne and our five daughters, Barbara, Caroline, Patricia, Aileen, and Chloe," glossing over the fact that Barbara was born of his first marriage with Irma and that Jeanne had brought daughter Caroline with her from a prior marriage.

Gavin's World War II journal makes clear that women found him very attractive, and that he in turn found that most enjoyable. That behavior pattern continued in later years.

Gavin's final book is a rich supplement to the journal, and of course the product of many years of reflection on the events both documents describe. By now, for example, Gavin is dead set on Berlin. "Since the war I have discussed the problem of Berlin many times," he notes, "and I have never been able to satisfy myself as to why we did not seize it. Now I know that we should have seized it."[39]

This final book was not the end of Gavin's interest in or attempts to influence development of better battlefield systems, however. In a letter dated May 14, 1980, to Army Chief of Staff General "Shy" Meyer, Gavin urged the development of an airborne tank. "As an amateur anthropologist," he reported, "I have always been aware that it is the soft furry animal that has survived and not the triceratops and dinosaur, nor the armadillo."

***

There might have been a sixth book, a memoir with the working title *Beyond the Stars*. It was never published but was clearly completed through the stage of a final draft.

In Gavin's correspondence files there is much about such a volume back and forth between him and Sterling Lord and, subsequently, between him and a Walter Fox (who tells Gavin he has been assigned by the Sterling Lord Agency to edit the manuscript). In a June 25, 1986, letter to Gavin, Fox tells him: "At long last, we now have the final manuscript."

But, over a year later, Gavin writes to Lord discussing a number of potential revisions. Among them: "I would like to add a couple of pages to the end of the first chapter. Being an orphan in the American society makes one a second-class citizen and I would like to say why this is so and what we can do about it."[40]

Gavin died February 23, 1990, in a Baltimore nursing home and was appropriately buried at West Point, where his experience as a cadet had, he always said, more than anything else molded his mind and body.

***

A constant over the years was Gavin's search for his birth mother, an effort that never came to closure. Gavin termed that the great disappointment of his life.

In his 1958 book Gavin wrote that his family lived on Deane [elsewhere he renders it Dean] Street in Brooklyn, and "I was born in a hospital several blocks away on the same street. Both of my parents were Irish immigrants, and both died before I reached the age of two. Through the intercession of the Church, I was adopted by an Irish family, the Gavins, again both from the Ould Sod."[41]

Gavin tried many avenues of exploration to learn more. One was the previously mentioned retention of the legal firm of Donovan, Leisure, Newton & Irvine to trace the various leads. Gavin concluded that the Catholic Church was determined to protect information about his mother, motive unclear, as seemed to be validated when his file was moved from Brooklyn to the Vatican. The law firm advised that further inquiries would be expensive and probably unavailing.

In a 1980 letter to Sterling Lord, Gavin told him that people at the Burns International Agency, a prominent detective agency, "have been working on this case altogether for 40 years, and they have been unproductive."[42]

Later Gavin told Lord that he had "considerable information; enough to establish the woman, 'Catherine (Katie) Ryan,' as a Nun. She lived in the Ozanam House [for Friendless Women] which is still in Brooklyn."[43] That turned out to be, despite Gavin's persistent and energetic and heart-breaking efforts to learn more, the end of the trail.

***

James Maurice Gavin lived one of the more colorful and interesting lives of his times. May he rest in peace.

Lewis Sorley

Notes

1 Gavin, "Foreword," in McNally, *As Ever, John.*
2 McNally, *As Ever, John,* pp. 83–84.
3 Gavin, *Airborne Warfare,* p. viii.
4 William C. Lee in Gavin, *Airborne Warfare,* xii
5 The DSC and Silver Star citations may be found following this Epilogue.

6   McNally, *As Ever, John*, Dedication.
7   Sorley, *Westmoreland*, p. 25.
8   Gavin, *Crisis Now*, p. 40.
9   In referencing this matter later Gavin gave this citation: *Study of Airpower: Hearings Before the Subcommittee on the Air Force of the Committee on Armed Services*, United States Senate, Eighty-fourth Congress, Second Session, Airpower, April 16-June 1, 1956, Parts I-XI, Volume I, pages 860–862.
10 *The Best and the Brightest*, p. xx.
11 *War and Peace in the Space Age*, pp. 3–4.
12 Trauschweizer, *Maxwell Taylor's Cold War*, pp. 1–2.
13 Trauschweizer, *Maxwell Taylor's Cold War*, p. 91.
14 Gavin, August 31, 1981, letter to Sterling Lord, GP Box 8.
15 Gavin, *Crisis Now*, p. 17.
16 Gavin later noted that the 1961 parade was the last of the great military reviews. It was made up of 15,000 military, 10,000 civilians, 40 floats, and 32 pieces of military equipment, including missiles, aircraft, 26 armored vehicles, and an actual PT boat that probably was the largest single entry in any inaugural parade. The whole thing took three hours and 11 minutes to pass the reviewing stand.
17 Gavin recalled a one-on-one conversation with President de Gaulle in which he said the following: "You know, Mr. Ambassador, those Foreign Legion regiments that I have in North Africa are like the Roman Legions of old, they are more loyal to each other than they were to Rome. Our legions have been away and at war so long that they are more loyal to their own regiments than they are to France."
18 Kennedy, January 4, 1962, letter to Gavin, GP Box 26.
19 Gavin, June 26, 1980, letter to Sterling Lord, GP Box 8.
20 Except on her tombstone, where the spelling reverts to Jean.
21 The school, subsequently named The Arthur D. Little Management Education Institute, was in 1973 granted authority to award a Master of Science degree in Management.
22 William C. Gibbons, Congressional Research Service, July 21, 1986, letter to Gavin, GP Box19.
23 Gavin, *Crisis Now*, p. 39.
24 Gavin, *Crisis Now*, p. 54.
25 Gavin, *Crisis Now*, p. 56.
26 Gavin, *Crisis Now*, pp. 62–63.
27 Gavin, *Crisis Now*, p. [185].
28 Gavin, *Crisis Now*, pp. v–vi.
29 Sorley, *Vietnam Chronicles*, p. 139.
30 Sorley, *Vietnam Chronicles*, p. 662.
31 Gavin, June 26, 1980, letter to Sterling Lord, GP Box 8.
32 Gavin, December 6, 1976, letter to Sterling Lord, GP Box 8.
33 Gavin, December 6, 1976, letter to Sterling Lord, GP Box 8.
34 Gavin, November 27, 1974, letter to Sterling Lord, GP Box 8.
35 Gavin, October 28, 1975, letter to Sterling Lord, GP Box 8.
36 Gavin, November 27, 1974, letter to Sterling Lord, GP Box 8.
37 Gavin, March 1, 1976, letter to Sterling Lord, GP Box 8.
38 Gavin, January 3, 1977, letter to Sterling Lord, GP Box 8.
39 *On to Berlin*, p. xiii.
40 Letter of August 5, 1987, GP Box 8.
41 *War and Peace in the Space Age*, p. 22.
42 Letter of May 14, 1980, Gavin Papers, Box 8.
43 Gavin, March 23, 1984, letter to Sterling Lord, GP Box 8.

Citations

Distinguished Service Cross

JAMES M. GAVIN, O-17676, Colonel, Infantry, U.S. Army. For extra-ordinary heroism in action lasting throughout daylight on July 11th, 1943, approximately five (5) miles West of Vittoria, Sicily. Colonel Gavin, Regimental Commander, 505th Parachute Infantry, 82nd Airborne Division, together with a small portion of his regiment, held and drove back a superior force of German Infantry and tanks in the face of heavy gunfire and counterattack, led by tanks, which reached to within 50 yards of his Command Post. This successful action enabled the 182nd Infantry, 45th Division, which had been held up all that day, to resume its advance. Colonel Gavin displayed cool courageous leadership of the highest order throughout the day's fighting, encouraging and inspiring his men, and by his heroic example achieved decisive success in the face of greatly superior odds. Entered military service from Mt. Carmel, Pennsylvania.

Distinguished Service Cross

1st Oak Leaf Cluster

For extra-ordinary heroism in action against the enemy on 9 June 1944, in France. In a battalion attack upon the town of LeMotey extremely heavy and intense enemy artillery fire inflicted heavy casualties among the officers and men, causing disorganization in the battalion. General Gavin, observing the results of this action, went immediately to the front lines. There he took charge and personally affected a re-organization of the battalion and directed it to a renewed attack upon the town. General Gavin, in order to better control the assault, moved to an exposed position in a wheat field. Although enemy fire was particularly intense at this point, General Gavin remained in this position until the battalion had completed a successful assault upon the town. The courage, personal bravery and outstanding leadership of General Gavin, reflect great credit upon himself and were in keeping with the highest traditions of the Armed Forces.

Silver Star

Major General JAMES M. GAVIN, O-17676, United States Army, for gallantry in action in the vicinity of MOOK, HOLLAND, on September 20, 1944. When two simultaneous attacks by enemy forces against the thinly held sector in the vicinity of BEEK and MOOK were made by the enemy, Major General (then Brigadier General) GAVIN moved the division reserve to a position of vantage and went personally to MOOK, the most critical sector. Upon arrival at the railroad overpass immediately west of the village, he came under intense artillery and mortar fire. Pressing on to obtain a more accurate picture of the situation, he came upon elements of a defending infantry unit which had lost many of their leaders. Major General GAVIN directed and carried out the reorganization and disposed the unit to affect a counter-attack. The ensuing attack broke the desperate bid of the enemy to break through. General GAVIN's presence with the assault echelon encouraged and inspired our troops and his personal leadership at a critical moment resulted in the shattering of the enemy attempts to break through our lines. The courage and inspiring leadership displayed by Major General GAVIN at MOOK were in keeping with the highest traditions of the United States Army. General GAVIN entered military service from Pennsylvania.

Silver Star

1st Oak Leaf Cluster

For gallantry in action against an enemy of the United States during the period December 21–25, 1944. Moving his division into a fluid situation caused by the German counter-offensive of December 16, 1944, Major General Gavin, by his personal courage and outstanding leadership, contributed materially to the success of his division. Constantly with the forward elements of his command, Major General Gavin imparted to his troops the positive, aggressive spirit which stopped the German in his offensive effort and inflicted punishing losses upon him. Throughout the period the heroic and fearless leadership of Major General Gavin was a source of inspiration to the troops he commanded.

Glossary

A A/B A	Allied Airborne Army
AA	anti-aircraft
AB	airborne
A/B	airborne
AC	Air Corps
Adj	Adjutant
AEAF	Allied Expeditionary Air Force
AFHQ	Allied Forces Headquarters
AFN	Armed Forces Network
AG	Adjutant General
AG	advance guard
AG	Army Group
AGF	Army Ground Forces
AGO	Adjutant General Office
AHEC	Army Heritage and Education Center
AMGOT	Allied Military Government for Occupied Territories
AR	Army Regulation(s)
ARC	American Red Cross
Armd	armored
Arty	artillery
AS	air support
ASO	Air Support Officer
Asst	assistant
AT	anti-tank
ATC	Airborne Training Center
AVM	Air Vice Marshal
AWOL	absent without leave
BA	British Army
BD	Berlin District
BG	brigadier general
Bn	battalion
BUPS	Beacon, Ultra Portable S-Band

CG	Commanding General
Cir	Circular
CM	Court(s) Martial
CO	Commanding Officer
Co	Company
CofS	Chief of Staff
Comdr	Commander
COSSAC	Chief of Staff, Supreme Allied Commander
CP	command post
CPX	command post exercise
CS	Chief of Staff
C/S	Chief of Staff
CT	Combat Team
DCS	Deputy Chief of Staff
Dept.	Department
Div	division
DP	displaced person(s)
DR	dead reckoning
dragged	Cadet slang for "dated"
DSC	Distinguished Service Cross
DSO	Distinguished Service Order
DZ	drop zone
EBS	Eastern Base Section
EG	Engineer Group [?]
EGB	[replacement unit]
Eng.	Engineer
Engr	Engineer
ETOUSA	European Theater of Operations, United States Army
Evac	evacuation
FA	Field Artillery
FAA	First Allied Army
FAAA	First Allied Airborne Army
FAA/BA	First Allied Airborne Army
FM	Field Marshal
FO	forward observer
ft	feet
FUSAG	First United States Army Group
FX	field exercise
G1, G2, G3, G4	Under the US Army staff system, the staff at Division and above is designated as G1 (Personnel), G2 (Intelligence), G3 (Operations) and G4 (Logistics)

GAF	German Air Force
GCC	Ground Control Center
Gen. R	General Ridgway
GHQ	General Headquarters
GI	soldier
gl	glider
GO	General Order(s)
GP	Gavin Papers (at USAHEC)
Gp	Group
Grp	Group
HE	high explosive
Hqrs	Headquarters
hrs	hours
IG	Inspector General
Inf	Infantry
IP	initial point
JA	Judge Advocate
J/M	jumpmaster
Ln	liaison
Lt	light
LZ	landing zone
MATS	Military Air Transport Service
Mech	Mechanized
MG	machine gun
MG	major general
MP	Military Police
MTs	mountains
NAAF	Northwest Africa Air Forces
NATOUSA	North African Theater of Operations, United States Army
NCO	non-commissioned officer
OCS	Officer Candidate School
OD	Officer of the Day
OD	olive drab
Para	parachute/parachutist
P/F	pathfinder
PI	photo interpreter
P/JM	parachutist/jumpmaster
plat	platoon
plt	platoon
PM	afternoon

PM	Provost Marshal
PND	"mouse detector"
PPI	personnel parachute inspection
Prop Blast	airborne initiation ceremony
Prov	Provisional
PW	prisoner of war
QM	Quartermaster
R	Ridgway
RAF	Royal Air Force
RE	[equipment]
Rebecca	radar navigation system used by airborne forces
Recon	reconnaissance
Regt	Regiment
RR	railroad
S1, S2, S3, S4	Subordinate organizations, brigade and battalion, the staff is designated as S1, S2, S3, S4.
SAC	Supreme Allied Commander
SHAEF	Supreme Headquarters Allied Expeditionary Force
SNAFU	Situation Normal, All [Fouled] Up
SOP	Standard Operating Procedure
SOS	Service of Supply
SP	self-propelled
TC	Troop Carrier
TCC	Troop Carrier Command
TD	Tank Destroyer
TE	Table of Equipment
Tnk	tank
TO	Table of Organization
Trp	troop
UK	United Kingdom
USAHEC	U.S. Army Heritage and Education Center
WD	War Department
WPA	Works Progress Administration

Selected Bibliography

Books by General Gavin

Airborne Warfare. Washington: Infantry Journal Press, 1947.
War and Peace in the Space Age. New York: Harper & Brothers, 1958.
France and the Civil War in America, with André Maurois. New York: Atheneum, 1962.
Crisis Now, with Arthur T. Hadley. New York: Random House, 1968.
On to Berlin: Battles of an Airborne Commander, 1943–1946. New York: Viking Press, 1978.

Some Related Works of Interest

Atkinson, Rick. *The Day of Battle: The War in Sicily and Italy, 1943–1944.* New York: Henry Holt, 2007.
Biggs, Bradley. *Gavin: A Biography of General James M. Gavin.* Hamden, CT: Archon Books, 1980.
Booth, T. Michael and Duncan Spencer. *Paratrooper: The Life of General James M. Gavin.* New York: Simon & Schuster, 1994.
Dawson, Buck [W. Forrest]. *Saga of the All American.* Fort Lauderdale: Hoffman Publishing Company Reprint, 1995. Originally published 1946 by 82nd Airborne Division Association.
Fauntleroy, Barbara Gavin. *The General & His Daughter: The Wartime Letters of General James M. Gavin to His Daughter Barbara.* New York: Fordham University Press, 2007.
Galvin, John R. *Air Assault: The Development of Airmobile Warfare.* New York: Hawthorn Books, 1969.
Gavin, Lieutenant General James M. Oral History, Senior Officers Debriefing Program. Carlisle Barracks, PA: U.S. Army Military History Institute, 1975.
Halberstam, David. *The Best and the Brightest.* New York: Random House, 1969.
Hastings, Max. *Warriors: Portraits from the Battlefield.* New York: Alfred A. Knopf, 2006.
LoFaro, Guy. *The Sword of St. Michael: The 82nd Airborne Division in World War II.* Cambridge, MA: Da Capo, 2011.
McNally, John V. *As Ever, John: The Letters of Col. John V. McNally to His Sister, Margaret McNally Bierbaum, 1941–1946.* Foreword by Lt. Gen. James M. Gavin. Fairfield, CT: Roberts Press, 1985.
Nordyke, Phil. *All American, All the Way: A Combat History of the 82nd Airborne Division in World War II: From Sicily to Normandy.* Osceola, WI: MBI Publishing, 2010.
Sorley, Lewis. *Vietnam Chronicles: The Abrams Tapes, 1968–1972.* Lubbock: Texas Tech University Press, 2004.
Sorley, Lewis. *Westmoreland: The General Who Lost Vietnam.* Boston: Houghton Mifflin Harcourt, 2011.
Summers, Harry. *On Strategy: A Critical Analysis of the Vietnam War.* Novato, CA: Presidio Press, 1982.
Taylor, Maxwell. *The Uncertain Trumpet.* New York: Harper and Brothers, 1959.
Trauschweizer, Ingo. *Maxwell Taylor's Cold War: From Berlin to Vietnam.* Lexington: University Press of Kentucky, 2019.

Index

References to maps are in *italics*.